irreverent guides

Washington, D.C.

other *Irreverent* titles: **Amsterdam, Boston, Chicago, London, Manhattan, Miami, New Orleans, Paris, San Francisco, Sante Fe, Virgin Islands (U.S.)**

irreverent guides

Washington, D.C.

BY

THEODORE FISHER

A BALLIETT & FITZGERALD BOOK

MACMILLAN • USA

Where to spot Bubba at dinnertime...

Red Sage, see Dining

See the biggest Mass in the Lower 48...

Washington National Cathedral, see Diversions

Get inside *and* keep your kids happy...

White House, see You Probably Didn't Know

Remember...

Vietnam Veterans Memorial, see Diversions

Admire Nixon's "plumbing"...

Watergate Hotel, see Accommodations

Panda to the electorate...

National Zoological Park, see Diversions

Fund the arts...

Arena Stage, see Entertainment

Address the tastes of the Union...

America, Union Station branch, see Dining

Get modern on the Mall...

Hirschhorn Museum, see Diversions

Explore the *other* kind of mall...

Georgetown Park, see Shopping

Sleep with antiques.

Morrison-Clark Inn, see Accommodations

what's so irreverent?

It's up to you.

You can buy a traditional guidebook with its fluff, its promotional hype, its let's-find-something-nice-to-say-about-everything point of view. Or you can buy an Irreverent guide.

What the Irreverents give you is the lowdown, the inside story. They have nothing to sell but the truth, which includes a balance of good and bad. They praise, they trash, they weigh, and leave the final decisions up to you. No tourist board, no chamber of commerce will ever recommend them.

Our writers are insiders, who feel passionate about the cities they live in, and have strong opinions they want to share with you. They take a special pleasure leading you where other guides fear to tread.

How irreverent are they? One of our authors insisted on writing under a pseudonym. "I couldn't show my face in town again if I used my own name," she told me. "My friends would never speak to me." Such is the price of honesty. She, like you, should know she'll always have a friend at Frommer's.

Warm regards,

Michael Spring

Michael Spring
Publisher

a disclaimer

Prices fluctuate in the course of time, and travel information changes under the impact of the varied and volatile factors that influence the travel industry. Neither the author nor the publisher can be held responsible for the experiences of readers while traveling. Readers are invited to write to the publisher with ideas, comments, and suggestions for future editions.

about the author

Theodore Fischer is the author of *Cheap/Smart Travel*, *Cheap/Smart Weekends*, *Fodor's Pocket Guide to New York City*, and literally billions of magazine travel stories. Like most Washington residents, he moved there from someplace else.

photo credits

Page i: © f-stop Fitzgerald Inc.; Page ii: courtesy of the Washington, D.C. Convention and Visitors Association; Page iv: top courtesy of Red Sage, middle and bottom © f-stop Fitzgerald Inc.; Page v: © f-stop Fitzgerald Inc.; Page vi: top courtesy of Watergate Hotel, middle and bottom courtesy of the Washington, D.C. Convention and Visitors Association; Page vii: top courtesy of America, bottom © f-stop Fitzgerald Inc.; Page viii: top courtesy of the Washington, D.C. Convention and Visitors Association, bottom courtesy of Morrison-Clark Inn.

Balliett & Fitzgerald, Inc.
Series editor: Holly Hughes / Executive editor: Tom Dyja / Managing editor: Duncan Bock / Production editor: Howard Slatkin / Photo editor: Maria Fernandez / Editorial assistants: Jennifer Lebin, Iain McDonald
Macmillan Travel art director: Michele Laseau

Design by Tsang Seymour Design Studio

All maps © Simon & Schuster, Inc.

Air travel assistance courtesy of Continental Airlines

MACMILLAN TRAVEL
A Simon & Schuster Macmillan Company
1633 Broadway
New York, NY 10019

ISBN 0-02-860884-4
ISSN 1085-4738

special sales

Bulk purchases (10+ copies) of Frommer's Travel Guides are available to corporations at special discounts. The Special Sales Department can produce custom editions to be used as premiums and/or for sales promotions to suit individual needs. Existing editions can be produced with custom cover imprints such as corporate logos. For more information write to: Special Sales, Simon & Schuster, 1633 Broadway, New York, NY 10019.

Manufactured in the United States of America

contents

introduction

There's nothing new about irreverent views of Washington—they've been pouring in since day one. An early surveyor, Major Andrew Ellicott, sneered that "this country intended for the Permanent Residence of the Congress, bears no more proportion to the country about Philadelphia... for either wealth or fertility, than a crane does to a stall-fed ox." Thomas Jefferson called it "that Indian swamp in the wilderness," a slur that stuck, although it's really a Potomac River flood plain. Charles Dickens dubbed Washington "head-quarters of tobacco-tinctured saliva," and Civil War-era visitor G.A. Sala called it "a vast practical joke... the most 'bogus' of towns—a shin-plaster in brick and mortar with a delusive frontispiece of marble."

Washington Confidential, by Jack Lait and Lee Mortimer, a guidebook-cum-exposé that came out in 1951, described Washington as "a made-to-order architectural paradise with the political status of an Indian reservation, inhabited by 800,000 economic parasites; no industries but one, government, and the tradesmen and servants and loafers and scum that feed on the highest average per capita income in the world, where exist the soundest security, the mightiest power, and the most superlative rates of crime, vice, and juvenile delinquency anywhere." (Things are different now; there are only about 600,000 parasites).

Poet Dylan Thomas enigmatically remarked, "Washington isn't a city, it's an abstraction." JFK's famous put-down—"A city of southern efficiency and northern charm"—was downright inspired. You could go on in that vein forever: a city of Republican compassion and Democratic frugality, of yuppie spontaneity and redneck subtlety, of bureaucratic ingenuity and entrepreneurial conscience, of gay decorum and fundamentalist irony, of liberal piety and conservative angst, of Eastern Seaboard egalitarianism and Middle American chic... you get the idea.

Suffice it to say that Washington is a special place, both in the dictionary sense of "unusual" and "extraordinary," and in the Church Lady sense of "Isn't *that* special." The U.S. Constitution made sure it would forever be a special place by ordering Congress to establish and "exercise exclusive legislation in all cases whatsoever" over a "seat of the Government of the United States," a weird political setup that's caused trouble ever since.

This squishy lowland at the convergence of the Potomac and Anacostia Rivers became the capital thanks to the kind of big-time insider horse-trading that would soon become the Washington way of life. Two pre-Beltway sharpies, New Yorker Alexander Hamilton and Virginian Thomas Jefferson, brokered the deal. They convinced the South to finally pay off the soldiers who won the Revolutionary War, in return for which they promised that the capital would *not* be one of the big cities of the North—New York, Philadelphia, or (God forbid!) Boston.

The first European visitor to the neutral site, which President Washington himself chose for the capital in 1789, was supposedly Captain John Smith (otherwise known as the male lead in Disney's *Pocahontas*). The District of Columbia was originally a ten-mile-square diamond straddling the Potomac, the unofficial border of North and South; it encompassed 69 square miles of Maryland and 31 square miles of Virginia. (The Virginia section was retroceded back to the state in 1846.) D.C. originally included Washington City, the thriving river towns of George Town, Maryland (later Georgetown), and Alexandria, Virginia, and a few other villages. Nowadays, the District of Columbia and Washington City are one and the same.

An imperious Frenchman named Pierre L'Enfant ("Langfang" in the local argot) was hired to plan the new capital. L'Enfant didn't last long—he was history by 1792—but his plan to overlay an orderly American-style street grid with the verdant roundabouts and broad boulevards of Paris was eventually carried out. City-planning-wise, the other major contribution came in the early 20th century from the Senate's McMillan Commission, which amplified l'Enfant's plan by laying out the National Mall, showplace site of the major monuments and museums.

The city of Washington has always had a stormy relationship with its Congressional masters. Citizens of Washington have no representation in Congress, which makes them frequently yell "Taxation Without Representation" and launch noisy campaigns for D.C. statehood. D.C. had home rule, with an elected mayor and council, from 1802 until a presidential Commission decided to take over in 1874. A Constitutional amendment granted Washingtonians the right to vote for president in 1961; full home rule, with an elected mayor and city council, was restored in 1975, though the arrangement is pretty unwieldy—Congress still has the right to approve the entire city budget.

Home Rule II has been a mixed blessing, partly due to the character of the elected home rulers themselves. Mayor Marion S. Barry was elected to his fourth four-year term in 1994, even though following his third term he served time in a federal prison, after being found guilty of drug possession. During Barry's absence, city council president John Wilson committed suicide for reasons unknown. By 1995, D.C. had become such a municipal basket case—bloated payrolls, invisible services, ridiculous schools—that Congress appointed a financial control board to run its affairs. For the foreseeable future, this mostly black, overwhelmingly Democratic city will be totally in thrall to appointees of a mostly white majority Republican Congress that Washingtonians had no voice in electing. Lousy governance, but great political theater.

However, the City of Washington itself is just the hub of a metropolitan area of nearly 4 million, the eighth largest population cluster in the U.S. It sprawls across Virginia and Maryland suburbs and exurbs and sends commuter tentacles as far as West Virginia and southern Pennsylvania. The people of the Washington area are 95 percent the same as everybody else—but it's that other five percent that makes them a bizarre race unto themselves.

For one thing, Washingtonians (which we'll call everyone who lives in the capital—they're not really capitalists) are pretty damn affluent. The metro area's average annual salary is nearly $33,000, ranking it tenth among 284 U.S. metropolitan statistic areas. The Washington area ranks first in percentage of families with incomes between $100,000 and $150,000 a year, and fourth in the $150,000+ class.

Washington is also a city of paper pushers (okay, computer inputters now). It produces hardly anything except laws, policy, and opinions. Washington has 15,000 lobbyists and only 5,000 journalists to keep an eye on them; it also has 56 lawyers for every 1,000 residents, compared to a mere 8 per 1,000 in New York City.

If you live around Washington, you work for the federal government or for a private business whose existence depends directly on federal government business. Or your spouse does. Or your children or close relatives do. Or your best friend or neighbors do. Or your customers do. Where other Americans see waste, fraud, and graft, Washingtonians see money in their own pockets or in the pockets of someone near and dear. When Washingtonians hear loudmouth politicians trash some federal program as a criminal squandering of almighty taxpayer dollars, they wonder if the agency is still hiring or still taking bids.

Washingtonians are smart enough not to flaunt this minority view in mixed company (i.e., among outside-the-Beltway aliens). Time is on their side—they know they'll survive this gang of government bashers just like all the others. But be forewarned that ad hominem attacks on "bureaucrats" and "tax-and-spend policies" and "big government" won't go down very well. Let loose with such sentiments around here and you're likely to get a pretty icy response.

Washington also seems more racially heterogeneous than a lot of other places. This is partly a federal thing: since the feds have pushed nondiscriminatory hiring, minorities permeate the government and occupy positions of authority. Private enterprise follows suit. But it's also a District thing: since the city is about 70 percent black, this "minority" maintains undisputed control of the local government now and for the imaginable future. Blacks don't feel threatened here. The races for the most part don't live together, but they work together and to some extent play together, and in general they seem fairly comfortable with each other. Pretty much the same holds true for Washington's large and conspicuous gay/lesbian community; best to leave remarks about Biblical abominations against nature out there in the boondocks.

Tolerance extends across political party lines, too. Washingtonians know better than to mouth off about politics until they know where their listener stands. This helps people of different parties coexist, but it does lend a don't-ask-don't-tell blandness to human interaction around here.

Washingtonians can afford to be tolerant because, down deep, they know how good they've got it. There are definitely some perks to living in this "special" city. Congress might fiddle while the District goes down the tubes, but it will never allow the Nation's Capital part of town to degenerate—congresspeople need a place they can show off to constituents. Washingtonians have access to some of the world's greatest museums—free access, I might add, so they can afford to pop in for a minute to check out a single exhibit or maybe a single work of art. Riding the partially federally funded Metrorail system is one of Washington's great pleasures. The American taxpayer also picks up the tab for Washington's parks; and federal security forces supplement the budget-busted, woebegone D.C. Police. (And don't think we're not grateful. As a Washingtonian, I want to personally thank all of you Americans for your generous tax support.)

But although almost everyone who lives here comes from someplace else—another state, or another country—you can hardly say that Washington is cosmopolitan. Except for the Hispanic neighborhoods around Adams-Morgan and a few Asian enclaves in the suburbs, there are no neighborhoods lined with intriguing shops, no charming offbeat restaurants that have been there forever. Beyond the Mall—which *Washington Confidential* likened to the white marble mausoleums of a well-kept cemetery—you might expect to find a vibrant, sophisticated city. Forget it. Washington is not a Great City like New York or Paris. It has no high-profile charisma. Washington is an Important City à la Brussels and Zurich, a lackluster place where people take care of weighty business.

Yes, Washington is a special place, and yes, it's fun to visit. You come here to walk in the footsteps of history (corny as it sounds), to behold soul-stirring monuments, to observe close-hand the workings of government, to visit august museums of art and of the sciences.

But if it's urban electricity you're after, you'd be better off in Cleveland.

Washington, D.C. Neighborhoods

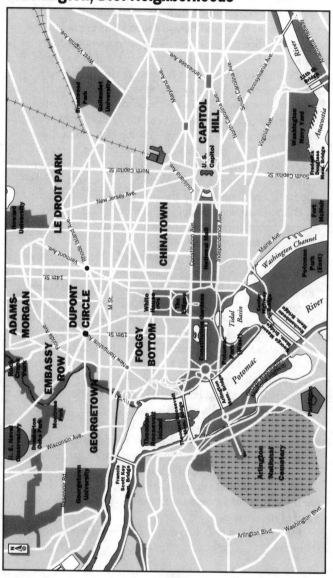

you
probably
didn't know

What the locals call the place... Seldom "Washington"—too big a mouthful, laden with negative implications of Big Government, and too easy to confuse with that state out there. More common locutions: "D.C." or "The District."

Which attractions require advance planning... During high season, which despite anti-Washington fervor now extends from March through November, it's nearly impossible to see some of the most popular visitor attractions unless you've done something about it in advance— making phone calls, writing letters, spending money, or using the influence of friends in high places (in other words, business as usual around here). As soon as you decide to visit Washington, request tickets for a VIP tour of the **White House** from your congressperson (U.S. House of Representatives, Washington, DC 20515) or senator (U.S. Senate, Washington, DC 20510). VIP tours, beginning between 8:15 and 9am, jump the visitor center lines and also take in more White House than the UIP (Unimportant People) tour. The trick is to write early—*at least* a month in advance—because representatives receive a limited allotment of tickets. Remind them that you're a tourist—

and you vote. (And you might as well ask them to toss in tickets to the **Bureau of Engraving and Printing**, the galleries of the **U.S. Capitol**, and a VIP tour of the **FBI**, which is just the same as the nobody's tour except that you don't have to wait in line.) Only the Permanent Exhibition of the **U.S. Holocaust Memorial Museum** requires advance planning; reserve tickets through TicketMaster (tel 800/551–7328, 202/432–7328) up to three months in advance. A fee ($2.75/ticket plus $1.25/order) is charged to your credit card, and tickets are held at the "will call" desk (at the Holocaust Memorial's 14th St. entrance). The only area of the **State Department** open to visitors holds the Diplomatic Reception Rooms, and that's only on guided tours, only if you make reservations in advance—absolutely no walk-ins or stand-bys. You can make a reservation up to 90 days before your visit—and should do it at least two weeks in advance during peak season. Call 202/647–3241, fax 202/736–4232, TDD 202/736–4474, leaving a voice-mail message or fax detailing when you'd like to come; someone will call back to confirm. You'll need a picture ID for admission; tours may be canceled with no notice when the reception rooms are required for affairs of state. At the **Washington Monument**, a limited number of set-time tickets are distributed to those who've been savvy enough to call a special TicketMaster number (tel 800/505–4040) up to 9pm the day before. Tickets costs $1.50, plus a 50¢ surcharge. The rest of the tickets are given away on a first-come basis each day beginning at 8:30am.

How to get Redskins tickets... The Redskins owe their phenomenal popularity to the fact that the team is one of the only subjects about which all factions here—Democrats/Republicans, blacks/whites, men/women—can have civil conversations. This despite the raging controversy over whether the name "Redskins" is a vile racist slur (as most Native Americans contend) or "a tribute to a valorous people" (as team owner Jack Kent Cooke insists). Consequently, Redskins tickets are impossible to obtain using normal procedures. There is no box office; season tickets for every seat have been sold in perpetuity, and if you're old enough to read this you won't live long enough to get off the waiting list. Nonetheless, you can always get a Redskins ticket if you want one badly enough and are willing to pay the price. Ticket agencies may have them (see Entertainment), but each ticket is likely to cost in the low three figures. For last-minute impulses, there are always scalpers working illegally but quite openly in the four-block strip between the Stadium/Armory Metrorail station and RFK Stadium, starting about two hours before game time. Ticket availability and prices are determined by market forces that factor in seat location, weather conditions, opposing team, and the Redskins' position in the standings. Prices can range from below list price to three or four times that. (Lately, scalper tickets have been plentiful and fairly cheap.) Bring a seating chart and be prepared to comparison-shop and haggle.

What the president's doing today... The only comprehensive daily run-down of *everything* going on in Washington—presidential movements; the activities of Congress, the courts, and federal agencies; new economic reports; other meetings around town; and guests on local and national talk shows—appears in the **"Washington Daybook"** of the *Washington Times*, the right-wing daily published by the Unification Church (Moonies). If you're sure that Anita Hill was lying and that Vincent Foster was murdered

---

Washington's Best Internet Sites
• **Planet Earth Home Page, D.C. Info** (*http://www.nosc.mil/planet_earth/washington.html*). *The mother of all home pages accesses all government agencies, the Metro system and the airports, what's new in Washington, even job openings.*
• **White House** (*http://www.whitehouse.gov*). *Speeches, letters, briefings, even a note from Socks; updated daily.*
• **U.S. House of Representatives** (*http://www.house.gov*). *Wide range of House documents plus direct access to individual members' home pages.*
• **THOMAS** (*http://www.thomas.loc.gov*). *Gingrich-inspired compendium of pending legislation, committee reports, and other congressional documents, plus C-SPAN schedules and congressional e-mail addresses.*
• **FBI** (*http://www.fbi.gov*). *Ten Most-Wanted list, chronologies of cases in progress, visitor info.*
• **CIA** (*http://www.odci.gov/cia*). *No secrets, but as close to The Agency as you're likely to get.*
• **Treasury Department** (*http://www.ustreas.gov*). *Virtual visit to Bureau of Printing and Engraving—if you've got the graphics capability.*

WASHINGTON, D.C. | YOU PROBABLY DIDN'T KNOW

(probably by Hillary Clinton), you might be able to handle the rest of the paper.

How to find out what's really going on with the D.C. government... Tune in to the "D.C. Government Hour" on the "Derrick McGinty Show," Fridays at noon on WAMU radio (FM 94.7). You'll be treated to a spirited discussion (i.e., shouting match) between McGinty, WAMU political analyst Mark Plotkin, guest journalists, and local pols who drop by or call in.

How to ride an escalator, Washington style... Washington's Metrorail system has some of the world's longest escalators—the five-minute-plus ride at the Wheaton station is reputedly the world's second longest. Washington also has some of the world's most self-important and impatient people. Consequently, Washingtonians do not *ride* on escalators, they *walk* on escalators. Standees are expected to cling single-file to the righthand railing while movers and shakers whiz past on the left. Only tourists stand on the left or, worse yet, stand side-by-side to obstruct passers-by.

Where to eat cheaply and well on the Mall... With a few exceptions (see Dining), museum cafeterias around here are crowded, crummy, and exorbitantly expensive. Avoid them by walking a block or two to one of the attractive, reasonably priced cafeterias located in your federal government's office buildings. Along with the opportunity to rub elbows with ID-wearing bureaucrats, cafeterias almost always have deli counters, by-the-ounce salad and pasta bars, and pizza; many have food stations catered by real restaurants. Best and most convenient: the **Department of Agriculture** (enter on the north side of C Street, SW, between 12th and 13th streets); the **Department of Energy, Forrestal Building** (second level—climb stairs on west side of 10th Street, SW [l'Enfant Promenade], between Independence Avenue and C Street); the **Department of Commerce** (enter on east side of 15th Street, NW, between Constitution Avenue and E Street); the **Department of the Interior** (enter on north side of C Street, NW, between 18th and 19th streets). Note: picture ID (driver's license or passport) may be required for entrance.

How much to fear the parking cops... The Washington city government may have its problems (to say the least), but one island of lofty morale and Prussian efficiency is its parking police. If you doubt that, leave your car in one of the metered spaces on downtown streets *after* the 4–7pm rush-hour parking ban goes into effect. By 4:03, you *will* be ticketed—everybody will be ticketed—and the fine is a hefty $50.

Where to rub (and bend) elbows with politicos... On the Senate (north) side of the Capitol, try **La Colline** (tel 202/737–0400; 400 North Capitol St., NW), a forthright bar in a French-country restaurant, or **The Monocle** (tel 202/546–4488; 107 D St., NE), a portrait-festooned nerve center of the Old Boy Network. Over the Hill, check out the raucous (for Washington) scene at **Bullfeathers** (tel 202/543–5005; 410 1st St., SE) and **Tune Inn** (tel 202/543–2725; 331 1/2 Pennsylvania Ave., SE) where low-level staffers go slumming.

How to hobnob with Washington society... For information on balls, galas, premieres, fashion shows, house tours, regattas, and charity benefits all over the Washington area, check out the "Benefits" section of the monthly *Washingtonian* magazine, or the "Datebook" column in the *Washington Post* "Sunday Style" section on the last Sunday of every month. Events listed are open to any members of the public willing to fork over from $5 to well up into the hundreds.

Security Clearance

The level of security in Washington has a lot to do with the latest headlines. As soon as the Persian Gulf War broke out in 1991, security checkpoints quickly popped up in buildings you could previously enter without challenge. Within days of the Oklahoma City bombing in April 1995, the priceless Gutenberg Bible was spirited away from the Library of Congress to parts unknown, and tours of the NASA Goddard Space Flight Center were suspended (they resumed in July). At all times, you must pass through metal detectors to enter most government buildings. In addition, many visitor attractions require adults to show a picture ID; a passport or a driver's license with photograph will do the trick. Such measures wouldn't keep out anybody less conspicuous than maybe Saddam Hussein, but if there is trouble, at least they have a name on record. Attractions that require ID: FBI, State Department, Treasury Building, Pentagon. You also have to show a driver's license to drive onto a military installation (Washington Navy Yard, Fort McNair).

Where else to see cherry blossoms... When the traffic gets so clogged that you can't make it to the Tidal

Basin area in cherry blossom time, locals drive out to the Kenwood section of Bethesda, Maryland, where cherry trees build a canopy of blossoms over the street. The Kenwood peak season (late March–early April) begins and ends a week or so later than the Tidal Basin peak. To get there, take Wisconsin Avenue north, turn west on River Road, then north on Brookside Drive—then follow your nose.

How not to be a crime victim... Washington is a dangerous place, but its astronomical crime rate is somewhat misleading. This is a relatively small city—68 square miles, population 600,000 and falling—and all the vast, relatively crime-free neighborhoods that normally modulate crime rates in other big cities happen to lie outside the District, in the Maryland and Virginia suburbs. Washington's disproportionate amount of inner city is where most of the perps and victims live and most crime takes place. Violent crime against visitors is rare, though not rare enough. The areas most frequented by visitors— The Mall, Dupont Circle, Foggy Bottom, Georgetown, Adams-Morgan—are patrolled by a plethora of city, federal, and private police forces, so they're pretty safe by day and night. Some parts of town are okay by day but best to avoid after dark; other sections are to be avoided at all times. Unfortunately, some 24-hour "bad neighborhoods" begin a block away or around a corner from popular attractions and hotels.

Here's a crude but effective way to redline out the scary parts of Washington. Get a street map of the city; start at the top of the diamond, where 16th Street, NW, crosses the city limits into Silver Spring, Maryland. Draw a line along 16th Street south to Massachusetts Avenue, NW. Draw your line east on Massachusetts past Union Station to 8th Street, NE. Then south along 8th Street to I-395 (it's the Eisenhower Freeway but nobody calls it that) and then west along the freeway to the Potomac River. Keep to the west and north of that line, and you should be fine. With only a few exceptions, all the attractions and virtually all restaurants and entertainment spots described in this book lie within this golden polygon.

The true meaning of "Watergate"... The real Watergate is a curving ceremonial staircase that rose out of the Potomac north of Memorial Bridge and due east of the Lincoln Memorial. Originally, foreign emissaries, conquering heros, and returning explorers disembarked from their ocean-going vessels there. Up through World War II, Waterside Drive, which passes between the steps and the river, was closed to traffic; soldiers and war workers could use the roadway and steps as seating for National Symphony concerts performed from a floating bandstand. Well, the steps between the roadway and the water are gone now; the riverside concerts have been discontinued. In the 1960s, the name "Watergate" was appropriated for a luxury hotel-apartment-office complex a half-mile downriver—and the rest is history.

Washington's best mystery series... Good mysteries tell you what goes on beneath the city's surface, and two mystery writers' series are by lifelong insiders. Margaret Truman, daughter of "Give 'em Hell" Harry, writes the Capital Crime Series, so far nearly a dozen books on Murder in/at/on landmarks like the Pentagon, Kennedy Center, Capitol Hill, and Embassy Row. Although FDR's son Elliott Roosevelt died in 1990, his publisher keeps posthumously releasing thrillers about murders committed in various White House venues (Blue Room, Oval Office, Pantry, etc.) and solved by his mother, First Lady Eleanor Roosevelt. With no pedigree whatsoever, Richard Timothy Conroy writes witty whodunits (*Mr. Smithson's Bones, The India Exhibition*) set deep in the bureaucratic bowels of the Smithsonian Institution. Warren Adler's improbable shamus is Fiona FitzGerald, gorgeous daughter of a U.S. senator, who labors as a D.C. homicide cop. In George P. Pelecanos's trilogy, electronics-salesman-turned-private-dick Nick Stefanos acts like Washington is just like any other scumbag-laden, decaying urban American sinkhole; *Down By the River Where the Dead Men Go* is his latest and best.

accomm

1

odations

Even as respect
for the federal
government
declines,
Washington's
popularity as a
visitor destination

just keeps growing. (Maybe folks just want to see the enemy up close.) But staying in the capital, even for a few days, can become a serious financial matter. Washington hotels charge an average daily rate of over $120, higher than any other major U.S. city except, of course, New York. Add a 13 percent occupancy tax (not to mention the measly $1.50 per night surcharge) and you're talking major bucks. There's no shortage of rooms, of course—Washington has nearly 24,000 hotel rooms. Accommodations here range from legendary seats of power to borderline fleabags. The capital is also uniquely well-endowed with apartment houses built in the first third of the 20th century and at some later date converted into transient hotels. These converts, available in all price categories, generally offer larger-than-normal rooms with non-cookie-cutter furnishings, often include kitchen facilities, and are situated in what were and are the city's prime residential neighborhoods. What Washington lacks are great numbers of good, clean, budget-priced hotels or motels in good, clean, safe neighborhoods. Hotels like that can be found in the suburbs and in outlying areas, but there are very few in the heart of the city. Rooms for under $100 per weekday night usually entail some fairly major form of human sacrifice.

Another thing Washington hotels lack is free parking. Unless listings indicate free parking or no parking at all, the hotel charges between $7 and $15 a night for parking. There's really no way around this.

On the other hand, it has become de rigueur in Washington's most expensive hotel rooms to have three phones (including one in the bathroom), dataports for modems, room safes built into closets, and ironing boards with irons.

Winning the Reservations Game

Hoteliers here seem to suffer Jekyll-and-Hyde mood swings—when you inquire about vacancies, their responses range from "No way in hell" to "Attention, Shoppers!" Just as Washington's political operators adjust rapidly to minute changes in the political climate, Washington hotels are adept at juggling rates according to shifts in demand. Ask a Washington hotelier how much a room costs and instead of a number you get a dissertation that begins in one of three ways. "It depends on the…

"… Season." April, May, and June are traditional high season, thanks to school trips, patriotic family spring vacations, and the best weather of the year. Congress is still in session, and if there's also a big convention is town, it may be almost impossible to find a room. And high season now laps over onto both shoulders, with ever increasing occupancy rates in March and July. August is weaker, even though the weather is no more miserably hot or humid than it was in July. Tourist business and business business pick up in September and October. Few vacationers come from November through February, so rates then are at their lowest and heavily advertised bargain packages abound. Check the travel sections of the *New York Times*, *Boston Globe*, *Chicago Tribune*, and *Washington Post*.

"… Day of the week." Washington is essentially a business travel sort of town, and hotels empty out during the weekend. The grander they are, the farther the rates fall.

"… Things you wouldn't think mattered about or couldn't know." Washington also has these mini–seasons only hotel people know about. The week after Labor Day, for instance, is dead. The week after the week after Labor Day begins one of the hottest seasons of the year. The city all but hibernates after the leaves fall in November.

So if it's off-season, or some special knowledge leads you to believe demand may be slack, get ready to haggle.

What if you have called around, tried the hotel discounters and bed & breakfast reservation services (see below), and still come up empty? Call a friend in Washington, maybe a friend you don't know you have. *Everyone* has three elected friends in Congress—two in the Senate, one in the House of Representatives—and all of them employ aides to provide "constituent services." They're supposed to help you if they can. Call the main switchboard at the Congress (tel 202/224–3121) and ask to be connected to your senator or representative. If you're not an American citizen, someone at your embassy may be willing to help. If you can't provoke an act of Congress, call the Washington office of your trade association or professional society. Washington is the home office for more associations and professional societies than anyplace else, and all of them have "membership relations" staff on the payroll. These aren't necessarily institutionalized services—you're just banking on the fact that, as local residents who deal with a lot of travelers, these staffers will know something or someone you don't. The worst thing they can say to you is "no"—and, if you've tried to find a hotel room during inauguration, the Cherry Blossom Festival, or some other impossible time, you're already used to hearing that.

Hotel discounters are the semiclandestine "bucket shops" of the lodging industry. They can sell empty rooms the hotels can't sell themselves, at steeply reduced rates—as much as 70 percent less than the rate you'd get from the hotel's reservation desk—as long they don't make too much noise about what they're doing. They're especially useful for last-minute reservations. Most of the time, hotel discounters can offer a choice of four or five hotels in your price range and preferred location. Call around to various discounters (toll-free) for the best deal. Services are free, but each discounter has its own procedures for guaranteeing and canceling reservations. Services operating only in the Washington area (D.C. and suburban Maryland and Virginia) include: **Capitol Reservations** (tel 800/847–4832, 202/452–1270, fax 202/452–0537) and **Washington D.C. Accommodations** (tel 800/554–2220, 202/289–2220, fax 202/483–4436). National/international services that handle Washington accommodations are **Accommodations Express** (tel 800/444–7666), **Hotel Reservations Network** (tel 800/964–6835), **Quikbook** (tel 800/789–9887), **RMC Travel** (tel 800/782–2674), and **Room Exchange** (tel 800/846–7000).

Bed & breakfast reservation services are the lodging-industry yentas who match guests with the absolutely perfect private home, apartment, or small inn. Locate the B&B on a map before you commit; if you're not sure about the neighborhood, seek a disinterested opinion. **Bed & Breakfast Accommodations, Ltd.** (tel 202/328–3510, fax 202/332–3885, e-mail bnbaccom@aol.com) books over 80 homes and inns in Washington, Maryland, and Virginia, as well as rooms in private homes, from $45 per night. **Bed & Breakfast League/ Sweet Dreams & Toast** (tel 202/483–9191) handles rooms and suites in D.C. private homes and apartments.

Is There a Right Address?

Deciding where to stay in Washington is, like Washington politics, a matter of making the least painful compromises. Almost all D.C. hotels are clustered within a triangle that fans northwest from Union Station to Georgetown and Woodley Park. But the differences between these neighborhoods—in terms of price, safety, inherent appeal, and nighttime activity—are pronounced.

Several hotels claim **Capitol Hill** locations, but that's somewhat misleading. "Capitol Hill," in local parlance, refers to the geographical elevation originally known as Jenkins Hill and for the last 200 years surmounted by the Capitol Building. Capitol Hill is also the name of the slowly gentrifying town house neighborhood to the east and south of the geographical Capitol Hill. These so-called Capitol Hill hotels, however, are all southwest of Union Station at the bottom of the Hill, four to six blocks north of the Capitol. They're generally reasonably priced, and they do offer proximity to the Capitol, the east end of the Mall, and Union Station. There's not a lot going on after dark around here, however, and safety becomes an issue once government workers close up shop.

The hotels north and east of the **White House** have history, elegance, and high voltages of Washington "juice." It's the most expensive part of town and quiet after dark, but, with all kinds of cops patrolling, the area is very, very safe. There's lots of lodging variety around the **Convention Center** (9th and H streets), from mega-convention properties to charming boutique hotels and historic B&Bs. They're fairly near Mall attractions and the Metro, but the area is dead at night, and the northern fringe (Massachusetts Avenue) borders a raunchy part of town. **Dupont Circle** is what used to be called a "swinging neighborhood," full of bars and restaurants and sidewalk cafes and street traffic at all hours. Dupont hotels run the gamut from the Ritz to the pits—The Ritz-Carlton and the shared-bath Brickskeller Inn are both on the same

JFK (and Jackie) Slept Here

• *Apartment 502, The Dorchester House, 2480 16th Street, NW.* Ensign JFK's bachelor pad while with the Office of Naval Intelligence, October 1941–January 1942. He was transferred out of town after involvement with Danish reporter Inga Arvad, a suspected German spy.
• *1528 31st Street, NW.* JFK's Georgetown digs in 1947–48, his first term in the House of Representatives.
• *3271 P Street, NW.* Home of Senator John F. Kennedy, 1953.
• *3321 Dent Place, NW.* Where newlyweds JFK and Jackie lived January–June 1954.
• *3307 N Street, NW.* Town house JFK purchased in 1957, where he and Jackie lived during the election campaign, moving into the White House in early 1961. Check out the plaque that reporters placed on the house across the street (3302 N Street), thanking its owners for a warm haven during "the cold winter of 1960–61."
• *3038 N Street, NW.* Home of socialite Pamela Harriman, wife of former New York governor W. Averell Harriman, where Jackie lived immediately after JFK's assassination in 1963.
• *3017 N Street, NW.* Town house Jackie lived in after the assassination, until the crush of tourists and paparazzi forced her to flee to New York.

ACCOMMODATIONS | WASHINGTON, D.C.

block, for example. It's a good place to find family-friendly all-suite properties. Safe and vibrant, within walking distance of many attractions, and with a Metro station under the circle itself, Dupont Circle is a good place to be. Ever heard of **Scott Circle** (or its namesake, Mexican-American War hero General Winfield Scott? Ever heard of the Mexican-American War?)? Well, Scott Circle itself is just a convoluted traffic circle where 16th and N streets, and Massachusetts and Rhode Island avenues collide. At the circle, a statue of Scott himself parades (on a horse that was sculpturally altered from mare to stallion following vehement complaints by Scott fanciers). But it's close to desirable spots like the White House, Dupont Circle, and Metro stations, and it's safe as long as you stay south of Rhode Island and west of 16th. For price and convenience, it's a good compromise, with mostly chain hotels on or near the circle.

Foggy Bottom is a residential and academic (George Washington University) coda between the K Street business district and the bright lights of Georgetown. Many Foggy Bottom hotels (with the notable exception of The Watergate) are converted apartment buildings, offering suites with kitchen facilities for the same rates as regular rooms elsewhere. No nightlife, but Georgetown is within walking distance along safe streets and there's a Metro station at hand. **Georgetown** is a nice place to visit *and* a nice place to live—but you wouldn't want to park there. Washington's oldest neighborhood, it has no Metrorail service. So one of the best reasons for choosing a Georgetown hotel is that you can walk to its many restaurants, bars, and clubs. Safe at all hours, quiet once you get off the main drags (Wisconsin Avenue and M Street), it's your best shot at an authentic Old Washington experience. That said, there are few hotels here, and their rates are high.

Woodley Park is an upper-middle-class residential neighborhood with two large convention hotels, a handful of B&Bs, and nothing in-between. The National Zoo and large swatches of Rock Creek Park are in Woodley Park. There are plenty of good restaurants near the Metro station on Connecticut Avenue and even better ones in nearby Adams-Morgan.

Arlington, Virginia, just across the Potomac from downtown D.C., has two hotel clusters. Rosslyn, within walking distance of Georgetown across the Key Bridge, flaunts the lofty office towers forbidden by Washington's height restrictions, and the hotels here are mostly high-rise chain properties (close to the Rosslyn Metro station), as well as budget motels along Route 50. Crystal City consists of several large business and convention hotels in a developed area between the Pentagon and National Airport. **Old Town Alexandria,**

Virginia, has shops, restaurants, bars, plenty of museums and galleries, and other cobblestone-streetside attractions. Unfortunately, most Alexandria hotels are chain properties situated about 10 blocks north of Old Town, beyond walking distance from the historic charm and nowhere near a Metro station. But these hotels have good-for-Washington rates and operate free shuttles to the places guests most want to go.

Suburban hotels near Metro stops are found in **Silver Spring**, **Bethesda**, and **Chevy Chase, Maryland**, directly north of the District. Beyond that, hotels are located at various interchanges of the Capital Beltway, some of them in or near shopping malls. The **Tysons Corner, Virginia**, area, around the northwest curve of the Beltway, has the best selection of first-class hotels. Chain hotels and motels along the Beltway in **Prince George's County, Maryland**, east and south of D.C., have the lowest rates. Why would anybody come all the way to Washington and stay out in some mall beside the interchange for the road to Palookaville? It's the rates, stupid. Hotel rates in Fairfax County, Virginia, for example, which surrounds Arlington and Alexandria and includes nearly the entire Virginia section of the Beltway, average nearly $40 a night less than D.C. rates. Plus, they give you free parking.

The Lowdown

Democracy's dowagers... Washington's grandest older hotels, the ones where powermongers stay, within shooting distance of the White House, all have a European ancestor in common: The **Hay-Adams**, **The Carlton**, and **The Jefferson** were all built in the 1920s, either as hotels or as apartment buildings, by Englishman Harry Wardman. Before he lost everything in the stock market crash of 1929, Wardman was responsible for scores of ornate Washington buildings, including the British Embassy. The **Hay-Adams** is so named because its prime Lafayette Square site was once occupied by the adjoining homes of John Hay, Lincoln's private secretary and later a Secretary of State, and statesman/historian Henry Adams, author of *The Education of Henry Adams*. **The Carlton** sits at the nexus of presidential Washington (16th Street) and lawyer/lobbyist Washington (K Street), while **The Jefferson** is in the 16th Street Corridor, five blocks north of the White House—close enough to be involved in the action but far enough away to harbor strategic retreats. The only other hotel that approaches Wardmanian pomp, the **Willard Inter-Continental**, has also known reversals in fortune. The "old" Willard, an amalgamation of row houses a block from the White House, was where the Pinkertons hid Lincoln before his inauguration, and where Julia Ward Howe composed "The Battle Hymn of the Republic." The "new" Willard opened in 1901, closed in 1968 (shortly after Martin Luther King Jr. wrote his "I Have a Dream" speech in a room here), but reopened in 1986 with its corridors-of-power ambience totally restored.

Top o' the polls... Two places keep leapfrogging one another in annual magazine polls of Washington's finest hotels, though neither one is what you'd call typically Washingtonian. The **Four Seasons Hotel** is in Georgetown, it's one of the newer hotels in town (1979), and the lobby has more palms than pols. The décor—tasteful antiques and reproductions from various eras—is opulent enough, but the real draw is its service, the product of a two-to-one staff/guest ratio and Javier Loureiro, the *Andrew Harper's Hideaway Report* Concierge of the Year (1994). Washington's other top-rated hotel isn't even *in* Washington: the **Morrison House**, off a brick alley in Old Town Alexandria. Though it was actually built in the Reagan era, the Morrisons—Robert and Rosemary—designed their 45-room inn to blend in with the Federal period architecture of the rest of Old Town, and filled it with Early American antiques and reproductions. It's got a perfect combination of classic decor and up–to–the–minute amenities—you can lie here in a four-poster bed *and* use a remote to change cable TV channels.

Ain't what they used to be... The **Renaissance May-flower Hotel** has loads of history—fully documented and illustrated in a coffee-table book—but revolving-door managements that let in a bit of dowdiness around the edges has driven the smartest money elsewhere. Originally opened in 1901, the **Willard Inter-Continental** closed in 1968, then reopened in 1986—only to discover that the locus of Washington power had shifted from Pennsylvania Avenue to K street. The **Sheraton Washington** has a split personality: though part is a classy twenties-era former home to three future presidents and others of note, most of it is a newish convention holding-pen with the largest room inventory in the city.

Scenes of the crimes... "Watergate" comes immediately to mind, specifically the June 17, 1972, burglary of the Democratic National Committee campaign headquarters, in an office building within the ultraluxury riverfront Watergate Complex. The complex's saw-toothed balconies conceal costly condos, a glitzy boutique mall, and the **Watergate Hotel**, brimming with the overstated elegance esteemed by the nabobs of international business and diplomacy. The Plumbers actually surveyed the situation from the distinctly more plebeian **Howard Johnson Lodge** across Virginia Avenue, first from Room 419 and then from Room 723, which had a better view. On March 30, 1981, President Reagan was shot by John Hinckley after delivering a speech at the **Washington Hilton**. In the early 1980s, Ollie North wined and dined prospective Contra contributors in the bar and restaurant of the cushy **Hay-Adams Hotel**, across Lafayette Square from his Old Executive Office Building lair. While it wasn't exactly a crime, there was one widely reported instance of outrageous conduct at the **Capital Hilton** in 1961 when, during his inaugural ball, JFK reputedly snuck up to Frank Sinatra's suite for a tryst with Angie Dickinson. Turning to local news, on January 18, 1990, the FBI used Room 727 of the **Vista International Hotel** as a studio for a videotaped demonstration by Mayor Marion S. Barry Jr. on how to smoke crack cocaine. Barry left office, served a brief term in prison—and was re-elected mayor in 1994. But the hotel, despite a change in name to the **Washington Vista Hotel**, still suffers the stigma, and consequently charges surprisingly low rates for such luxury digs.

Foreign affairs... The **Hotel Sofitel** was converted in the mid-1970s from a 1906 apartment building, but it wasn't until it was taken over by the French Sofitel chain in early 1994 that it acquired its many Gallic affectations. Three floors of designated *chambres fumeurs* are sometimes simply not enough for all the foreign smokers here who want them. The "center of Irish hospitality in America," the **Phoenix Park Hotel** used to be the Commodore, until it was bought in 1982 by Dan Coleman—his Dubliner

Restaurant and Pub next door was such a smash, he decided to add a hotel, and name it after Dublin's grandest park. Expect Irish wool carpets, Waterford crystal chandeliers, and a staff comprised of about 40 percent FBI (Foreign Born Irish). All parties in the Irish troubles—including controversial Irish Republican Army political leader Gerry Adams—stay here while in Washington. The **Barceló Hotel Washington** betrays its Spanish roots with wrought-iron exterior trims, the terrific tapas bar in its restaurant, Gabriel, and a lobby infused with the atmosphere of heavy smokers. Think Costa del Sol rather than patrician Madrid, however—Barceló Hotels is best known for fun-in-the-sun Mediterranean resorts, and the hotel occupies a converted 1968 apartment building. Eastern European middle managers, not to mention Czech Republic president Vaclav Havel, and other intriguing characters lurk around the below-ground-level lobby of the **Embassy Row Hotel**; it's said that many a coup has been plotted in a secluded corner here, while "invisible security" is provided by the anonymous private security forces of the many nearby embassies.

Spurious foreign affairs... The **Canterbury Hotel** sounds Olde Englishe (it's actually owned by a hotel chain based in Bombay), but the theme is limited to 18th-century English prints in guest rooms, the Union Jack pub serving British brews, and Chaucer's restaurant, serving dishes like ploughman's lunch and bangers-and-mash. The Merchant-Ivory thing is pulled off more successfully at the **Henley Park Hotel**, which was converted in the 1980s from a Tudor-style 1918 apartment building. Expect reproductions of 18th-century hunt club prints, afternoon tea served beside a roaring fire, and the overall tweedy hush of an English country estate. Despite the name, the **Normandy Inn** doesn't seem particularly French, perhaps because it's actually owned by Ireland's Irish Inns. The **ANA Hotel**, formerly the Westin, is owned by Japan's All Nippon Airways, but the only hint of the Japanese connection is the Japanese Breakfast (grilled mackerel, miso soup, seaweed, pickled vegetable, melon, omelet, green tea) on the menu of the Parisian-style Bistro restaurant.

For the tasseled-loafer set... When out-of-town lobbyists and lawyers wearing tasseled loafers (and female fashion equivalents still clad in power suits) come to Washington, there are certain hotels in which they feel compelled to stay, to encounter local counterparts in hotel "juice" bars. The Town and Country Lounge off the lobby of the **Renaissance Mayflower** pours heavy martinis and Manhattans no matter who's in office, and boasts of passing more bills than Capitol Hill. The Mayflower has been a hub of extracurricular political activity from the moment it opened in 1925, and even more so since the nexus of power has gravitated in its direction toward K Street and Connecticut. Nixon lived here before he was president; Truman, while president, snuck over for poker; the young (and recently married) Senator John F. Kennedy maintained a suite (No. 812) that Secret Service agents referred to as "JFK's playpen." The Starbuck's espresso bar along the block-wide lobby is one of the best (and cheapest) places to spot brand-name politicos and newshounds from the ABC bureau next door. The term "lobbyist" was coined with a snarl of contempt by President Grant in reference to would-be power brokers in the public areas of the old Willard, an amalgamation of row houses a block from the White House; today The Round Robin in the **Willard Inter-Continental**, with a smallish round bar and view of Pennsylvania Avenue, often serves as a kind of neutral zone for confrontations between the press (the National Press Club is across the street) and politicians. A bit farther removed from the hurly-burly, **The Jefferson** is a site for discreet encounters, in its clubby restaurant decorated with memorabilia from Jefferson and other American solons (don't touch—the precious documents are protected by an alarm system). On Capitol Hill, lobbyists tend to convene at the Powerscourt restaurant in the **Phoenix Park Hotel**, that bastion of Irish affability, or in the long lobby bar at the sleek **Washington Court on Capitol Hill**.

More funky than quaint... Washington's smallest hotel (seven rooms), the **Swiss Inn**, located in a circa 1900 red-brick town house, could almost be a B&B, except that they only provide the bed. Guests can prepare meals on the full-sized appliances in every room and eat them at breakfast bars. It's easy to find—look for the mural covering the entire west side wall. Painted by prominent local muralist G. Byron Peck, it depicts the life of African American abolitionist leader Frederick Douglass.

For those who hate surprises... Two efficient, moderately priced chain hotels around Scott Circle—**Holiday Inn Central** and **Doubletree Park Terrace**—provide nothing to complain about. The **Governor's House**, just off Scott Circle (on the safe southwest edge of the area), is a former Holiday Inn, with only minimal changes made since its declaration of independence from that dependable chain. The new name refers to Governor Gifford Pinchot of Pennsylvania, first chief of the Forest Service, who once lived on this site. The **Hotel Washington** has a power-central location half a block from the White House, but somehow it feels like the main hotel in a small midwestern city: Both the Rotary (Wednesday) and the Kiwanis (Thursday) meet here. One senses that somebody could do a lot more with it, but I for one hope they leave features like executive floors and chrome-plated lobbies to the big chains. Dowdiness has its charms, too.

Indoor backpacking... Many hotels aspire to "European style," but only the **Allen Lee Hotel** knows what it really means: small rooms, grubby furniture, bathrooms down the hall. Popular with foreigners because, opines management, "Our name begins with 'A,' so we're the first one listed in the budget-hotel guides." It's on George Washington University's Foggy Bottom campus, so students should feel at home. The **Brickskeller Inn**, a converted 1910 apartment house formerly called the Marifex Hotel, doesn't have many frills (few private bathrooms or TVs) but you can count on the three C's: clean, convenient (two blocks from Dupont Circle), and cheap (singles from $35 per night). Twelve-person double-bunked dorm rooms (single-sex) and shared baths are standard at the tidy and efficient **Washington International Youth Hostel**, but rates are rock bottom, and unlike many hostels, they'll let you hang around all day in the lounge, perusing free newspapers from around the world. Unlike other Washington hotels, the hostel's peak season is mid-July through September, when young Western European students on summer break occupy most of the $25-a-night bunks.

Suite deals... In Foggy Bottom, the all-suite-est part of town, Kennedy Center artistes, George Washington University academics, and State Department bureaucrats mingle at the **Inn at Foggy Bottom**. G.W., which owns the place, has laid on a Williamsburg motif befitting the college's team name (the Colonials), but don't expect period charm in this 1960s midrise. Upper-strata business types prefer the **St. James**, also in Foggy Bottom, which has even larger rooms, some with balconies—it was converted from an apartment building in the late 1980s, which explains why the reception area is hidden in a rear corner of the discreet lobby. One former U.S. president called **One Washington Circle** "one of the most truly outstanding hotels in the nation"—all right, so it was Nixon, but he liked the hotel enough to make the eighth-floor Suite Grande Classe his post-Watergate Washington outpost. (Some rooms have a view of the Watergate complex in the distance.) If the Nixon connection doesn't reel you in, this suite hotel is also a magnet for traveling musicians and show folk, and its West End Café has a popular jazz bar— identify all the photographs of artists, writers, and musicians on the wall and you get some sort of prize. In Dupont Circle, the **Embassy Square Suites** (not to be confused with the more costly Embassy Suites a few blocks away) is a budget-priced hotel catering mainly to long-term guests from developing countries and American families on short-term stays. All rooms at the **Canterbury Hotel** are what they call "junior suites"—others might call them rooms with alcove kitchens. This converted 1960s apartment building is a bit shabby around the edges, but at least the rates are reasonable. The **Georgetown Dutch Inn**, usually filled with Europeans and (for reasons the management can't quite fathom) South Americans, is nothing fancy, but it's as close as you get to a bargain in Georgetown—and it's one of few Washington hotels with free parking. Outside of central D.C., the **Embassy Suites—Chevy Chase Pavilion** is coolly efficient but expensive, while the somewhat bland **Sheraton Suites Alexandria**—a bit out-of-the-way on the northern tip of Alexandria—tosses in buffet breakfasts.

Family values... The **Embassy Square Suites** has a lot of what families are looking for in a D.C. hotel: large suites ranging from efficiencies to two bedrooms, a safe and convenient location two blocks from the Dupont Circle Metro, an outdoor pool, free breakfast, room-service pizza, low regular rates, and lots of discount deals. The **J.W. Marriott**, steps from the Mall and attached to a food court, has an indoor pool and has yanked out all those kid-tempting guest room minibars; over weekends, when the business contingent absents itself, the place halves its rates to draw in families. Both the **Holiday Inn Central** and **Howard Johnson Lodge** have low rates, safe locations, rooftop outdoor pools, and game rooms. Two-room suites at the **Sheraton Suites Alexandria** makes it a conspicuous bargain for families willing to negotiate the transportation (there's a free shuttle service to Old Town Alexandria and the Metro), and it has an indoor pool. If you're willing to pop for high rates, **The Carlton** caters to youngsters under 12 with free ice cream with dinner, milk and cookies at bedtime, and unlimited access to the toy chest.

For Democrats... Democrats seem like downright rightwingers among the progressive activists who favor the **Tabard Inn**. Plush as it is, the **Ritz-Carlton** has been a Democratic clubhouse for years: Al Gore's family owned it (when it was the Fairfax) and little Al practically grew up there. The namesake of the **Jefferson Hotel** founded the Democratic party, and the Clinton-Gore campaign made it its headquarters. The **Embassy Inn** and **Windsor Inn** accommodate Democratic-style alternative lifestyles more comfortably than Republican-style family values.

For Republicans... In return for pomp, Republicans overlook the unpleasant circumstances associated with the **Watergate Hotel** (besides, all the s-word happened in the office building next door). After the fall, Nixon always stayed at **One Washington Circle**, his suite overlooking the Ronald Reagan Institute of Emergency Medicine at (Federalist) George Washington University. The **Henley Park Hotel** scores with G.O.P. types, with its décor inspired by British aristocracy and its location directly across the street from a conservative think-tank, the Cato Institute. The **Georgetown Inn** represents what Republicans seem to want for the whole country: modern conveniences in the clubby privileged style of the good old 18th century.

For Perotistas... The **Swiss Inn**: no frills, and only seven rooms.

Likeliest to have royalty... While royalty on official visits usually mooch rooms at the government's Blair House, sometimes they have to stay in hotels. The Duke and Duchess of Windsor and Japanese Prince Takamatsu stayed at the venerable **Renaissance Mayflower**. Queen Elizabeth II made the grande dame hotel **The Carlton** her headquarters during a 1991 visit. King Hussein of Jordan and the royal family of Spain opted for somewhat newer costly digs at the **Four Seasons** in Georgetown. Since reopening in 1986, the **Willard Inter-Continental** has entertained 54 heads of state (28 presidents, 11 prime ministers, three kings, two queens) and two U.N. Secretaries General. And King Arthur—or at least Robert Goulet, while playing King Arthur in a revival of *Camelot*—occupied the $2,100-a-night Presidential Suite at the **Ritz-Carlton**. He liked the color scheme so much that he appropriated it for his New York apartment.

May I get that for you, sir?... The multinational staff of the **Hotel Lombardy**—including the operator of the throwback non-automatic elevator—speaks a combined 29 languages and treats guests like they're participating in some experiment in international goodwill. This converted 1929 apartment building on the cusp of Foggy Bottom and K Street has the raffish air and international flavor of a hostel for grownups; many guests come from abroad to do business with the World Bank, Eximbank, and the Peace Corps, whose headquarters is just around the corner. The staff at the hippie-dippie **Tabard Inn** assume you must be good people or you wouldn't be staying with them: Flash them a peace sign. Staying at the **Embassy Inn** (or its close sibling, the **Windsor Inn**), feels like staying with friends—real good friends who let you know what's happening all over town but still clean your bathroom and make your bed. Lacking parking facilities, for example, they cheerfully give you a hand-out, "Musical Cars: The Perils of Rush Hour Parking." The **Phoenix Park Hotel** staff is almost aggressively friendly, like ambassadors-at-large for the entire Irish nation.

Snootiest staff... The **Watergate Hotel** rolls out the red carpet for senators, ambassadors, and dukes (or higher), while others may get a polite version of the bum's rush. Some of the staff at the **Morrison-Clark Inn** look as though they're just waiting for you to bust one of their antiques. Owned and largely occupied by the French, **Hotel Sofitel** makes snootiness de rigueur—no extra charge.

Deluxe addresses, bargain rates... The **Bellevue Hotel** has the lowest rates in convenient Capitol Hill—near Union Station, the Capitol, east Mall agencies and associations—plus a complimentary breakfast buffet. The Bellevue's two decorating motifs are Packards and the Senators, Washington's twice-lost major league baseball team. The non-innlike **Inn at Foggy Bottom**, near K Street offices and a block from the Metro, is another converted apartment building with good-sized rooms; an older, shabbier version is the **Hotel Lombardy**, on the eastern edge of Foggy Bottom even closer to the towers of K Street. A former Holiday Inn, the **Governor's House** has some bargain-priced kitchenettes and junior suites a few blocks from K Street. It's popular with midlevel government business travelers, both U.S. (to whom it guarantees a low per diem rate year-round) and foreign, especially those attached to the nearby Australian, Philippine, and Peruvian embassies. The **Hotel Washington** is somewhat more costly, as you'd expect from its prime location—across the street from the Treasury Building and a half-block from the White House—but it's got the lowest rates in this high-rent district, and it offers plenty of discount programs to soften the blow. One block of cut-rate rooms along an underground corridor of Georgetown's **Latham Hotel** has shutters and stoops and period doorways that mimic real Georgetown town houses. The catch? No views *at all*, because they don't even have exterior windows. If you're game to try the suburbs, the **Quality Hotel Silver Spring** offers substantially more luxury for the buck than most places in D.C., plus Metro convenience and easy access to the Beltway.

Well-kept secrets... You can hardly tell that the eight-year-old **St. James** is an all-suite luxury hotel—even when you're standing in the lobby. No signs, no advertising, except for a couple of magazine blurbs posted on the lobby wall. Quirky **H.H. Leonard's** keeps its 12 rooms occupied almost all the time (even by some celebrities), exclusively via word-of-mouth. No exterior signs even hint that this is, in fact, an inn. The unassuming **Embassy Inn** and **Windsor Inn** are considered special Washington places by Europeans, gay people, and visitors to the environmentally minded organizations—like the Audubon Society and the Wildlife Federation—quartered nearby.

Few brewster boosters quaffing the Brickskeller's 550-plus beers realize they could sleep it off in a decent cheap hotel right over their heads, the **Brickskeller Inn**.

Best of the burbs... The best hotel in the suburbs is one regularly voted the best hotel in the Washington area: the ersatz 1790s **Morrison House** in the heart of Old Town Alexandria. Another reason for leaving D.C. is that you can have a view of its landmarks from afar, which is the case at the 18-story **Ritz-Carlton Pentagon City** in Arlington. It also happens to be the most lavish and expensive hotel outside D.C. limits, loaded with antiques and art. The best qualities of **Quality Inn-Iwo Jima** are free parking and a five-minute walk to the Rosslyn Metro, the Orange and Blue lines' first stop in Virginia. Nothing that special about this three-story roadside motel, but rates are low and it's extremely logistically correct. As the name promises, it's around the bend from the Marine Corps War Memorial ("Iwo Jima Monument"), for what that's worth. Okay, the blandly upscale **Embassy Suites-Chevy Chase Pavilion** is technically within D.C., but Western Avenue, outside its front door, marks the border with Maryland.

Gym dandies... How good is the Fitness Center at the **ANA Hotel**? Good enough for Ah-nold, whenever he comes to town pursuing his many political connections. Easily the best in the city, it has a cafe which serves reasonably but not fanatically healthy food, a large indoor pool, virtual-reality bikes, and treadmills equipped with personal TVs, VCRs, and phones. The **Four Seasons** in Georgetown has a trilevel fitness center with a lap pool, exercise bikes, treadmills, and StairMasters equipped with individual TVs, VCRs, and personal stereos. Yet another way in which the **Ritz-Carlton Pentagon City** tries harder than its swank Embassy Row older sibling is by having a fitness center with many more exercise machines and a lap pool.

When everything else is filled... Irreverent does not equal irrational, so presumably you're not crazy enough to arrive in Washington with no place to stay. But not all needs can be anticipated, and when our friend could find no room at any other inn after a snowstorm cancelled just about everybody's flight out of town, he was welcomed at the **Canterbury Inn** near Dupont Circle, which delivered a small suite for a decent price. The **Best Western Arlington**, lost in a twilight zone off I-395 betwixt the Pentagon and the Beltway, almost always has a few vacancies, possibly because it's so incongruously large—325 rooms in a two-story motel or seven-story hotel tower. The rooms have no character, but hey, if you're stuck…. If you're really desperate, a board beside Gate G at Union Station advertises a dozen or so low-priced hotels and B&Bs, and there's a phone with direct free connections to any of them.

The Index

$$$$$	over $200
$$$$	$150–$200
$$$	$100–$150
$$	$50–$100
$	under $50

Price ranges apply to standard double rooms, midweek, peak season—the highest price you could pay. These rates do include the 13 percent combined D.C. sales and occupancy tax and $1.50/room/night surcharge.

Allen Lee Hotel. The location is great—in Foggy Bottom on the George Washington University campus—the neighborhood's safe, and the price of under $50 for the *best* room in the house is very right. All rooms air-conditioned, with phone and TV. No restaurant (unless you count vending machines), but a lively international scene in the lobby…. *Tel 202/331–1224, 800/462–0186. 2224 F St., NW, 20037, Foggy Bottom–GWU Metro, Taxi zone 2A. 85 rms., 30 with private bath. $*

ANA Hotel. The ANA Hotel ("ay-en-ay", not "Anna"), owned by Japan's All Nippon Airways, appeals to upper-strata

American and international businesspeople with large quiet rooms and a broad and inviting greenery-filled lobby. It's located in the "West End," a tony-sounding name for an otherwise anonymous strip on the cusps of Dupont Circle, Foggy Bottom, and Georgetown. The fitness center is tops.... *Tel 202/429–2400, 800/ANA–HOTELS, fax 202/457–5010. 2401 M St., NW, 20037, Foggy Bottom–GWU or Dupont Circle Metros, Taxi zone 2A. 415 rms. $$$$$*

Barceló Hotel Washington. Two blocks from the Dupont Circle Metro, this Spanish-owned hotel appeals to U.S. and foreign business travelers and vacationers, with its large rooms and sensible rates. Gabriel, its Spain-meets-Santa Fe restaurant, packs them in for its weekend early-evening all-you-can-eat tapas bar. Outdoor pool, exercise room.... *Tel 202/293–3100, 800/333–3333, fax 202/857–0134. 2121 P St., NW, 20037, Dupont Circle Metro, Taxi zone 1B. 298 rms. $$$$*

Bellevue Hotel. A converted 1928 apartment house around the corner from Union Station, the Bellevue offers large rooms and proximity to the station, the Capitol, and government bureaus; a full American buffet breakfast is included in its rate. Free parking on weekends.... *Tel 202/638–0900, 800/327–6667, fax 202/638–5132. 15 E St., NW, 20001, Union Station Metro, Taxi zone 1D. 144 rms. $$$*

Best Western Arlington. Rooms are comfortable and spacious, the neighborhood is safe, and rates are comparable to far more remote locations. Shuttle service from National Airport, but you'll feel stranded without your own wheels. Free parking, outdoor pool, exercise room.... *Tel 703/527–4400, 800/426–6886, fax 703/685–0051. S. Glebe Rd. and I-395 (exit S. Glebe Rd. north), Arlington, VA 22206. 325 rms. $$*

Brickskeller Inn. Virtues include a convenient and safe Dupont Circle location and rates so low that business travelers on a per diem stay here and pocket the difference. The three floors of rooms have air conditioning, TVs, sinks, private baths, views of Rock Creek Park—but not all at the same time. State your priority at check-in because management won't ask. No parking.... *Tel 202/293–1885, fax 202/293–0996. 1523 22nd St., NW, 20037, Dupont Circle Metro, Taxi zone 1B. 44 rms., 2 with private bath. $*

Canterbury Hotel. All "junior suite" accommodations, which means one largish room with separate kitchenettes and with queen, double queen, or king beds; some have fold-out sofas. Prime location on a quiet residential block off Dupont Circle. Complimentary continental breakfast, access to YMCA fitness center one block away.... *Tel 202/393–3000, 800/424–2950, fax 202/785–9581. 1733 N St., NW, 20036, Dupont Circle Metro, Taxi zone 1B. 99 rms. $$$*

Capital Hilton. The former Statler and Statler Hilton lacks the character and history of its older, grander White House-area neighbors—it's an upper-level convention and business hotel esteemed more for convenience and efficiency than ambience. Well-equipped health club and maps to three "Monumental Miles" jogging courses.... *Tel 202/393–1000, 800/445–8667, fax 202/639–5784. 16th and K streets, NW, 20036; Farragut North, Farragut West, or McPherson Square Metros, Taxi zone 1B. 543 rms. $$$$$*

The Carlton. The Carlton—a 1920s version of an Italian palazzo—boasts of making special arrangements for particular guests. Japanese guests get a yukata (Japanese robe), the *Yomiuri* Japanese newspaper, and a traditional Japanese breakfast; when Cher stays here, she gets Pepperidge Farm Goldfish, plain M&Ms, and a guest room converted into a personal gym. All meals are served in the Mediterranean-style Allegro restaurant. Health club.... *Tel 202/638–2626, 800/325–3535, fax 202/638–4231. 16th and K streets, 20006; Farragut North, Farragut West, or McPherson Square Metros, Taxi zone 1B. 197 rms. $$$$$*

Doubletree Hotel Park Terrace. This spiffy, sharply run business hotel works well for visitors to nearby associations and to National Geographic headquarters, a block away, as well as European tour groups and executives of General Electric (a partner in Doubletree Hotels). Fitness center.... *Tel 202/232–7000, 800/222–8733, fax 202/332–7152. 1515 Rhode Island Ave., NW, 20005, Dupont Circle or Farragut North Metros, Taxi zone 1B. 219 rms. $$$$*

Embassy Inn/Windsor Inn. Twin sisters in the outermost orbit of Dupont Circle. Rooms at the Embassy are mostly small, suited only for singles or couples; the Windsor looks a bit spiffier and offers a variety of room sizes (including a private-entranced, nine-room annex for large parties). Both feature complimentary continental breakfast and sherry in the salon from 5 to 9. No parking.... *Tel 800/423–9111, fax 202/234–3309. Embassy Inn: tel 202/234–7800; 1627 16th St., NW, 20009; 38 rms. Windsor Inn: tel 202/667–0300; 1842 16th St., NW, 20009; 45 rms. Dupont Circle Metro, Taxi zone 1B. $$*

Embassy Row Hotel. A block from Dupont Circle at the threshold of Embassy Row, this 25-year-old independent property teems with foreign visitors. Rooftop outdoor pool, tiny fitness center, and the Bistro Twenty Fifteen restaurant on site.... *Tel 202/265–1600, 800/424–2400, fax 202/328–7526. 2015 Massachusetts Ave., NW, 20036, Dupont Circle Metro, Taxi zone 1B. 200 rms. $$$$*

Embassy Square Suites. Options include Embassy Suites (efficiencies), Attaché Suites (one-bedrooms), and Diplomat Suites (two bedrooms/two baths); families who want a semblance of privacy and elbow room are advised to spring for the bedroom. Complimentary continental breakfast. No restaurant, but there is room service. Small health club.... *Tel 202/659–9000, 800/424–2999, fax 202/429–9546. 2000 N St. NW, 20036, Dupont Circle Metro, Taxi zone 1B. 250 rms. $$$*

Embassy Suites-Chevy Chase Pavilion. Part of Chevy Chase Pavilion, a fairly posh shopping mall, on the borderline between the Chevy Chase section of D.C. and Chevy Chase, Maryland. Not much going on in the immediate neighborhood, but the mall has a Metro station, a 14-minute ride to the center of D.C.... *Tel 202/362–9300, 800/EMBASSY, fax 202/686–3405. 4300 Military Rd., NW, 20015, Friendship Heights Metro, Taxi zone 4B. 198 rms. $$$$*

Four Seasons Hotel. Washington's highest room rates are charged at this deluxe property, opened in 1979 on the threshold of Georgetown, with rooms overlooking Rock Creek and the C&O Canal. Rooms have tasteful antiques and reproductions from various eras but the fitness center is all nineties. Cocktails, tea, Sunday jazz brunch served in junglelike Garden Terrace lobby restaurant; formal dining at Seasons.... *Tel 202/342–0444, 800/332–3442, fax 202/342–1673. 2800 Pennsylvania Ave., 20007, Foggy Bottom–GWU Metro, Taxi zone 2A. 196 rms. $$$$$*

Georgetown Dutch Inn. One- and two-bedroom suites (some bilevel) fill this seven-story property just off M Street in Georgetown. Each suite has a full kitchen with stove and coffeemaker, plus two TVs. Complimentary continental breakfast, free underground parking.... *Tel 202/337–0900, 800/388–2410, fax 202/333–6526. 1075 Thomas Jefferson St., NW, 20007, Foggy Bottom–GWU Metro, Taxi zone 2A. 47 rms. $$$*

Georgetown Inn. Double-paned windows insulate streetside rooms from the raucous Wisconsin Avenue late-night scene. The 30-some-year-old inn creates a haven of delicate civility amid the Georgetown nightlife scene, a reminder of what Georgetown maybe used to be. The clientele is split pretty evenly between business travelers and leisure guests.... *Tel 202/333–8900, 800/424–2979, fax 202/625–1744. 1310 Wisconsin Ave., NW, 20007, Foggy Bottom–GWU Metro, Taxi zone 2A. 95 rms. $$$$*

Governor's House Hotel. Most of the larger-than-normal Holiday Inn-style rooms have pull-out sofas; good bargains available for kitchenette suites. Outdoor pool and complimentary access to YMCA fitness center across the street. Herb's restaurant boasts the city's largest patio.... *Tel 202/296–2100, 800/821–4367, fax 202/331–0227. 17th St. and Rhode Island Ave., NW, 20036, Farragut North or Dupont Circle Metros, Taxi zone 1B. 152 rms. $$$*

H.H. Leonard's. Nonguests can wander this quirky little inn's dimly lit warren of Victorian chambers and purchase whatsoever strikes their fancy. Complimentary continental breakfast. No restaurant; outdoor pool.... *Tel 202/659–8787, fax 202/659–0547. 2020 O St., NW, 20036, Dupont Circle Metro, Taxi zone 1B. 12 rms. $$$$*

Hay-Adams Hotel. Guest rooms re-create the color schemes of 23 cheery English country houses, and within its hushed Italian Renaissance lobby you'd never guess that a big government was going on just outside the door. Lafayette restaurant serves three meals and tea.... *Tel 202/638–6600, 800/424–5054, fax 202/638–3803. 16th & H streets, NW, 20006, McPherson Square or Farragut West Metros, Taxi zone 1B. 137 rms. $$$$$*

Henley Park Hotel. Across the street from conservative think-tank the Cato Institute, this ersatz-English country estate is the sort of place where you take tea beside a roaring fireplace. Some rooms have four-poster beds, and the Coeur de Lion restaurant offers the ambience (though, thank goodness, not the cuisine) of an English baronial estate. Access to exercise facilities at Morrison-Clark Inn (see below) a half-block away.... *Tel 202/638–5200, 800/222–8474, fax 202/638–6740. 926 Massachusetts Ave., NW, 20001, Metro Center Metro, Taxi zone 1C. 96 rms. $$$$*

Holiday Inn Central. Rooms are big, bright, cheerfully furnished, and almost new: the place was totally rebuilt in 1991. It has a convenient and safe Scott Circle location (as long as you turn right at the front door if you go out at night). Guests get a free continental breakfast and access to one of the city's few rooftop pools, all for rates almost always under three figures. All-you-can-eat buffets at every meal in the Avenue Café.... *Tel 202/483–2000, 800/248–0016, fax 202/797–1078. 1501 Rhode Island Ave., NW, 20005, Dupont Circle or Farragut North Metros, Taxi zone 1B. 213 rms. $$*

Hotel Lombardy. Rooms in this friendly Foggy Bottom hotel are spacious and most have apartment-sized kitchens; about 50 rooms have been renovated and refurnished, and they're about $20 per night more expensive. Intimate Café Lombardy features northern Italian cuisine. Health club access.... *Tel 202/828–2600, 800/424–5486, fax 202/872–0503. 2019 I St., NW, 20006, Foggy Bottom–GWU or Farragut West Metros, Taxi zone 1B. 126 rms. $$$*

Hotel Sofitel. Situated across Connecticut Avenue from the Washington Hilton, its rooms are unusually large, with former apartment kitchenettes inconveniently adapted into small studies. Foreign (mostly French) guests account for much of the clientele, from 40 percent in May and June up to 70 percent during summer. Complimentary admission to Washington Sports Club across the street. Bistro-style Trocadero serves three meals a day.... *Tel 202/797–2000, 800/424–2464, fax 202/462–0944. 1914 Connecticut Ave., NW, 20009, Dupont Circle Metro, Taxi zone 2A. 145 rms. $$$$*

Hotel Washington. It's the hotel closest to the White House and, opened in 1913, the oldest continuously operating hotel in town. The lobby looks like it could use a break, but it's nearly a block wide with lots of comfortable places to sit, and there's a good people-watching bar at one end. The rooms, some with Mall/Monument views, have classy two-poster beds and lace curtains. Health club. No parking, but public lot nearby.... *Tel 202/638–5900, 800/424–9540, fax 202/638–1595. 15th St. and Pennsylvania Ave., NW, 20004, Metro Center or McPherson Square Metros, Taxi zone 1A. 350 rms. $$$$*

Howard Johnson Lodge. HoJo brings its roadside ambience to prim Foggy Bottom with a lobby full of videogames and chow served up at Bob's Big Boy. Free indoor parking.... *Tel 202/965–2700, 800/654–2000, fax 202/965–2700, ext 7910. 2601 Virginia Ave., NW, 20037, Foggy Bottom–GWU Metro, Taxi zone 2A. 192 rms. $$*

Inn at Foggy Bottom. Hardly your antique-crusted cutesy inn, this is a mid-1960s-era nine-story building located mid-block on a quiet residential street near the G.W. campus and the State Department. Complimentary continental breakfast. Access to Watergate Hotel fitness center two blocks away.... *Tel 202/337–6620, 800/426–4455, fax 202/298–7499. 824 New Hampshire Ave., NW, 20037, Foggy Bottom–GWU Metro, Taxi zone 2A. 95 rms. $$$*

J.W. Marriott Hotel. The flagship of over a dozen Marriotts bestrewn around the Washington area, the J.W. Marriott is an efficient modern downtown business and convention hotel in a fantastic location, within walking distance from all Mall attractions. As part of the National Place complex, it's connected to the National Press Club and the Shops at National Place mall. It has one of the city's biggest indoor pools, a fitness center, and four restaurants on site.... *Tel 202/393–2000, 800/228–9290, fax 202/626–6991. 1331 Pennsylvania Ave., NW, 20004, Metro Center Metro, Taxi zone 1A. 773 rms. $$$$$*

The Jefferson. A clubby atmosphere prevails here, with rooms of various configurations arranged in a U-shape around a courtyard, each ostentatiously furnished with pieces acquired at various junctures since 1923. The Jeffersonian connection is apparent only in the restaurant at the Jefferson—named The Restaurant at The Jefferson. Access (paid) to nearby University Club fitness center.... *Tel 202/*

347–2200, 800/368–5966, fax 202/331–7982. 16th and M streets, 20036, Farragut North Metro, Taxi zone 1B. 100 rms. $$$$$

Latham Hotel. Two red-brick buildings inconspicuously occupying a slope between Georgetown's bustling M Street and the pastoral C&O Canal. Standard rooms have canal, river, or Georgetown "treetop" views, and there are also nine bilevel carriage suites and four poolside bungalows. Its three-meal restaurant is the acclaimed casual California-French-style Citronelle. Outdoor pool.... *Tel 202/726–5000, 800/368–5922, fax 202/337–4250. 3000 M St., NW, 20007, Foggy Bottom–GWU Metro, Taxi zone 2A. 143 rms. $$$$*

Morrison-Clark Inn. With sweeping verandas and a girdle of greenery, the antique-laden Morrison-Clark exposes Washington's southern soul. It's popular for weddings and honeymoons. Massachusetts Avenue-side rooms with porches have more character, but inner courtyard rooms are quieter and more cozy. Complimentary continental breakfast service in the Club Room of the popular Morrison-Clark restaurant. Exercise room.... *Tel 202/898–1200, 800/332–7898, fax 202/289–8576. 1015 L St., NW, 20001, Metro Center Metro, Taxi zone 1C. 54 rms. $$$*

Morrison House. Though it looks like a place where George Washington did sleep, it's really some 200 years newer. Ye olde country inn ambience of smallish rooms with 2- or 4-poster beds is modulated with up-to-date touches like hair dryers, remote-control TVs, and bathroom phones. Elysium restaurant features Mediterranean cuisine and lively piano bar; afternoon tea served from 3 to 5. Health club privileges.... *Tel 703/838–8000, 800/367–0800, fax 703/684–6283. 116 S. Alfred St., Alexandria, VA 22314, King Street Metro. 45 rms. $$$$$*

Normandy Inn. This tidy, sedate hotel occupies a converted circa 1960 private-school dorm on a safe, quiet street in Kalorama Heights, above Dupont Circle and Embassy Row. No restaurant. Guests can use the outdoor pool at the nearby Washington Court hotel (see below) at no charge, or pay to use the equally convenient Washington Sport Club.... *Tel 202/483–1350, 800/424–3729, fax 202/387–8241. 2118 Wyoming Ave., NW, 20008, Woodley Park–Zoo or Dupont Circle Metros, Taxi zone 2A. 75 rms. $$$*

40

One Washington Circle. Five classes of suites are available, all with full kitchens and balconies; some overlook a statue of G.W. himself in the hub of Washington Circle. The West End Café is a popular jazz bistro. Outdoor pool, access to health club.... *Tel 202/872–1680, 800/424–9671, fax 202/887–4989. One Washington Circle, NW, 20037, Foggy Bottom–GWU Metro, Taxi zone 2A. 151 rms. $$$$*

Phoenix Park Hotel. This trim 9-story former Commodore Hotel, built in 1927 a (blarney) stone's throw from Union Station, today owes its good fortune to what it calls "Irish hospitality." A new wing opens May 1996.... *Tel 202/638–6900, 800/824–5419, fax 202/393–3236. 520 North Capitol St., NW, 20001, Union Station Metro, Taxi zone 1D. 151 rms. $$$$*

Quality Hotel Silver Spring. This plush 13-story former Sheraton Inn is a handy place to stay, near the City Place outlet mall and three blocks from the Metro. Free parking. Indoor pool, exercise room with sauna.... *Tel 301/589–5200, 800/228–5151, fax 301/588–1841. 8727 Colesville Rd. (from I-495, go south on Colesville Rd. [U.S. 29]), Silver Spring, MD 20910, Silver Spring Metro. 254 rms. $$*

Quality Inn-Iwo Jima. This fairly standard chain motel sits three blocks from the Rosslyn Metro and within medium walking distance over the Key Bridge to Georgetown, and parking is free. Outdoor pool; exercise room.... *Tel 703/524–5000, 800/221–2222, fax 703/522–5484. 1501 Arlington Blvd. (U.S. 50, exit N. Queen St. north), Arlington, VA 22209, Rosslyn Metro. 141 rms. $$*

Renaissance Mayflower. Lobbyists and politicians of all parties swill Manhattans and martinis in the Town and Country Lounge. Now owned by Hong Kong-based Renaissance Hotels International, the Mayflower has spacious rooms and bellmen who remember Nixon as a good tipper. Small fitness club, passes to YMCA available.... *Tel 202/347–3000, 800/HOTELS–1, fax 202/466–9082. 1127 Connecticut Ave., NW, 20036, Farragut North Metro, Taxi zone 1B. 659 rms. $$$$$*

Ritz-Carlton. The jet set's most refined wing stays at this Embassy Row landmark, in reasonably large guest rooms furnished with Federal and Empire antiques and reproductions. The hotel was completely renovated in 1993, though the Jockey Club restaurant, designed by Al's cousin Louise Gore, has hardly changed an English hunt club-style hair since it opened in 1961, the night before JFK's inauguration. Fitness center.... *Tel 202/293–2100, 800/241–3333, fax 202/293–0641. 2100 Massachusetts Ave., NW, 20008, Dupont Circle Metro, Taxi zone 1B. 206 rms. $$$$$*

Ritz-Carlton Pentagon City. This highrise Ritz lacks the bloodlines of its Embassy Row sister, but it has twice as many rooms, public areas filled with valuable 18th- and 19th-century antiques, and, from many of its 18 floors, sweeping views of the National Mall. Fitness center.... *Tel 703/415–5000, 800/241–3333, fax 703/415–5060. 1250 S. Hayes St. (from I-395, go south on U.S. 1, west on 15th St., right on Hayes), Arlington, VA 22202, Pentagon City Metro. 345 rms. $$$$$*

Sheraton Suites Alexandria. This suburban red-brick highrise offers modern two-room suites with two TVs, two phones, and free American-style breakfast buffets. The Fin & Hoof restaurant is on site; there's an indoor pool and a weight room, plus free shuttle service to Old Town, National Airport, and National Airport Metro station.... *Tel 703/836–4700, 800/325–3535, fax 703/548–4514. 801 N. St. Asaph St. (George Washington Pkwy. south, east on First St.), Alexandria, VA 22314. 249 suites. $$$*

Sheraton Washington. Washington's largest hotel and mega-convention site strives to keep all its rooms occupied by offering some low-priced standard rooms and steeply discounted off-peak deals and packages. Two outdoor swimming pools, a fitness room, two restaurants, and a gourmet deli.... *Tel 202/328–2000, 800/325–3535, fax 202/234–0015. 2660 Woodley Rd. at Connecticut Ave., NW, 20008, Woodley Park–Zoo Metro, Taxi zone 2A. 1,505 rms. $$$*

St. James. One-bedroom, two-bedroom, and den suites here are as large as many Washington apartments, except that the kitchens are bigger and better equipped. Complimentary continental breakfast. Room service, but no restaurant. Fitness center.... *Tel 202/457–0500, 800/852–8512, fax*

202/659–4492. 950 24th St., NW, 20037, Foggy Bottom–GWU Metro, Taxi zone 2A. 196 rms. $$$$

Swiss Inn. Washington's smallest hotel is intimate and quirky, with funky furnishings, but small families and others prepared to rough it can save money by staying here. No restaurant, but kitchenettes.... *Tel 202/371–1816, 800/955–7947. 1204 Massachusetts Ave., NW, 20005, Metro Center Metro, Taxi zone 1B. 7 rms. $$*

Tabard Inn. For anyone seeking an adventure in lodging. Tabard Inn has been a hotel since World War I, when three contiguous Victorian town houses were turned into a vertical labyrinth of passages and stairways. Complimentary breakfast features homemade granola. No parking.... *Tel 202/785–1277, fax 202/785–6173. 1739 N St., NW, 20036, Dupont Circle Metro, Taxi zone 1B. 40 rms., 25 with private bath. $$–$$$*

Washington Court on Capitol Hill. High-end luxury near the Capitol. A terraced grand entrance slopes down to a vast glass–ceilinged atrium; traditionally furnished rooms, all with marble-appointed bathrooms and either bars or full kitchens. Exercise center with sauna.... *Tel 202/628–2100, 800/321–3010, fax 202/737–2641. 525 New Jersey Ave., NW, 20001, Union Station Metro, Taxi zone 1D. 264 rms. $$$$$*

Washington Hilton & Towers. The "Hinckley Hilton" is an exuberant curving mid-1960s structure on a hillside above Dupont Circle—just the type of big-city, suit-infested property against which hotels which refer to themselves as "boutiques" or "Eurostyle" are positioning themselves. It ain't quaint, but it's still a major nerve center of Washington life. Large fitness center.... *Tel 202/483–3000, 800/445–8667, fax 202/265–8221. 1919 Connecticut Ave., NW, 20009, Dupont Circle Metro, Taxi zone 2B. 1,123 rms. $$$$*

Washington International Youth Hostel. Unlike many youth hostels, this place lets you hang around all day, and credit cards are even accepted. Sleeping rooms accommodate up to 12; single-sex dorms prevail, so couples should try to wangle one of the four-bed family rooms if you don't want to be split up. No parking, no restaurant, but you can fix your own meals in a fully equipped kitchen (an onsite shop sells basic grub).... *Tel 202/737–2333, 800/444–6111. 1009 K St., NW, 20001, Metro Center Metro, Taxi zone 1C. 300 beds. AE, D, DC not accepted. $*

Washington Vista Hotel. Thanks to the stigma of Mayor Barry's drug arrest here, the Washington Vista charges somewhat below-market rates for luxury downtown. Bright, pretty, modern rooms—the suites were designed by Hubert de Givenchy—surround a foliage-packed lobby that simulates a town square. It's in a recently reformed red-light district; the neighborhood tradition persists on the other side of Thomas Circle: avoid it after dark. Health club with sauna.... *Tel 202/429–1700, 800/847–8232, fax 202/785–0786. Thomas Circle, 1400 M St., NW, 20005, McPherson Square Metro, Taxi zone 1B. 400 rms. $$$*

Watergate Hotel. Though the famous Watergate complex is totally modern, a distinct Olde English accent permeates the hotel's large rooms, which have either Potomac or interior garden views. Michelin two-star chef Jean-Louis Palladin thought enough of the restaurants to name both of them after himself. Vast fitness center. Complimentary limo service weekdays 7am–10pm.... *Tel 202/965–2300, 800/424–2736, fax 202/337–7915. 2650 Virginia Ave., NW, 20037, Foggy Bottom–GWU Metro, Taxi zone 2A. 235 rms. $$$$$*

Willard Inter-Continental. Incredibly, the joint was closed from 1968 until 1986, when real estate magnate Oliver Carr restored and reopened it under Inter-Continental management. Since then the imposing Beaux–Arts edifice has again become a major power address. The lobby has a circular cornelian velvet sofa surrounded by plush turn-of-the-century furniture under a ceiling decorated by the state seals. Guest rooms look 19th century, too, but cunningly conceal turn-of-the-next-century amenities. Fitness room and access to pool (for a fee) at J.W. Marriott across the street.... *Tel 202/628–9100, 800/327–0200, fax 202/ 637–7326. 1401 Pennsylvania Ave., NW, 20004, Metro Center Metro, Taxi zone 1A. 341 rms. $$$$$*

Windsor Inn. See **Embassy Inn/Windsor Inn.**

Washington, D.C. Accommodations

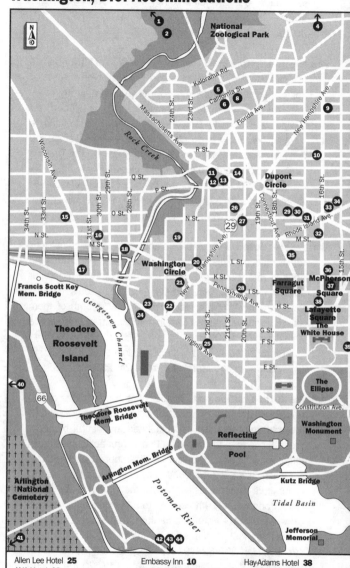

National
Zoological Park

Kalorama Rd.

California St.

Florida Ave.

New Hampshire Ave.

Massachusetts Ave.

Rock Creek

R St.

Q St.

Dupont
Circle

P St.

16th St.

Connecticut Ave.

Rhode Island Ave.

Wisconsin Ave.

34th St. · 33rd St. · 30th St. · 29th St. · 28th St.

31st St.

N St.

M St.

Washington
Circle

Farragut
Square

McPherson
Square

Francis Scott Key
Mem. Bridge

Georgetown Channel

Pennsylvania Ave.

Lafayette
Square

The White House

Theodore
Roosevelt
Island

New Hampshire Ave.

Virginia Ave.

The
Ellipse

66

Theodore Roosevelt
Mem. Bridge

Constitution Ave.

Washington
Monument

Reflecting
Pool

Arlington
National
Cemetery

Arlington Mem. Bridge

Potomac River

Kutz Bridge

Tidal Basin

Jefferson
Memorial

Latham Hotel **16**
Morrison House **44**
Morrison-Clark Inn **47**
Normandy Inn **5**
One Washington Circle **20**
Phoenix Park Hotel **54**
Quality Hotel Silver Spring **4**
Quality Inn-Iwo Jima **40**
Renaissance Mayflower **35**
Ritz-Carlton **13**

Ritz Carlton Pentagon City **42**
St. James **21**
Sheraton Suites Alexandria **43**
Sheraton Washington **2**
Swiss Inn **46**
Tabard Inn **29**
Washington Court
  on Capitol Hill **52**
Washington Hilton &
  Towers **8**

Washington International
  Youth Hostel **48**
Washington Vista Hotel **45**
Watergate Hotel **24**
Willard Inter-Continental **50**
Windsor Inn **9**

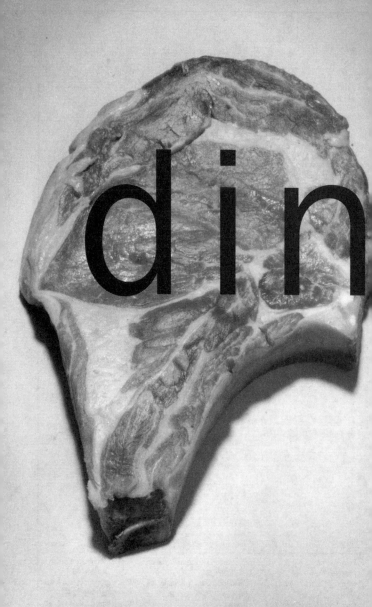

ing 2

In Washington,
this totally undar-
ing, all-things-to-
all-persons capital
city, restaurants
work pretty much
like you'd expect:

nothing new originates here, but just about every style of cooking in these here United States (not to mention the United Nations) is dutifully represented. Washington restaurants purvey regional American cuisine, from Boston steamed seafood to California sun-dried edibles, with stops along the way in the homestyle heart of Dixie, the spicy Cajun quarter, Tex-Mex fusion land, and the beefsteak belt of the Great Plains. You can also find the cuisine of every country under the sun, including countries that most geographically impaired Americans couldn't locate on a map. It is even said (by cab drivers, tour guides, concierges, guidebook scribes, and other professional know-it-alls) that a month after a coup takes place in some country you've never heard of, like clockwork a new strain of ethnic restaurant shows up in Washington.

Washingtonians' schedules demand that they eat out more than almost everybody else, and for that they pay a price. Restaurants here are more expensive than those in any other U.S. city except New York, San Francisco, and Miami. The comings and goings of celebrity chefs are breathlessly reported in local gossip columns and water-cooler chitchat. On the other hand, midpriced national chains—the Houlihans and California Pizza Kitchens—thrive, largely dominating the market between fast-food and fine dining; Washington is one culture where middle-of-the-road is actually considered a *good* quality.

At the high end, Washington's most distinctive restaurants exude a kind of federal authority—you feel you're eating among people who could make a lot of trouble for you if they wanted to. Such establishments serve "Vaguely Regional American" cuisine, and décor consists mainly of pictures of important people who have dined there (or undoubtedly would have, had the place been open when they were still alive).

Washington's other forte is **Asian restaurants**, especially Southeast Asian restaurants; in particular, Vietnamese. Why so many Vietnamese have settled in the capital of their erstwhile nemesis is a riddle for social psychologists; most Washingtonians prefer not to question why, but to feed away. Although the best ones are out in the burgeoning Asian communities in Virginia and Maryland suburbs, good somewhat-Americanized restaurants can be found in D.C.'s meager Chinatown and scattered around every other part of the city.

While food and presentation are top-notch, Washington lags way behind the curve in terms of wait staff. Diners complain that service is either rushed or glacially slow; that servers oversell specials but can't answer elementary questions about menu items or wines; and that they seldom give reliable recommendations. Unlike waiters in more established restaurant towns—New York, New Orleans, and San Francisco, among others—Washington wait staff often seem untrained and too inexperienced to understand what patrons expect when they pay serious money for a meal.

Only in D.C.

Washington lacks distinctive dishes, just as it lacks the distinctly ethnic neighborhoods from which those dishes usually come. The closest thing to local cuisine are "crabocentric" dishes that spill down from Baltimore. **Crab cakes**—crabmeat mixed with egg white, seasoning, and filler, served in sandwiches or as platters—are on virtually every menu, the quality of crab cake generally rising along with the proportion of crabmeat to Crab Meat Helper. **Hardshell crabs** are Chesapeake Bay blue crabs steamed and doused with Old Bay spice mixture. They are ordered by the bucket and consumed during lengthy ceremonies involving mallets and picks and paring knives on newspaper-covered tabletops, a very labor-intensive (and bee-intensive) activity that mines a few morsels of fresh crabmeat from mountains of claws and shell.

Dining at the Capitol

*There are over a dozen eating spots tucked into various nooks and crannies of the Capitol itself and its office buildings, any of which you can use (after all, you own them). The **Senators' Dining Room** on the Senate side of the Capitol (open to the public 1:30–3), is the most elegant. You'll need a note from your senator to get in, but it's the best place to spot C-SPAN superstars. Visitors of no note can pay less for the same food—Senate bean soup and apple pie are specialties—in the **Refectory** (first floor, Senate side). The Dirksen Building houses the excellent **North Servery** cafeteria, incorporating both the white-tablecloth, all-you-can-eat-for-$7.75 South Buffet, and the casual salad, deli, sausage, and frozen yogurt bars of Southside. The elegant royal-blue **Bennett Dining Room** on the House side of the Capitol features a Smart Heart Alternatives menu. Pluses in the Rayburn Building's **Rayburn Pizza Plus** include rotisserie chicken combos and gourmet coffee.*

WASHINGTON, D.C. | DINING

Places that serve hardshells are scarce in Washington—that's really an excuse for excursions to "Ball'mer" or the shore—but yuppie-friendly **softshell crabs** are available in many restaurants throughout the year. They're basically the same animal, only nailed during the molting stage; they're usually served lightly breaded and sautéed. You generally get two crabs to an order and you eat everything you get, including claws. Yes, shells and all.

Breakfast side dishes might have some vaguely local flavor, with either **grits** up from the South or **scrapple**, a fried meat-scrap-and-cornmeal mush, down from Pennsylvania Dutch country. Beyond that, the only only-in-Washington dish is the zesty sausage called **half smoke**, sold in food carts along the Mall and all over downtown. Half smokes, though, are absolutely no big deal. Nobody argues about who makes the best ones. Many Washingtonians have never tasted one and may not know they even exist. They just don't seem to be sold anywhere else, that's all.

How to Dress

Unless you live in New York or Europe, Washington is probably a bit dressier than the place you're coming from. Few places force a gentleman to don the house sport jacket before admitting him to the dining room, but in many of the better restaurants, every male will be wearing a jacket, probably a suit and tie. Those not dressed *comme il faut* will be identified as tourists who, as such, are more or less invisible to local residents—including servers. Unless a dress code is indicated in the listings below, feel free to dress as casually as you like, but never worry that people will stare if you overdress.

When to Eat

Breakfast is served early, sometimes before 6am to accommodate the many local workers whose workdays begin at 7 or 7:30. Lunchtime rush begins at noon; most places are empty by 1:30. Closing time for early-bird dinner specials is a clue to when "fashionable" dining commences—most of them end at 6:30 or 7, the close of a typical executive workday and time to grab dinner before heading home. Eight o'clock sharp is prime time for gracious dining; dinners seldom commence after 9pm; most kitchens are closed by 11.

Vast, all-you-can-eat Saturday/Sunday brunches run from 11am until almost dinner time—plan carefully and you can make this the only real meal you have to buy that day.

Getting the Right Table

With the demise of Larry King's former home-away-from-studio, Duke Zeibert's, none of the important restaurants is really spacious enough to have a Siberia section for tourists and local yokels. There are, however, many reasons for lobbying for preferential treatment: to obtain a favored table beside a window with a view, near the fireplace, in the ever diminishing smoking section, or out-of-doors. You might also wish to jump to the front of a long line to get in. In a traditional city like Washington, the old ways work best: slip a little something to the maître d'—but make it a $20 bill if you want to be noticed.

To get a reservation at the hottest restaurants, the person to contact is the concierge at your hotel (whom you tip humongously for all services rendered at the end of your stay). Concierges have "arrangements" with many restaurants that allow them to obtain a reservation when you can't get one yourself. Such arrangements often yield unexpected dividends, such as a free after-dinner drink "compliments of Victor/ Victoria your concierge at the Grand Plaza Tower Inn," paid for, of course, by the restaurant. Strangely enough, this is one game where everybody plays a winning hand.

Where the Chefs Are

New York, San Francisco, and New Orleans may have more snob appeal for serious foodies, but Washington is the only city in America with *two* chefs who have earned two-star *Guide Michelin* ratings (with restaurants they operated in Europe). Gascony-born **Jean-Louis Palladin** is perhaps most responsible for educating the collective native palate; since opening in 1979, his restaurant **Jean-Louis** at the Watergate Hotel proves night after night that people here appreciate the food enough to pay $150 for a meal. As a concession to nineties constraints, he opened **Palladin By Jean-Louis** upstairs at the Watergate, a bistro to which the word "budget" can be applied only in relation to the original Jean-Louis. Although two-star Jean-Louis oversees Palladin's menu, less stellar sous-chef **Larbi Dahrouch** is the one who actually plates the lamb *tagine*, *brandade* of cod, and other dishes here. Palladin also operates **Pesce**, a truly informal—if not exactly inexpensive—neighborhood seafood place, in partnership with celebrity chef **Roberto Donna** of **Galileo**, unquestionably the city's preeminent Italian restaurant. Donna, too, has spun off budget lines with his less formal **I Matti** (tel 202/462–8844, 2436 18th St., NW, Taxi zone 2B), his even less formal **Arucola** (tel 202/244–1555, 5534 Connecticut Ave., NW, Taxi zone 4B) and his downright cheapo **Il Radicchio** (see Index).

Back among the Michelin two-stars there's **Gerard Pangaud**, a somewhat recent newcomer who opened **Gerard's Place** in 1993 after stints at the Ritz-Carlton in Pentagon City and restaurants in New York. But the most dedicated foodies who make the pilgrimage to Washington have no Michelin stars in their eyes and they don't stay in town; their destination is **Patrick O'Connell's Inn at Little Washington** on the edge of Virginia's Blue Ridge Mountains, two hours from downtown D.C. If you haven't heard of it, you probably don't deserve to eat there.

Yannick Cam is this year's Comeback Kid. His Le Pavillon became a fashion victim of eighties excess a few years back, but he has recently scored big again with frenetic **Coco Loco** and refined **Provence**. Formerly at a place called Twenty-One Federal, **Bob Kinkead** has found his niche with the eponymous **Kinkead's**, an altar to haute seafood. Young, energetic **Jim Papovich** successfully reinvented himself when Embassy Row Hotel management converted his posh Lucie's into the chic but family-friendly **Bistro Twenty Fifteen**. **Peter Pastan** covers both high- and low-end Italian with the side-by-side **Obelisk** and **Pizzeria Paradiso**.

Michel Richard checks in monthly on California-French **Citronelle**, a clone of his L.A. restaurant Citrus, and Santa Fe's **Marc Miller** keeps an eye on his southwestern-trendy **Red Sage**, but neither stays in town full-time anymore. **Nora Pouillon**, the city's foremost female chef, shows Washingtonians that healthy, organic food never has to make excuses for itself, at **Nora** and **Asia Nora**.

Street Food

You'll see mobile food carts parked along the Mall and on virtually every corner of the downtown area. True, they're cheap and convenient—parks to eat in are usually close by—but they're woefully monotonous. A few dispense falafel, burritos, and espresso, but for the most part they sell hot dogs and half smokes. The street vendor's version of prix-fixe is one hot dog or half smoke with all the trimmings (relish, sauerkraut, onions), bag o' chips, and can o' soda, all for $2. All carts sell candy bars; some also sell coffee, muffins, egg rolls, popcorn, and cigarettes; but that's about the extent of it. Without a doubt, some carts have better food than others, but it'd be impossible to tell you where to find them on any given day, since, according to the law of the street, prime locations are snapped up every day on a first-come basis.

Info, Info, Info

Call **Menus by Fax** (tel 202/MENU-FAX) and they'll fax you menus from any of over 100 restaurants in D.C. and the near suburbs. **Post Haste** (tel 202/334–9000, access code

DINE), a multifaceted information service operated by the *Washington Post*, also sends restaurant menus by fax, plus verbal information and updates on specials. The *Washingtonian* magazine's Internet Web site—***Washingtonian Online*** (http://www.infi.net/washmag) lets you access lists of its restaurant critics' choices of the area's 100 very best dining establishments, 100 best bargain restaurants, results of recent readers' surveys of favorite places to eat out, and a calendar of upcoming D.C. food and wine events. For a complete list of "100 percent Vegetarian" and vegetarian-friendly restaurants in the area, contact the **Vegetarian Society of D.C.** (tel 301/589–0722, Box 4921, Washington, DC 20008).

The Lowdown

First Family sightings... Nothing against the White House chef, but the Clintons have dined out at more Washington restaurants than the last five presidents combined. At upscale Italian **Galileo**, we bet they didn't have to cool their heels at the bar as do most folks, even with reservations. The hunt club décor at the **Jockey Club**, Nancy Reagan's favorite hangout, may remind Bill of his Oxford days; the tone is more British colonialist at the **Bombay Club**, reportedly Chelsea's choice, a languorous space with dark shutters and ceiling fans, where the waiters sound like extras from *The Jewel in the Crown*. The Clintons have confronted more daunting culinary challenges, too: the overseasoned and overpriced southwestern fare at **Red Sage**, in its dazzling subterranean dining room with handcrafted light fixtures, antler sconces, and tree trunk fireplace; or the Amish quilt-filled townhouse of **Nora**, for organic food without the tofu and sprouts—duck-filled ravioli, lamb sausage and lentils, asparagus and morels.

Georgetown undergrad Bill Clinton frequented a neighborhood saloon called **The Tombs**, but President William Clinton moved upstairs to starchy **1789** (the name refers not to the price of a meal, fortunately, but the year in which Georgetown University was founded and the Constitution adopted). The First Couple have brunched with a Potomac view at **Sequoia**, where the president ordered tuna burgers, honey-marinated pork tenderloin, and Pete's Wicked Ale. (We would have had the duck dumplings or one of their fancy salads, but who elected us?).

They've also sampled the granolas at **Tabard Inn**, that power-to-the-people spot where agents of, say, Greenpeace concoct plots with their opposite numbers from the Sierra Club. But you have to get up pretty early in the morning to see this president—and camp out at the so-called **Presidential McDonald's**, around the corner from the White House on the west side of 17th Street between Pennsylvania Avenue and H Street.

Congressional hangouts... In his whodunit *Murder in the Senate*, no less an inside source than Senator William S. Cohen (R-ME) labels the **Monocle** "a watering hole for lobbyists, members, and Hill staffers... a place to discuss matters off the record." Standing all by its lonesome down the hill from Senate office buildings, this off-campus clubhouse for Congress members serves a traditional American menu with a veto-proof majority of steaks, chops, and seafood. When congressional cloakrooms get too crowded, stategy sessions may spill over into the rarified French country **La Colline**. Ladies get their hands kissed here—unless they're surrounded by Secret Service agents. The odd House member occasionally wanders into **Bullfeathers** (see Nightlife) for a drink, and sometimes for a bite to eat. But when pols just want to have fun they kick up their heels at **Tunnicliff's**, a year-round Mardi Gras owned by a real-live Cajun from Louisiana, Lynne Breaux, who opened this restaurant/bar on Capitol Hill because "Washington didn't have enough places to party and New Orleans had too many." Senator John Breaux (D-LA) (her unrelated fellow Louisianan) and cronies frequent the joint, as do the Newtster, Clinton nemesis Paula Jones, Clinton ass-saver Leon Panetta, and the occasional normal neighborhood person. **Two Quail**, a comfy, cozy little nest in a Capitol Hill rowhouse, is a popular spot for female Congress members who include Laura Ashley prints among the trappings of authority.

Seats of power... There are plenty of off-the-Hill restaurants where lobbyists take legislators, businesspeople take bureaucrats, and expense accounts take a beating. People love to hate **The Palm**, either because it comes out of New York, because they can't afford to eat there, or because they can't get in, but it's Clout Central now, especially after Duke Ziebert's demise (a temporary regrouping, quoth His Grace). King, Larry that is, is a regular; so are fun power couples Maury Povich/Connie Chung and James Carville/Mary Matalin. David Brinkley, Redskins owner Jack Kent Cooke, Democratic honcho Bob Strauss, and a guy named Bush mosey into the back room to sit beneath caricatures of those less famous than themselves. **Morton's of Chicago** is still the place for important meetings and important meat, though Rosty of Chicago—disgraced former Representative Dan Rostenkowski, who wielded megapower as the House Ways and Means Committee chairman—no longer holds court at his table here, designated Rosty's Rotunda by a brass plaque.

The diplomatic community hatches its devious plots amid the stately confines of **Maison Blanche**, a block from its Anglicized namesake. Crystal chandeliers, leather banquettes, velvet armchairs—it's so old-fashioned it's chic. Decision makers for international organizations like the World Bank and OAS (Organization of American States) congregate at **Taberna del Alabardero**, which did tapas before tapas went electric and became short-attention-span theater. Don't let the kitschy matador's costume in the window scare you off. When White House staff are let loose, they're apt to wind up at the **Old Ebbitt Grill** or the **Occidental Grill**, the nearest off-campus bars. The Occidental's framed photos of everybody who was ever anybody in Washington make it feel more insidery than, at this point in time, it really is—opt for the red leather-y ground-floor **Grill Room** for its mahogany bar and stronger in-crowd vibes. The nerve center of D.C. government power—something of an oxymoron during the reign of the Control Board—is **Georgia Brown's**. You may get a glimpse of His Permanence the Mayor; for a side order of urban irony, look out the window at about six o'clock and see the van pull up across the street at McPherson Square to feed D.C.'s homeless.

Historic surroundings... The John Wilkes Booth mob plotted the kidnapping and assassination of Lincoln and his cabinet at Mary Surratt's boardinghouse—a federal-style bulding that's now **Go-Lo's**, a run-of-the-mill Chinatown restaurant a few blocks from the Ford's Theatre crime scene. As President Andrew Johnson put it, Surratt "kept the nest that hatched the egg" of the assassination plot; her involvement was never clearly established, but she was convicted of conspiracy and expeditiously hanged. In 1962, the **Yenching Palace**, a

Chinese restaurant near the National Zoo, was the site of the secret talks between John Scali (an ABC reporter and later ambassador to the U.N.), and Aleksander Fomin of the Soviet Embassy—the first and last of a series of secret meetings that settled the Cuban Missile Crisis. In April 1972, the restaurant also hosted a press conference celebrating the arrival of China's giant pandas to the nearby National Zoo. In 1985, KGB defector Vitaly Yurchenko walked out on his CIA handlers (and his share of the bill) at the earthy Georgetown bistro **Au Pied de Cochon** and headed straight back to the always forgiving arms of Mother Russia. Milking the incident for all it's worth, the restaurant mounted an erroneously dated plaque marking the banquette of "Yurchenko's Last Supper in the USA" and the bar serves Original Yurchenko Shooters (Stoly and Grand Marnier).

Kid pleasers... You can't make your kids eat every meal in a food court, can you? Can you? Of course not. Take them to an **American Cafe**, a local chain with an imaginative American-style menu, although options diminish if you're not in the mood for something made with chicken or turkey. Earnest efforts at creating a distinctive stylish décor for each branch make these restaurants look more expensive than they are. At **America** kids get a kick out of all the action swirling around Union Station; opt for the noisy outdoor cafe-type seating in the Great Hall and no one will notice the row your kids make. They can order goofy unrestaurantlike items like Kraft USA (macaroni and cheese); Plains, Georgia (peanut butter and grape jelly); or Las Vegas (devil's-food cake). **Music City Roadhouse** is a big, noisy, converted foundry where hearty country-style entrees with bottomless side dishes are served family-style, and kids under 6 can share for free. The décor is honky-tonk hokey and the achy-breaky soundtrack is cloying, but the food's the real thing— crispy fried chicken, crusty barbecued ribs, batter-fried catfish, skillet corn bread, lumpy mashed potatoes, smoky greens, and hot cobbler. Elevated noise level, jokey menus, and ample portions at tolerable prices come with a Tex-Mex accent at **Austin Grill** (warn the kids: order dishes "hot" or "extra hot" at your peril) and with a New-Mex accent at **Las Cruces**, with its garish shrine to Elvis, Christmas lights a-blinking 12 months a year, and menus encased in out-of-date New Mexico license plates. For youngsters who want to act grown-up, **Bistro Twenty Fifteen** is, like, this really fancy restaurant in a hotel, y'know? But the special Family Fare menu offers less refined stuff like taco platters and spaghetti-and-meatballs—including bottomless soft drinks—all for under $10.

Vegging out... Strict vegetarians won't find much to write home about in Washington. One of the only purely vegetarian places, **Delights of the Garden**, is so pure that it doesn't even *cook* its food. The menu features hearty impostors that would be horrifying to some, all served in the raw: spaghetti and meatballs is actually sprouts and nuts; Monifa's chili bulks up with mushrooms; cookies use raw peanut butter to bind bananas, papaya, and other tropical fruit. Uncooks replace stoves with blenders, food processors, dehydrators, and *kuumba* (Swahili for creativity). **Balajee** earns zero for décor, but it serves meatless Indian food in the downtown business district—specialties like vegetable curries, yogurt-based soups, and lentil dishes, as well as lots of good breads. **Food for Thought** (see Nightlife) serves only vegetarian meals, but it's not totally opposed to carnal pleasures—there's a full bar along with live entertainment almost every night.

Within the mainstream, the highly evolved organic dishes at trendy-chic **Nora** and **Asia Nora** go far toward lifting the taint of second-class gastronomic citizenship, and **Tabard Inn** makes meat-haters feel right at home, with organic vegetables grown on their own farm, and lately, under the new chef, a fresh emphasis on seafood. Even the meats are additive-free in this p.c. hotel dining room. The **Red Sage Chili Bar**, attached to the trendy southwestern restaurant Red Sage, serves a fiery, fat-free, five-bean vegetarian version. **Trumpets** marks its meatless dishes with a yin-yang symbol, which sounds more Zenlike than this gay bar/restaurant really is—witness the artwork on the walls, heavy on stressed metal and rivets, and the ultra-high-decibel sound system. The cooking is enough to slap jaded palates silly: roasted corn, carrots, and goat cheese molded to look like a corncob; jerk pork tenderloin with chili spaetzle, and nachos made from artichokes served with black beans and avocado-lime aioli.

For committed carnivores... Morton's of Chicago fetches top dollar for dry-aged steaks, but its well-heeled clients never beef, and the portions are never small. Sides are downright colossal—baked potatoes weigh in at over a pound. A caricature-laden outpost of the New York-based chain, **The Palm** specializes in broiled steak and raw power: political honchos, media megastars, and sports moguls keep their ears to the ground in here. At **Fran O'Brien's**, a new place run by an old Redskin, the hearty atmosphere is palpably less stuffy than at the other fabled meat houses, as knowledgeable sports talk ricochets across the round bar. O'Brien serves the heaviest slab of beef in town—a 24-ounce New York strip steak. **Les Halles** is another imported steakhouse, a clone of the New York original, with French-cut steaks and *frites* that would do any Left Bank brasserie proud. But Les Halles also treats house-made sausages and roast chicken as more than just afterthoughts, and provides a special third-floor dining room for cigar smokers.

Something fishy... Washington lacks the kind of big midpriced seafood joints that flourish in Baltimore and on the shore. Noting the gap, Boston-based **Legal Sea Foods** in 1995 boldly planted its flag on the K Street Corridor, quickly becoming an in spot for long business lunches and early postwork dinners. For squid addicts, the fried calamari appetizer is mandatory; simple preparations of scrupulously fresh seafood, much of it flown down from New England, make the choicest entrees. Finish off with marionberry cobbler, which is not an in-joke but an actual fruit. Originally a fish store with a few tables for occasional eat-in customers, **Pesce** evolved into a restaurant with a display case for occasional fish buyers (apparently the natives refused to shop for anything more exotic than halibut or shrimp). This chalkboard-menued, bare-tabletopped eatery is owned jointly by two of Washington's best-known chefs, Jean-Louis Palladin and Roberto Donna, and serves the same kinds of fish you can get for a lot more money at their upscale restaurants. Pricey **Kinkead's**, in a landlocked Pennsylvania Avenue town house, keeps changing its superb menu—and keeps on getting better. Nowhere else in town could you find such winning dishes as sautéed cod cheeks, Portuguese seafood stew, skate with red wine sauce, or grilled squid with polenta. **Taberna del Alabardero** is known for its hake with green sauce, as well as for paella just like in Old Madrid (but you'll need two people to order it). Star chef Gerard Pangaud, at the pricey French **Gerard's Place**, can do incredible things with lobster.

Closer to earth, price-wise—and a stone's throw from the Potomac in Alexandria—**Union Street Public House** serves a creamy seafood stew containing lobster, oysters, scallops, shrimp, and fish over rice—just about everything that swims but Flipper. Get past the cutesy gaslights and "Ladies Invited" signs, and this self-styled "neighborhood tap and grill" actually has some waterfront flavor. A few blocks offshore, in an Alexandria rowhouse, **Le Gaulois** does fish and shellfish with saucy French flair. The Georgetown bistro **Au Pied de Cochon** serves a popular lobster special—a pound and a quarter for $12.95, the last time we checked. Freshest and cheapest of all, the **Market Lunch** serves seafood right beside the fish section of Capitol Hill's Eastern Market. Choose between two types of crab cake—spicy shredded and all-lump.

Nouveau southern... Valet-park your pickup outside **Georgia Brown's** for a fancy version of good home cookin'. Of course, you can take nouvelle southern only so far, the owners learned shortly after opening, when customers raised on their Dixie Mamas' home cooking squawked that the collard greens were *way* undercooked. Georgia Brown's held a cook-off, offering both quick-sautéed and slow-simmered greens on the menu. (Tradition won.) The newest of the nouveaus is **B. Smith's** in Union Station, owned by model Barbara Smith (she of the Oil of Olay ads). After successfully launching a nouvelle southern establishment in Manhattan's theater district, Smith has taken her act on the road, bringing sweet potatoes garnished with foie gras, grits dressed up like polenta, and hamhock-larded beans and rice closer to folks who say "y'all" naturally. **Vidalia,** a cozy subterranean dining room with extraordinary food, pays homage to the southern onion so sweet you can eat it like an apple. Especially in the late spring season, the menu features Vidalia onions baked into a goat cheese tart, fried into crisps to accompany the steak au poivre, creamed into a sauce that accompanies the salmon, or caramelized into a confit you spread on house-made breads. Smithfield ham flavors the green beans and the sweetbreads served with wild mushrooms.

Good evening, Vietnam... Vietnamese cuisine, with less flame and more seafood than Thai cooking, has captured the hearts, minds, and stomachs of Washington. The ambience and food in the relative old-timer **Saigon Gourmet** (and its Alexandria clone, East Wind) are often damned with faint praise as "reliable" and "consistent"; truth is, they're rather bland but unthreateningly suitable for beginners. Cinnamon beef (rolled flank steak) or crispy rice noodles topped with mixtures of meat, seafood, and/or vegetables are "dependable" entrees. **Miss Saigon** in Adams-Morgan puts on a better show, with a light, not-too-spicy menu and the dramatic décor of a black lacquer box. For real Hanoi home cooking, though, you need to track down one of the **Pho 75** outlets in the suburbs, where *pho* (correctly pronounced "fuh")—spicy rice noodle soup mixed with odd combinations of beef parts, Thai basil, and sprouts—is the only dish on the menu. You sit at long communal tables, close enough to observe how Vietnamese diners wield spoon and chopsticks to amplify *pho* with bean sprouts, sprigs of coriander and mint, lemon, lime, and hot sauces. No meal is complete without a dose of ultrastrong brewed-in-your-cup Vietnamese coffee. Be really authentic and order it with sweetened condensed milk; it may replace the latte in your life.

Elsewhere in Indochina... Most of the best Thai restaurants are in the suburbs that Thai communities call home: Wheaton and Rockville in Maryland, Vienna and Falls Church in Virginia. If you don't feel like making such a trek, though, here are some perfectly reasonable options. **Star of Siam** is named after the asterisks dotting the menu, indicating "hot and spicy" dishes—mainly, the Thai-style curries. (Red curry is hotter than yellow, and green is hottest of the hot.) **Cajun Bangkok**'s jungle-green Alexandria storefront next to a used-rug shop looks disappointingly ordinary for a restaurant that blends two fiery high-profile cuisines, but the kitchen delivers the goods, combining chili peppers, seafood, and greens in both classic and hybrid dishes. What is Burmese cuisine? As you can learn for yourself at **Burma**, a Chinatown hole-in-the-wall, it's less highly seasoned than Thai, uses less seafood than Vietnamese cooking, and like Indian cuisine, uses various amounts of curry, tamarind, and turmeric. In the exotic, batik-laden dining parlor of **Straits of Malaya**, you can sample the "straits cuisine" of multiethnic Singapore: blending meats, seafood, vegetables, and noodles with the spices of India and Malaysia (bamboo shoots, coconut milk, turmeric, chili, basil, ginger) and fast-cooking it Chinese-style in a wok.

Asian delights... Both locations of **Pan Asian Noodles & Grill** charter "Asia On Three Noodle Dishes A Day" tours of the continent: Asian Ravioli in spicy Taiwanese beef sauce; red-hot Singapore Curry Vermicelli with seafood, meat, or vegetables; gentle Korean green bean Chapchae Noodles with sauce served with rice; steamed Drunken Noodles with chicken in a spicy basil sauce. In a trendy townhouse among the West End hotels where Asians like to stay, **Asia Nora** purveys Asian-organic-fusion cuisine that sometimes comes off as confusion cuisine—Szechuan carpaccio, lemongrass sticky rice risotto, and other dishes that might inspire purists to commit hara-kiri. Still, since the owner is Nora Pouillon of **Nora** (see below), D.C. diners eat it up. If you have an appetite for simplicity, **Jing-Ga**, the first U.S. outlet of the upscale Seoul food chain, offers uncompromisingly authentic Korean tabletop cooking, though they've solved the usual problem of fume-filled rooms by using down-draft grills. Beef is best to barbecue, either *kalbi*, thin chunks of short rib, or *bulgogi*, paper-thin highly seasoned slices. Side dishes include the traditional *kimchi*, the pungent fermented cabbage that Koreans eat with every meal and many Westerners can't stomach. Warning: Don't confuse Jinro-Soju with some wimpy rice drink like sake—it's high-octane sweet-potato vodka.

Affordable French... Although most people think of provençale food as heart-healthy (all that garlic and olive oil), the best things on the provençale menu at **Lavandou**, near the National Zoo, are naughty: duck liver terrine, bacon-wrapped pork loin, salmon in puff pastry, mussels with crème fraîche. Fat-gram counters can take refuge in the herb-poached salmon in parchment, the chicken *piperade*, or the lamb stew with artichokes and beans. A Georgetown fixture since the mid-seventies, **Bistro Français** offers à la carte dishes such as duck with raspberry sauce, rabbit with thyme and mustard, and swordfish with green peppercorns for prices that aren't very *cher*. The main problem with **Bistrot Lepic**, the hot new kid on an upper-Georgetown block, is getting a reservation. This patron-and-patronne (mom-and-pop) bistro opened in 1995; Bruno Fortin cooks while Cecile Fortin works the front of the house, a bright but minuscule storefront on a quiet stretch of Wisconsin Avenue. Decorated with a mural depicting namesake Rue Lepic at the turn of the century, it offers quirky innovative takes on classic bistro fare—order calf liver or quail stuffed with goat cheese if available. **Le Gaulois** moved out to Alexandria when its D.C. site was urban-renewed into oblivion, but its hungry following tracked it down. The place is authentic down to the vigilant *patronne* and whimsical depictions inside and out of its namesake, Gaulois Man, a tough dude with a handlebar mustache sporting helmets with wings or horns. **Au Pied de Cochon** is probably the least pretentious, price- and palate-wise, but the 24-hour Georgetown bistro is full of students, tourists, noise, and fun.

Très cher French... If price is no object, you will find nothing at **Jean-Louis** in the Watergate Hotel to displease you. Showman/chef Jean-Louis Palladin acts a lot like the fussy French chefs in bad Hollywood films: he cooks according to whim, changing his handwritten menu daily, and never prepares a dish exactly the same way twice. Many folks praise the Watergate's upstairs bistro, **Palladin By Jean-Louis**, as "Jean-Louis cooking for half the price," but be wary—although Palladin designed the menu and maintains control, he's not the one at the stove. **Maison Blanche**, near the House White, has long been a diplomatic choice for stately celebrations and as a place to rub powerful elbows. The cuisine is called "modern French" (tuna steak with black peppercorns, sesame pork medallions, dessert soufflés), but nothing's too exotic. Similarly, **La Colline** on Capitol Hill is full of Congress members and their generous hosts who would probably enjoy the food better if the portions were larger and the sauces less classically French. On the cutting edge of Washington's French cuisine stands **Gerard's Place**, whose owner/chef Gerard Pangaud was the youngest ever to earn two stars from Michelin. A favorite of the French diplomatic corps, this jewel box of a restaurant is often misleadingly referred to as a bistro, but the persimmon walls, starched linens, and haute cuisine prices lure dealmakers and lobbyists, not unpublished novelists maxed out on their credit cards. The décor and aromas of **Provence** go by the book (Peter

Mayle's *A Year In Provence* and sequels), but don't expect rustic fare—Yannick Cam's bold menu takes off in all directions, with painterly dibs and dabs meant to evoke the feeling and flavors of that French province and current yuppie-happy hunting ground. You'll find *brandade* of cod with a whiff of garlic, pigeon atop celeriac purée, a multi-colored omelet with tapenade and tomato coulis. The wrought-iron chairs with femme fatale faces are a hoot.

Palazzo Italian... Top-of-the-line **Galileo** has gravity-defying prices and ofttimes diffident service, but it's capable of producing the best Italian meal of your life. This oversized palazzo is hardly about red sauce or designer pizza; think asparagus with black truffle sauce, ricotta gnocchi with pine nuts and raisins, or roast pigeon with red wine and juniper. Some of the best dishes are the simplest, like grilled swordfish or snapper seasoned only with a few herbs, lemon, and olive oil. **I Ricchi**, a shrine to sunny Tuscany, was put on Washington's culinary map when President Bush dined here right after his inauguration. Let the fragrant fire emanating from the wood-burning grill guide you through the short menu and long list of daily specials: grilled fish, lamb, beef, or sausage, along with the best focaccia in the area. The stone floors may evoke a Mediterranean palazzo but make for terrible acoustics—this is a noisy place. **Obelisk**, a casual 12-table cafe in a Dupont Circle walk-up, serves Italian cuisine for the Slim and Beautiful People—the coolly elegant décor and single-page prix-fixe menu are an exercise in minimalism.

Paisano Italian... **Il Radicchio**, with locations in Dupont Circle and Georgetown, has set the standard for stylish low-priced Italian—an all-you-can-eat spaghetti deal, pizzas, spit-roasted chicken, and daily specials like baked rabbit and stewed mussels for under $10. But Mama Mia, what lines! **Panevino** looks like a roadside diner, but a roadside diner in Tuscany—imported terra-cotta tiles, classic Mediterranean-trattoria chairs, food- and wine-themed original paintings. Designer pizzas, pastas, and a huge antipasti buffet are all just fine; this place should be more popular than it is. **Pizzeria Paradiso** has the principal trapping of a legendary pizza parlor: a long line outside at mealtimes. That's partly because the Neapolitan-style thin-crust pies are baked in a traditional wood-burning oven, and partly because Paradiso seats only 35, six at the counter in front of the open kitchen.

Top of the tapas... The tapas trend took almost a decade to drift down from New York to Washington (must have taken the Eastern shuttle), but it finally arrived—with a vengeance. **Taberna del Alabardero** did them before they were fashionable and may still do them best, but the atmosphere is, how you say, a bit stiff. It's more fun to do the tapas thing at **Jaleo**, the hottest spot in the up-and-coming downtown district called Penn Quarter (neighbors include the Navy Memorial, Shakespeare Theater, and the Insect Club). A young, artsy crowd nibbles at blood sausage, grilled quail, chorizo, and octopus, among many others. And Washingtonians have gone so cuckoo over **Coco Loco**, you'd think they'd never had tapas before. Well, truth is, most of them hadn't heard of the dainty noshes until Yannick Cam's amphetamine trip of a restaurant opened on the skirts of Chinatown. Sarong-wrapped women and overmuscled men crowd in to peruse the à la carte tapas menu, which features more than 30 unapologetically bogus scene stealers—chipotle-fried shrimp and bacon morsels, crab cakes in pumpkin seed sauce, garlic roasted until carmelized and served over black rice. **Gabriel** runs an all-you-can-eat tapas bar Wednesday through Friday from 5:30–8, with happy-hour drink prices. The food here is best described as Hispanofusion—chef Greggory Hill's menu begins like the conquistadors in Spain (with hot and cold tapas, manchego cheese), storms across the Mediterranean (hummus, fried calamari), infiltrates the Caribbean (smoked black bean soup), conquers Latin America (pancake-like Salvadorean *pupusas*) and Mexico (duck-filled tortillas), and ultimately settles into Tex-Mex border country (southwestern cabbage rolls). The tapas are Mediterranean à la Melrose Place at Adams-Morgan's hip **Tom Tom**, where you and a host of trendies rub elbows over little plates of pizzas, pastas, noshes and dips—grilled radicchio, couscous with pesto, lamb kebabs, roasted elephant garlic.

Beyond the Beltway... Both restaurants that invariably top Washington's best-restaurant lists lie beyond, well beyond, the Capital Beltway. At the **Inn at Little Washington**—located on the fringe of Virginia's Blue

Ridge Mountains, some 50 miles west of Big Washington—chef Patrick O'Connell gussies up prize local ingredients like Potomac rockfish and Shenandoah veal with the most exquisite sauces. Some say eating here is a life-changing experience. **L'Auberge Chez François**, the romantic Alsatian country inn, started out on Connecticut Avenue near the White House, but for the last 20 years it's been just outside the suburbs in Great Falls, Virginia. The remarkable menu is old-school French (cassoulet, Grand Marnier soufflé) with a sublime Alsatian accent (sauerkraut and sausage platter, shellfish in a Riesling sauce).

Al fresco... Weather permitting, you can find Washington restaurants that will feed you outdoors until Thanksgiving. Hands-down first choice is **Sequoia**, the anchor of the Washington Harbour, an office-residential-restaurant complex on the Georgetown waterfront. The place feels like a trim cruise ship, with three floors of indoor and outdoor terraces all offering spectacular views of the Potomac River. In Adams-Morgan, trendy **Tom Tom**'s hottest spot in fair weather is the balcony, for flaunting that *you* got in. Among Adams-Morgan's host of Asian exotics, there's rooftop dining at the **Star of Siam** (for hot Thai curries), and the nearby **Straits of Malaya** (for multiethnic Singaporean food); **Miss Saigon**, a Vietnamese charmer, has a few tables on a pleasant terrace just off a main drag, though indoor palm trees make the interior seem even more gardenlike. The refined cafe **Bistro Twenty Fifteen**, in the Embassy Row Hotel, has tables on a sheltered balcony one level above Massachusetts Avenue, and **Tabard Inn** serves its health-conscious food in an inner courtyard well-shielded from the bustle of the street. At **Patent Pending**, a charming self-service cafe in the old Patent Building, you can take your stuffed croissants over to tables in the sculpture garden of the National Portrait Gallery and the National Museum of American Art, on opposite wings of the building.

Institutions... Washingtonians wax wistful about restaurants departed—Harvey's (where J. Edgar Hoover dined almost daily), San Souci (where Gerald Ford enjoyed his only restaurant meal as president), Le Rivage, Le Pavillon, Duke Zeibert's (which shall return—maybe), Trader Vic's (anybody notice?). In fact, very few Washington restaurants have actually enjoyed longevity. **Old Ebbitt Grill** has been migrating around the downtown area since 1856 (serving future presidents Grant, Cleveland, and Theodore Roosevelt), before, in 1983, assuming its present site, a block from the White House. The old Washington name and Victorian American frippery have traveled well, though, and it's still a feel-like spot (as in "I feel like the Ebbitt Grill") for downtown workers. The clubby **Occidental Grill**, in operation along Pennsylvania Avenue between 14th and 15th streets since 1906, displays photos of 2,000 distinguished patrons willing to swap a picture for a free lunch. You might expect to find antiquey, museumy, fireplacey, pewtery restaurants all over D.C., but **1789**, in a Georgetown town house, is the only one—and it opened in 1962 (the furniture and antiques and Currier & Ives prints just make it seem historical). The **Jockey Club**, which looks more aristocratic British than democratic American, opened a year earlier, on the eve of JFK's inauguration. Chefs and menus come and go here, but "traditional" baked French onion soup, *pommes soufflés*, crusty rack of lamb, Dover sole, and delicate crab cakes are forever (Nancy Reagan always orders Cobb salad).

The soul of black Washington... The 50-year-old **Florida Avenue Grill** is a classic corner diner known for southern-style food, heavy on the four G's—grits, greens, gravy, and grease—and waitresses too familiar with the regulars to take any lip from them. The panfried chicken and ham hocks are excellent options, but the homemade corn muffins are mandatory. It's all cholesterol-free—there's no extra charge for the cholesterol larded into every dish. Since 1958, **Ben's Chili Bowl** has been a late-night hangout for African American entertainers (some from the historic Lincoln Theater across the alley), civil rights activists, and students from nearby Howard University, one of the nation's oldest and most prestigious black universities. Ben's anoints itself as "Bill Cosby's favorite place to eat in Washington, D.C."; Bill won't confirm, but they've got pictures to prove he's eaten there at least once. **Delights of the Garden** is only a couple of years old, and its strictly vegetarian uncooked cuisine is hardly classic, but, situated across the street from Howard U., it's quickly working its way into the local pantheon.

Where to pop the question... A drive in the rolling Virginia countryside, a table by the fireplace or, better yet, on the gardenside terrace at **L'Auberge Chez François**, a perfect soul-expanding French-Alsatian meal: her/his answer has to be yes. In town, arrange to snuggle up in one of the cozy nooks of the ornately Victorian-style **Morrison-Clark Inn**. The Mediterranean-flavored cooking—things like sautéed sea scallops with bouillabaisse sauce, veal tenderloin with tomato and pine nut risotto, free-range chicken over tabouleh—is light stuff that won't spoil an amorous evening. **Two Quail** may have a tad too much power/business/status buzz for some tastes, but in Washington that's what passes for romantic. The light's not too dim for a lady to show off a new rock on her ring finger. The odd but intimate **Mrs. Simpson's** is a memorabilia-crammed shrine to the lovebirds of the century, the Duke and Duchess of Windsor. The menu blends their purported favorites—kir royale and Negroni cocktails, chicken and watercress sandwiches, lemon mousse—with of-the-moment offerings like grilled lamb and tabouleh, Chinese-spiced duck, or salmon in parchment.

For dinner and dancing... The Art Deco **River Club**—all done up in etched glass, neon lightning bolts, scads of black and silver—plays big band music for mature hoofers. The menu is refreshingly simple, along the lines of veal chops from the grill, pan-roasted salmon, and smoked lobster, but prices are high; save some bucks by coming just to drink and dance. Sashay into **Melrose** on Friday or Saturday nights when a quartet plays big band music and you'll feel like an extra in a Fred and Ginger flick. (A lone pianist plays other nights.) Set in the Park Hyatt Washington hotel, the décor is old-new Italian, with a big splashy fountain in the courtyard, marble and muted colors inside. Young romantics come here to feel grown-up, while silver-haired twosomes glide around the floor to feel young. The French cuisine of the **Marquis de Rochambeau** (see Nightlife) is a bit common, but the late-night dance scene crosses the border to mondo bizarro. Only young feet can dance to the jazz/funk/hip-hop at **State of the Union** (see Nightlife), but the Russian-style food is suitable for mature stomachs.

Museum places... Most museum cafeterias are too crowded, too expensive, and too horrible to contemplate, but a few are worthy of exhibition. At the chic sit-down **Terrace Café** atop the East Wing of the National Gallery of Art, one side overlooks the museum's central courtyard and the large Calder mobile; the other side overlooks the Mall. What's on the menu has everything to do with what's hanging in the galleries: Armenian dishes during an Arshile Gorky exhibition, Dutch items for Vermeer—get the picture? A corridor connecting the National Portrait Gallery and National Museum of American Art briefly becomes **Patent Pending**, a self-service cafe so utterly decent that even museum staffers eat there. House-specialty stuffed croissant sandwiches and hot daily specials go down with espresso, microbrew beer, or American wine. The cafeteria atop the **Library of Congress** books outside restaurants—including good ones like Charlie Chiang's (Chinese) and Rooster's rotis-serie chicken—to serve lunch and late breakfast (after 9am). There's also deli stuff, pizza, a fruit bar, and a machine that brews cappucino for as little as 85¢. Look out upon a view of the Anacostia River, and while you're up there, take a glance at the exhibit in the Oval Gallery, and find out where your tax dollars are going by reading the job vacancies posted to the left of the cafeteria entrance. On the grounds of the **Hillwood Museum** (see Diversions), you can view Marjorie Merriweather Post's Russian decorative art treasures, then slip round to the cafe in the old stables for Russian/former Soviet lunch specialties (or English-style afternoon tea). The lunch menu changes twice a year, but count on some kind of borscht, blintzes, stuffed cabbage, and *lachmanjun* (red or white Armenian pizza). No food is available within Mount Vernon itself but **Mount Vernon Inn**, just out-side the entrance, supplements the cooking styles of old Virginia with modern touches like mesquite-grilled seafood. Expect costumed waiters, the whole works.

Prix fixe... Out in Great Falls, Virginia, the wonderful Alsatian country inn **L'Auberge Chez François** serves a five-course prix-fixe menu that isn't exactly cheap, but it's less than half the price of the city's most expensive restaurants. Coolly elegant designer-Italian **Obelisk** serves a full prix-fixe meal for under $35. The three-course fixed-price options at **La Colline** and **Maison Blanche**, two upscale French places, entice junior diplomats who otherwise couldn't get in the door; the more plebeian bistros **Lavandou**, **Bistro Français**, and **Au Pied de Cochon** have good early-bird prix-fixe deals, too. Lunch and dinner set-menus at **Bistro Twenty Fifteen**, the Embassy Row Hotel's classy dining room, won't save you a bundle, but they'll give you a taste of what's best. The Park Hyatt Washington Hotel's sleek restaurant, **Melrose**, offers a pre-theater menu of fussed-over modern American food, with an emphasis on seafood. The family-style menu at down-home **Music City Roadhouse** is an Americanized species of prix fixe: you pay flat per-person rates and get three entrees and three sides, with or without soup and/or salad.

How to get the best for less... Several Washington showcase restaurants let you sample the merchandise without paying all the freight. At southwestern trendsetter **Red Sage**, you save serious greenbacks by eating upstairs at the Chili Bar or lighter, healthier dishes in the Red Sage Café. **Kinkead's** serves nosh versions of its gourmet seafood in its downstairs bar/cafe. You can sneak in for the picture show at the **Occidental Grill**—2,000 personalized photographs line the walls—for under ten bucks if you order a burger or vegetable pita. Want to see what the **Jockey Club** looks like without selling the farm? Go for breakfast.

Caffeine scenes... The Coffee Revolution struck hard in Washington—all the gourmet coffee bars, cafes, and sidewalk espresso carts that were almost impossible to find four years ago are now nearly impossible to avoid. Besides tons of Starbuck's (including cafes inside the Renaissance Mayflower and the National Museum of American History), there's the locally owned Hannibal's Coffee Company chain, gobbling up smaller chains. But when you want fine coffee and something a bit more substantial than muffins or scones, go to the **Mudd House**, a modest M Street snackbar. The coffee is 100 percent organic, the plates are paper, and the menu is heavy on heart-healthy stuff like black bean salad, curry rice, and low-fat *panini*, Washington's sandwich of the moment—meat, cheese, and vegetables between grilled focaccia. Along with coffee, the **Dean & Deluca Café** in Georgetown serves Italian-style sandwiches, a daily pasta special, microbrew beers, and wines—or you can fetch for yourself any of the prepared foods and cheeses sold in D.C.'s most sophisticated grocery, a branch of the New York abfab food emporium. Seize one of the classic Parisian wicker cafe chairs, sit back, and watch the crowds streaming in and out of the Georgetown Park mall across the alley.

Best brunch... Both branches of rustic Italian **Panevino** serve a Tuscan brunch on weekends, and the Alexandria location even brings in opera singers on the first Sunday of the month. The country-style brunch at **Music City Roadhouse** presents live gospel music plus cheese grits with the power to heal. For brunch with a view of the Potomac, line up for a table at **Sequoia** or ascend to the **Roof Terrace** atop Kennedy Center (see Entertainment), where they lay out the Sunday buffet brunch in the kitchen. **Fleetwood's** (see Nightlife), the Alexandria jazz and blues club, has both a Sunday gospel brunch *and* a setting beside the Potomac. Brunch at **Tom Tom** means long lines and a full dose of the trendy Adams-Morgan morning-after scene. The hillies of Capitol Hill get live music with their brunch at **Bullfeathers** (see Nightlife), coffee with chicory and Cajun-style crayfish omelets at **Tunnicliff's**. **Austin Grill** (and Alexandria's **South Austin Grill**) specialize in hearty, spicy Tex-Mex hangover-killers. **America**, in bustling Union Station, has a special brunch menu (as if its regular all-50-states menu wasn't enough to cover all appetites). The chic French-California-style brunch at **Citronelle** is part and parcel of the late-rising Georgetown weekend scene. But the brunch to end all brunches (and possibly your life) has to be the all-you-can-drink vodka-or-beer Sunday brunch at **State of the Union** (see Nightlife).

All-you-can-eateries... What is it about people who work for the government that makes them salivate at the thought of a free feed? Various restaurants in town lure diners with open-trough policies—not free exactly, but the more you eat, the better your cost ratio. Make unlimited passes at an antipasto table groaning with grilled and marinated vegetables, and Italian meats and cheeses at **Panevino**, in either D.C. or Alexandria. The Brazilian *churrascaria* in back of cockamamie **Coco Loco** offers a mixture of rotisserie beef, lamb, pork, ribs, sausage, and chicken, accompanied by nearly two dozen antipasti, or lower-priced forays at the unlimited antipasto bar. At **Tony Cheng's Mongolian Restaurant** there's a $13.95 Mongolian barbecue: pick whatever meats, vegetables, and sauces you crave and hand it over to the chef, who cooks it up for you. La Spagheterria at **Il Radicchio** is quasi-all-you-can-eat: all the plain spaghetti you can eat "on the premises" for six bucks, plus 22 fresh sauces for various per-serving prices, from Pomodoro (tomato sauce with garlic and basil) for $1, to Al Fegatini (chicken livers and Marsala wine) for $2, to top-of-the-line Gamberi (shrimp with onions) for $4. For vegetarians, no-frills **Balajee** (downtown) lays out a meatless Indian buffet for lunch on weekdays.

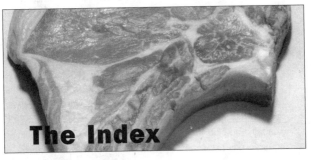

The Index

$$$$$	Over $40
$$$$	$30–$40
$$$	$20–$30
$$	$10–$20
$	Under $10

Per person, including appetizer, entree, and dessert, not including drinks, tax, or tip.

WASHINGTON, D.C. | DINING

America. In a bustling, dramatic four-level space in Union Station (in and around a former Turkish bath), this busy restaurant offers dishes named for various American locales. Table 83 in the Caviar Bay (on a landing behind the semiclad Roman legionnaire statues—see Diversions) has the best restaurant-table view of the Capitol dome. Same menu, less awesome surroundings in Tysons Corner.... *Tel 202/682–9555, First St. and Massachusetts Ave., NW, Union Station Metro, Taxi zone 1D. Tel 703/847–6607, Tysons Corner Center, Rte. 7, McLean, VA. D not accepted.* $$

American Cafe. Stylish local chain serves sit-down meals for prices just above fast-food. The hot artichoke dip appetizer is good to share. Many locations; the one at National Place is good for overcoming tourist fatigue near the Mall.... *Tel 202/626–0770, National Place, 13th and F streets, NW, Metro Center Metro, Taxi zone 1A. Tel 202/547–8500, 227 Massachusetts Ave., NE, Union Station Metro, Taxi zone 2D. $$*

Asia Nora. When New Wave started sounding like nostalgia, organic chef Nora Pouillon (see **Nora**, below) reinvented City Café with her bankable moniker, a pan-Asian fusion-cuisine gimmick, and much higher prices. Easy to find: When you see the anachronistic City Café mural on the outside wall and smell jasmine and ginger, descend the stairs and settle into a Zen state.... *Tel 202/797–4860. 2213 M St., NW, Foggy Bottom–GWU or Dupont Circle Metros, Taxi Zone 2A. AE, D, DC not accepted. $$$*

L'Auberge Chez François. Local critics may award higher praise to the Inn at Little Washington or Jean-Louis at the Watergate, but Washingtonians who pick up the tabs flock to this totally charming French-Alsatian country hideaway when they have something to celebrate (which is why it's usually booked four weeks in advance). There's a five-course prix-fixe menu. In warm weather, drop-ins vie for a spot on the terrace, which doesn't take reservations.... *Tel 703/759–3800. 332 Springvale Rd., Great Falls, VA. Reservations essential. D not accepted. $$$$*

Au Pied de Cochon. Not the best French restaurant in town, but likely the cheapest, and the one most evocative of Left Bank student bistros. Not everyone can stomach the namesake pig's feet, but the daily menu features solid bistro fare (with early-bird specials until 8pm), crepes, lobster specials. Open 24 hours.... *Tel 202/333–5440. 1335 Wisconsin Ave., NW, Taxi zone 2A. D not accepted. $$*

Austin Grill. Good-time places with pastel-tinted Tex-Mex dinner booths and food served as hot as you can stand it. Always long lines to get in, but generous margaritas or Austin-brewed Celis Pale Bock could make you care less.... *Tel 202/337–8080. 2404 Wisconsin Ave., NW, Taxi zone 2A.* **South Austin Grill:** *Tel 703/684–8969, 801 King St., Alexandria, VA. Reservations not accepted. $$*

B. Smith's. This New York import cashes in on Washington's rediscovery of its southern roots. The Union Station location, with its soaring columns and comfortable rattan chairs, feels like the richest plantation this side of Tara.... *Tel 202/ 289–6188. Union Station, First St. and Massachusetts Ave., NE, Union Station Metro, Taxi zone 1D. Reservations recommended. $$$$*

Balajee. This self-service restaurant near Farragut Square offers the purest and cheapest vegetarian food in the downtown area. All-you-can-eat buffet, weekdays from 11am– 2:30pm.... *Tel 202/682–9090. 917 18th St., NW, Farragut North or Farragut West Metros, Taxi zone 1B. Closed Sun. No credit cards. $*

Ben's Chili Bowl. At this black hangout near Howard University, Ben serves mainly chili con carne: straight up, on burgers, on dogs, or half smokes. Hell, he'll even slather chili on your fries and add cheese if you want it. Ben's Big Breakfasts feature eggs, grits, biscuits, accompanied by the usual breakfast meats or scrapple, salmon cakes, or half smokes. No alcohol.... *Tel 202/667–0909. 1213 U St., NW, U Street–Cardozo Metro, Taxi zone 1C. Open daily to 2am; Fri–Sat to 3am. No credit cards. $*

Bistro Français. When workaholic Washington turns into a pumpkin at midnight, this Georgetown haunt kicks into high gear. Budget-priced three-course specials appeal to early-birds (5–7pm) as well as night owls (10:30pm–1am), and include a glass of wine.... *Tel 202/338–3830. 3128 M St., NW, Taxi zone 2A. $$$*

Bistrot Lepic. The secret's out on this classic French bistro that opened in 1995 in upper Georgetown. Quirky, innovative takes on the usual bistro dishes.... *Tel 202/333–0111. 1736 Wisconsin Ave., NW, Taxi zone 2A. Reservations essential. $$$*

Bistro Twenty Fifteen. A hotel dining room that doesn't apologize for itself. Lots of blond wood and comfortable tapestry–upholstered chairs encourage lingering. Regular menu offers refined fare, like soft-shell crabs with capers, house-made sausages, and miniature dessert souffles; a much-lower-priced "Family Fare" offers homey stuff like spaghetti, tacos, and burgers.... *Tel 202/939–4250. Embassy Row*

WASHINGTON, D.C. | DINING

Hotel, 2015 Massachusetts Ave., NW, Dupont Circle Metro, Taxi zone 1B. $$$$

Bombay Club. Sahib-class Indian restaurant has a menu that spans the subcontinent. Specialties include chicken, lamb, and fish baked in a tandoor oven and an outstanding selection of upscale vegetarian dishes.... Tel 202/659–3727. 815 Connecticut Ave., NW, Farragut West or Farragut North Metros, Taxi zone 1B. Reservations recommended. D not accepted. $$$

Burma Restaurant. Washington's only Burmese restaurant. One exotic entree is kaukswe thoke, noodles mixed with a tangy sauce of ground shrimp, cilantro, and peanuts. Pickled green leaf tea salad and golden fingers (rice-battered squash sticks) make good starters or sharers. Service is sometimes so inconspicuous you may wonder if you have a waiter at all.... Tel 202/393–3453. 740 6th St., NW, Gallery Place–Chinatown Metro, Taxi zone 1D. $$.

Cajun Bangkok. Louisiana's Cajun country and Thailand may be far apart geographically, but they're related by the marriage of hot sauces, seafood, and greens, as this restaurant proves. An appetizer called meang kham mingles coconut and ginger with collard greens, but the best entrees are straight Cajun (roasted pecan catfish, crawfish meat with spring onion) or Thai (green curry chicken or beef, seafood stir-fry with basil). Likewise the beer: Thailand's Singha or Blackened Voodoo Dixie.... Tel 703/836–0038. 907 King St., Alexandria, VA. D not accepted. $$

Citronelle. After achieving fame for Citrus in L.A., Michel Richard successfully cloned California-French chi-chi in Santa Barbara, San Francisco, Philadelphia, Baltimore, and now Washington. He breezes in from the coast monthly to make sure hand-picked successors do not deviate from his culinary ideals: eye-pleasing arrangements, inventive combinations, and a light touch with the seasoning. Pre-theater three-course menu ($30) until 6:30, five- and six-course tasting menus, and chef's tables in the kitchen.... Tel 202/726–5000. Latham Hotel, 3000 M St., NW, Taxi zone 2A. Reservations recommended. $$$$$

Coco Loco. Part Brazilian churrascaria (unlimited rotisserie meats and salads), part unlimited antipasto bar, part pan-

Latin tapas bar, a pulsating nightclub after midnight, Coco Loco is Carmen Miranda and MTV rolled into one.... *Tel 202/289–2626. 810 7th St., NW, Chinatown–Gallery Place Metro, Taxi zone 1C. Reservations recommended. $$$*

La Colline. Country-French Capitol Hill fixture, so close to the Senate you can almost hear the filibustering. Business-people like the quiet, spacious tables where they can enjoy the Béarnaise sauce without guilt. Pricey, but three-course prix-fixe dinner is a trophy for bargain-hunters.... *Tel 202/ 737–0400. 400 N. Capitol St., NW, Union Station Metro, Taxi zone 1D. D not accepted. $$$$*

Dean & Deluca Café. The indoor/outdoor (in summer) self-ser-vice café clings to the outer wall of a dramatic market hall housing the Dean & Deluca gourmet food shop. Limited menu has casual Italian flavor—pasta of the day, salads, sandwich-es, pizzettes (baby pizzas), pastries. Not enough? Go inside and retrieve any of the prepared foods, breads, or cheeses sold in the market. Live music Friday, Saturday nights.... *Tel 202/342–2500. 3276 M St., NW, Taxi zone 2A. $*

Delights of the Garden. The principled kitchen of this tiny cafe opposite Howard University prepares strictly vegetarian food: no meat, no dairy, no cooking at all. If you like the grub, buy their book, *The Joy of Not Cooking*. No alcohol.... *Tel 202/588–0648. 2616 Georgia Ave., NW, U Street–Cardozo Metro, Taxi zone 2B. No credit cards. $*

Florida Avenue Grill. A 50-year-old corner diner beloved for old-time southern cooking, located between the U Street Corridor and Howard University. Photo collection above counter commemorates outstanding Washingtonians, not all of them African American, in sports, entertainment, and pol-itics. No alcohol.... *Tel 202/265–1586. 1100 Florida Ave., NW, U Street–Cardozo Metro, Taxi zone 2B. Closed Sun–Mon. AE, D, DC not accepted. $*

Fran O'Brien's Steak House. O'Brien, a Redskins' lineman in the 1950s and a restaurateur for more than 30 years, took over the vast space in the Capital Hilton basement after Trader Vic's sank slowly in the west. This place combines the best elements of a serious steakhouse and a raucous sports bar; choose big or small cuts of all meats on the menu.... *Tel 202/STEAK–99. Capital Hilton, 6th and K streets, NW;*

WASHINGTON, D.C. | DINING

Farragut North, Farragut West, or McPherson Square Metros, Taxi zone 1B. $$$$

Gabriel. The restaurant in the Spanish-owned Barceló Hotel Washington looks pure Spanish, with tan stucco walls, cafe curtains, and a dark mahogany bar, but the food ranges from classic Spanish to Caribbean to Tex-Mex. Popular cocktail hour for area office workers, later scene for P Street gay crowd.... *Tel 202/956–6690. Barceló Hotel Washington, 2121 P St., NW, Dupont Circle Metro, Taxi zone 1B. Reservations recommended. $$$*

Galileo. If you can bear the snooty service accorded to all but regulars, Galileo may offer you an Italian meal you'll never forget. Expense accounts go through heavy-impact aerobics here, and the crowd dresses up.... *Tel 202/293–7191. 1110 21st St., NW, Dupont Circle Metro, Taxi zone 1B. Reservations recommended. $$$$$*

Le Gaulois. Substantive French *bourgeois* fare for moderate prices in a handsome brick rowhouse on the west end of Alexandria Old Town. Menu highlights include the house-made paté platter, a duck and lamb cassoulet from the south of France, plenty of seafood selections depending on the season. *Cuisine minceur* dieter's menu is available but their heart's not in it. Intimate country-style decor.... *Tel 703/739–9494. 1106 King St., Alexandria, VA. Reservations recommended. $$$*

Georgia Brown's. The menu hankers toward Carolina low-country fare: shrimp and grits, Hoppin' John (black-eyed peas and rice to Yankees), and smothered pork chops in sausage gravy.... *Tel 202/393–4499. 950 15th St., NW, McPherson Square Metro, Taxi zone 1B. Reservations recommended. $$$*

Gerard's Place. Chef Gerard Pangaud's signature dishes include confit of pork cheeks, cod with potatoes, rabbit roulade, and sweetbreads with bacon. Very haute French.... *Tel 202/737–4445. 915 15th St., NW, McPherson Square Metro, Taxi zone 1B. Reservations recommended. DC not accepted. $$$$$*

Go-Lo's Restaurant. An outside plaque summarizing this site's connection with Lincoln's assassination is the main thing that distinguishes Go-Lo's from all the other storefront restaurants in Washington's scruffy Chinatown. Specialty dishes include stir-fried mussels and Kingdom pork ribs. Kid's meal deals.... *Tel 202/347–4656. 604 H St., NW, Gallery Place–Chinatown Metro, Taxi zone 1D. $$*

Les Halles. *Mais oui*, they have *onglet* (hangar steak), that butcher's choice cut, along with flank steak, rib steak, steak tartare, house-made sausages and patés, roast chicken, frisée salad, onion soup, celery Rémoulade, marinated leeks, creme brulée and chocolate mousse. If you order wisely, you can eat here for nearly half the price of Washington's American-style steakhouses.... *Tel 202/347– 6848. 1201 Pennsylvania Ave., NW, Federal Triangle or Metro Center Metros, Taxi zone 1D. $$$$*

Hillwood Museum Café. This museum cafe in a converted stable serves breakfast, mostly Russian specialties for lunch, and an English-style afternoon tea from 2 to 4:30. No alcohol. Admission and reservations required to enter museum grounds.... *Tel 202/686–8893. 4155 Linnean Ave., NW, Van Ness–UDC Metro, Taxi zone 3B. Museum closed Feb. Reservations recommended. D, DC not accepted. $*

Inn at Little Washington. The *International Herald Tribune* has ranked Patrick O'Connell's cozy little establishment two hours west of downtown D.C. as one of the 10 best restaurants in the world, and his other national accolades would fill pages. The menu is prix fixe-only and approaches three figures per person on Saturdays—not including wine, tax, and tip.... *Tel 703/675–3800. Middle and Main streets, Washington, VA. AE, D, DC not accepted. Reservations essential. $$$$$+*

Jaleo. *Jaleo* means uproar, and this corner tapas bar, with tables along streetside windows, is indeed full of music and pre-theater/post-theater chatter (mid-theater it quiets down a bit). Valet parking.... *Tel 202/628–7949. 7th and E streets, NW, Gallery Place–Chinatown Metro, Taxi zone 1D. No prime-time reservations. $$$*

Jean-Louis at the Watergate. This is the place to splurge if you've never tasted real foie gras, truffles, woodcock, sea urchin, or squid ink, which Jean-Louis Palladin elevates into the next stratosphere, along with the check. The menu has five- and six-course prix-fixe options, plus a four-course pre-theater one. The Watergate's upstairs bistro, **Palladin By Jean-Louis** (tel 202/298–4455, $$$$) has a menu designed by Jean-Louis, though other chefs do the cooking.... *Tel 202/298–4488. Watergate Hotel, 2650 Virginia Ave., NW, Foggy Bottom–GWU Metro, Taxi zone 2A. Reservations essential. Jacket/tie required. $$$$*

Jin-Ga. A prime spot for Korean barbecue, where table-grilled entrees come with *miso* soup and five side dishes. Aim for table overlooking traditional landscaped rock garden. Bargain lunches; free valet parking with dinner.... *Tel 202/785–0720. 1250 24th St., NW, Dupont Circle or Foggy Bottom–GWU Metros, Taxi zone 1B. Closed Sun. Reservations recommended. $$$*

Jockey Club. The Ritz-Carlton restaurant closed in 1992 for nine months, only to be reborn later with every dark-wood-and-pewter jot and tittle intact. A place to appear for international power brokers and Hollywood types; Nancy Reagan (who was both) considered it her own special place. The menu is traditional Continental.... *Tel 202/659–8000. Ritz-Carlton Hotel, 2100 Massachusetts Ave., NW, Dupont Circle Metro, Taxi zone 1B. Jacket/tie required. $$$$$*

Kinkead's. This top-notch two-story seafood restaurant has a cavernous dining room upstairs with an open kitchen, which discloses no trade secrets—chef Bob Kinkead and his line cooks communicate amid the din via NFL-style headsets. The downstairs cafe/bar is for smaller appetites and smaller spenders.... *Tel 202/296–7700. 2000 Pennsylvania Ave, NW, Foggy Bottom–GWU Metro, Taxi zone 1B. Reservations recommended. $$$$*

Las Cruces. Named after a town in New Mexico, it stands in tacky polar opposition to the Santa Fe and Taos chicdoms. The chef, a Las Cruces High grad, imports tortillas and chilies from home for Tex-Mex–New-Mex standards like jalapeño fritters, stolen–by–Texas tacos, pancake-style enchiladas, grenade-sized chile rellenos. Friday dance party features eighties hits.... *Tel 202/328–3153. 1524 U St., NW, U Street–Cardozo Metro, Taxi zone 1B. Closed Mon. $$*

Lavandou. French sans sticker shock. Close to National Zoo, prix-fixe menu attracts flocks of early-birds each day.... *Tel*

202/966–3002. 3321 Connecticut Ave., NW, Cleveland Park Metro, Taxi zone 3B. Reservations recommended. D not accepted. $$$

Legal Sea Foods. Outlets of the famed Boston seafood chain, with more refined décor and slightly higher prices (but the food's just as good and portions are even larger).... *Tel 202/496–1111. 2020 K St., NW, Farragut North or Farragut West Metros, Taxi zone 1B. Tel 703/827–8900, Tysons Galleria, 2001 International Dr., McLean, VA. Reservations recommended. $$$*

Library of Congress Cafeteria. Sixth-floor dining area overlooking the seldom-seen Anacostia River is mostly catered by outside restaurants.... *Tel 202/707–8000 or TDD 202/707–6200. Madison Building, First St. and Independence Ave., SE, Capitol South Metro, Taxi zone 1D. Open weekdays for breakfast and lunch only. No credit cards. $*

Maison Blanche. "Modern French" cuisine, a block from the White House, attracts celebrity pols and Cabinet makers and shakers. Mostly à la carte, but the three-course prix-fixe menu is a good deal. Cheaper yet are the free hors d'oeuvres during weekday happy hour in the circular glass cocktail lounge.... *Tel 202/842–0070. 1725 F St., NW, Farragut West Metro, Taxi zone 1A. $$$$$*

Market Lunch. The ultimate fate of Capitol Hill's Eastern Market, the city's only permanent indoor/outdoor food market, remains clouded in controversy, but lines keep forming at Market Lunch in the market's northeast corner. The longest lines are on Saturday mornings, for hearty servings of ham and eggs and grits; weekday lunches feature crab cakes and smoky North Carolina barbecue. Self-service, and no lingering, because someone badly needs your counter space or table.... *Tel 202/547–8444. 7th and C streets., SE, Eastern Market Metro, Taxi zone 2D. Closed Sun–Mon. No credit cards. $*

Melrose. Seafood dominates the menu in this upscale hotel dining room: faux ravioli of gravlax and crabmeat, ricotta gnocchi with shrimp and Smithfield ham, angel hair pasta with lobster and tomato, and some of the best crab cakes in town.... *Tel 202/955–3899. Park Hyatt Washington Hotel, 24th and M streets, NW, Foggy Bottom–GWU or Dupont Circle Metros, Taxi zone 2A. $$$$*

WASHINGTON, D.C. | DINING

Miss Saigon. As dramatic as its Broadway namesake, with shiny black walls, windows open to the street on two sides, and sheltering palms. Headliners on the menu are tiny roast quail, served as an appetizer or entree soup, grilled seafood, and the vegetarian Buddha's Delight.... *Tel 202/ 667–1900. 1847 Columbia Rd., NW, Woodley Park–Zoo Metro, Taxi zone 2B. $$*

The Monocle. This traditional Hill hangout serves steaks, chops, and seafood. It's a good place to make the acquaintance of crab cakes and, since Congress members come here when they're picking up their own tab, prices are reasonable.... *Tel 202/546–4888. 107 D St., NE, Union Station Metro, Taxi zone 1D. Reservations recommended. Closed Sun. $$$*

Morrison-Clark Inn. Quaint (with a capital curlicue), heavily tchotchke'd and ornately mirrored, this Victorian-era dining room of a historic landmark inn is swoony enough for dates, refined enough for women dining alone, and quiet enough for businesspeople pondering sheafs of contracts over house-blend coffees. The vaguely Mediterranean menu changes seasonally.... *Tel 202/898–1200. 11th St. and Massachusetts Ave., NW, Metro Center Metro, Taxi zone 1C. Reservations required. D not accepted. $$$$*

Morton's of Chicago. Prime aged beef for larger-than-life egos with larger-than-life charge limits. The porterhouse steak, which comes in one-and-a-half and three-pound slabs, shines on.... *Tel 202/342–6258, 3251 Prospect St., NW, Georgetown, Taxi zone 2A. Tel 703/883–0800, Fairfax Square, 8075 Leesburg Pike, Vienna, VA. Reservations recommended. $$$$$*

Mount Vernon Inn. Just outside the gates of Mount Vernon, the Inn keeps up the spirit with colonial fittings and furniture, waiters decked out in ruffles and knee stockings, and native Virginia dishes George Washington might have served his guests.... *Tel 703/780–0011. South end of George Washington Memorial Pkwy., Mount Vernon, VA. Reservations recommended. $$$*

Mrs. Simpson's. Before Marge, Homer, and a certain ex-football player sullied the name in perpetuity, the most famous Simpson was the almost-local Mrs. Wallis Warfield Simpson of Baltimore, a commoner who snagged a king, Edward VIII of England. He abdicated and they lived thronelessly ever after as the Duke and Duchess of Windsor. Knickknacks, photographs, magazine covers, coronation souvenirs, and other memorabilia crammed into this white tablecloth retreat pay homage to them. Menu is mostly light stuff.... *Tel 202/332–8300. 2915 Connecticut Ave., NW, Woodley Park–Zoo Metro, Taxi zone 2B. $$$$*

The Mudd House. Unassuming snack shop, done up in mudlike terra-cotta paint, timber walls, and desert prints. Coffee bar in front serves organic coffee drinks; after 3pm prices for scones, bagels, and muffins are cut in half.... *Tel 202/822–8455. 1724 M St., NW, Farragut North Metro, Taxi zone 1B. Breakfast, lunch only. No credit cards.$*

Music City Roadhouse. Country cookin', served family-style in a spacious converted Georgetown foundry. College kids come in to carbo-load and guzzle bargain-priced pitchers of beer, while somewhat older kickers sip microbrews and a big selection of small-batch bourbons. Free parking (in Georgetown!) weekdays after 5, all day Saturday, Sunday.... *Tel 202/337–4444. 1050 30th St., NW, Taxi zone 2A. $$*

Nora. Austrian-born, classically trained Nora Pouillon was doing organic back when it was the near-exclusive domain of the Vita-Mix set. Vegetarians will have plenty of choices, but artfully interpreted (additive-free) meat, fish, and fowl dominate the menu.... *Tel 202/462–5143. R St. and Florida Ave., NW, Dupont Circle Metro, Taxi zone 1B. AE, D, DC not accepted. $$$$*

Obelisk. For about $33, the chic young things who dine here choose from two appetizers, two first courses, three main courses, an optional cheese course, and dessert. The room seats 30 if no one exhales. Chef Peter Pastan also owns the jam-packed Pizzeria Paradiso next door (see below).... *Tel 202/872–1180. 2029 P St., NW, Dupont Circle Metro, Taxi zone 1B. Reservations recommended. D not accepted. $$$$*

Occidental Grill. Around the corner from the White House, this venerable clubby power hangout charges high prices for what you get. Make a meal of appetizers or order low on the menu (Occidental Burger, $7.95) just to get in and see the place.... *Tel 202/783–1475. 1475 Pennsylvania Ave., NW, Metro Center Metro, Taxi zone 1A. Reservations recommended. $$$*

Old Ebbitt Grill. Bursting with tourists—make a reservation or you'll wind up wandering around the White House area with a beeper on your belt like some Secret Service agent. Menu features federally approved favorites like leg of lamb, pork chops, pepperpot beef.... *Tel 202/347–4801. 675 15th St., NW, Metro Center or McPherson Square Metros, Taxi zone 1A. Reservations recommended. $$*

Palladin by Jean-Louis. See **Jean-Louis at the Watergate**.

The Palm. Where Washington's political/media/sports power cabal migrate. What's for dinner? Shut up and eat your steak.... *Tel 202/293–9091. 1225 19th St., NW, Farragut North or Dupont Circle Metros, Taxi zone 1B. Reservations recommended. $$$$*

Pan Asian Noodles & Grill. A stylistic cut above more nationalistic typical noodle houses, it offers a 15-dish tour of the Asian noodlery; the grill is an afterthought, a couple of chicken dishes and Crying Tiger, a steak with a "tear-bringing" dipping sauce. Vermont Avenue location popular for mildly festive workday lunches and workaholic dinners; P Street gets Dupont Circle neighborhood denizens.... *Tel 202/783–8899, 1018 Vermont Ave., NW, McPherson Square Metro, Taxi zone 1B. Tel 202/872–8889, 2020 P St., NW, Dupont Circle Metro, Taxi zone 1B. $$*

Panevino. Underappreciated country-Italian ristorante, for designer pizzas and unusual pasta specialties. Sluice it down with a pitcher of their exclusive Villa dell'Ugo chianti. Fixed-price four-course seafood feast Fridays; Tuscan brunch weekends.... *Tel 202/223–0747, Embassy Suites Hotel, 23rd and N streets, NW, Foggy Bottom or Dupont Circle Metros, Taxi zone 2A. Tel 703/838–9600, 1755 Duke St., Alexandria, VA, King Street Metro. $$*

Patent Pending. Charming self-service cafe between the National Portrait Gallery and the National Museum of American Art on opposite wings of the old Patent Building.

No MSG added to soups and sauces; beer and wine; outdoor seating in the sculpture garden.... *Tel 202/357–2700. Block of 8th, 9th, F, and G streets, NW, Gallery Place Metros, Taxi zone 1D. Lunch only. No credit cards. $*

Pesce. Owned jointly by two of Washington's best-known chefs, Jean-Louis Palladin and Roberto Donna, this simple eatery serves the same skate, soft-shell crab, and sardines they charge lots more for in their white tablecloth locations. Meatiest crab cakes in town.... *Tel 202/466–3474. 2016 P St., NW, Dupont Circle Metro, Taxi zone 1B. $$$*

Pho 75. Most Vietnamese restaurants serve their versions of *pho*, a noodle soup in an anise-flavored beef broth, but in these bustling strip-mall mess halls it's the only thing on the menu. *Pho* comes in two sizes, large and small, but in 16 combinations of beef, from ordinary flank steak and brisket to exotica like soft tendon and bible tripe. No alcohol; ice coffee mixed with condensed milk is drink of choice. Closes at 8pm daily.... *Tel 703/525–7355, 1711 Wilson Blvd., Arlington, VA, Rosslyn Metro. Tel 703/ 204–1490, 3103 Graham Road, Falls Church, VA. Tel 301/ 434–7844, 1510 University Blvd. E., Langley Park, MD. No credit cards. $*

Pizzeria Paradiso. The ten fundamental *pizze* at this wildly popular Dupont Circle spot are imaginative but not self-consciously outrageous. Add the usual suspects plus capers, eggplant, potatoes. Many folks prefer to order the *panini*, roasted pork, lamb, vegetables, or cheese stuffed into homemade foccacia. Drink beer or wine, a concoction of lemonade and soda, or semisweet Tuscan Sangria, the sangria for people who hate sangria.... *Tel 202/223–1245. 2029 P St., NW, Dupont Circle Metro, Taxi zone 1B. No reservations. $$*

Presidential McDonald's. So-called (unofficially) because it's closest to the White House, this joint sells the same Big Macs and Happy Meals as any other McD's.... *Tel 202/ 828–8311. 750 17th St., NW; Farragut West Metro, Taxi zone 1A. Reservations not accepted. $*

Provence. Designer French food, in a setting that's more *Architectural Digest* than Arles—heaping baskets of dried herbs, wooden shutters, and stone floors. No matter, it's too noisy to carry on a conversation anyway.... *Tel 202/296–1166. 2401 Pennsylvania Ave., NW, Foggy Bottom–GWU Metro, Taxi zone 2A. Reservations recommended.* $$$$

Il Radicchio. The gimmick that makes these Dupont Circle and Georgetown trattorias so wildly popular is La Spagheterria, an all-you-can-eat spaghetti deal with a host of sauces to choose from. Pizza offers similar à la carte overkill: two sizes, 14 combinations of cheese and sauce, 25 toppings. Kids enjoy cosmopolitan clutter and bottomless spaghetti bowl, but not the bottomless wait for tables, especially on weekends.... *Tel 202/986–2627, 1509 17th St., NW, Dupont Circle Metro, Taxi zone 1B. Tel 202/337–2627, 1211 Wisconsin Ave., NW, Taxi zone 2A. Reservations not accepted.* $$

Red Sage. The most talked-about restaurant of 1992, culinary cowboy Mark Miller's concept-riddled Red Sage has faded faster than bleached denim. Save serious money at the **Chili Bar** or the **Red Sage Cafe** (both $$, no reservations), with lighter, healthier dishes: shrimp in green chili rice, Caesar salad six ways, wild mushroom and roasted corn pizza. Use a trip to the restroom as a pretense to peek downstairs, and you'll enjoy the best of both worlds.... *Tel 202/638–4444. 14th and H streets, NW, Metro Center Metro, Taxi zone 1A.* $$$$

I Ricchi. This upscale northern-Italian-style trattoria elevates cooking on a wood-burning grill to the level of performance art. Anything prepared here is likely to be superb.... *Tel 202/835–0459. 1220 19th St., NW, Dupont Circle or Farragut North Metros, Taxi zone 1B.* $$$$

River Club. Come here for forties big band music and nineties big wallet prices. Many just skip dinner, order champagne, and dance the night away. Complimentary valet parking.... *Tel 202/333–8118. 3223 K St., NW, Taxi zone 2A. Jacket/tie required.* $$$$

Saigon Gourmet. The attractive setting and helpful service in this Woodley Park Vietnamese spot make it more tourist-frendly than its brusquely authentic competitors in the 'hoods. **East Wind**, a clone in Old Town Alexandria (tel 703/836–1515, 809 King St.), has a nearly identical menu.... *Tel 202/265–1360. 2635 Connecticut Ave., NW, Woodley Park–Zoo Metro, Taxi zone 2A. D not accepted.* $$

Sequoia. Popular casual spot in Washington Harbour complex, with terraced dining overlooking the Potomac. Accentless American favorites like duck–pignoli dumplings, beer–batter onion rings, cedar planked salmon, and whole wheat spaghetti. Nice riverside walk to or from Kennedy Center.... *Tel 202/944–4200. 3000 K St., NW, Taxi zone 2A. $$$*

1789. A distinguished and quite formal establishment in a Georgetown town house. Two menus a year—spring/summer and fall/winter—feature classic renderings for regional game like quail, duck, and the outstanding Chesapeake Bay Hot Pot, an American bouillabaisse served in an iron skillet. Pre-theater dinner, $25.... *Tel 202/965–1789. 1226 36th St., NW, Taxi zone 2A. Reservations recommended. Jacket required. $$$$$*

Star of Siam. For spicy Thai curry. Use the downtown location for a quiet business lunch; the one in Adams-Morgan swings, with seating outdoors on the roof and soft chair-shaped cushions within.... *Tel 202/785–2839, 1136 19th St., NW, Farragut North Metro, Taxi zone 1B. Tel 202/986–4133, 2446 18th St., NW, Woodley Park–Zoo Metro, Taxi zone 2B. Tel 703/524–1208, International Plaza, 1735 N. Lynn St., Arlington, VA, Rosslyn Metro. $$*

Straits of Malaya. Situated on the Straits of 18th Street between Dupont Circle and Adams-Morgan, it's the place to eat Singapore's multiethnic "straits cuisine," and to drink your first Singapore Sling (theirs has layers of gin, lemonade, cherry brandy, melon liqueur), Singapore's acclaimed Tiger beer, or 15 types of tea.... *Tel 202/483–1483. 1836 18th St., NW, Dupont Circle Metro, Taxi zone 1B. $$$*

Tabard Inn. English country inn setting in funky hotel offers healthfully correct menu; count on several outstanding vegetarian entrees. Outdoor courtyard seating and strapping (but healthful) breakfasts.... *Tel 202/833–2668. 1739 N St., NW, Dupont Circle Metro, Taxi zone 1B. Reservations recommended. AE, D, DC not accepted. $$$*

Taberna del Alabardero. A dignified dining destination for those who wish to celebrate grandly—the classic Spanish food is a refreshing alternative to the ubiquitous fancy French and Italian. Entrance on 18th Street; free valet parking at dinner.... *Tel 202/429–2200. 1776 I St., NW (enter* on 18th St.), Farragut West Metro, Taxi zone 1B. Reservations recommended. $$$$

Terrace Café. Sit-down restaurant in the 20th-century East Wing of the National Gallery of Art. The menu changes constantly to reflect the country of origin of artists currently on exhibit. Wine and beer.... Tel 202/7789–3201. 4th St. and Pennsylvania Ave., NW, Archives Metro, Taxi zone 1D. Lunch only. Reservations recommended. D, DC not accepted. $$

Tom Tom. A prime site in the Adams-Morgan pickup scene. No entree—not even the wine—costs over ten bucks, which explains the 45-minute wait most nights. (Watch out for sneak attacks; the basket of bread they offer isn't free).... Tel 202/588–1300. 2333 18th St., NW, Woodley Park–Zoo Metro, Taxi zone 2B. Reservations not accepted. $$

The Tombs. Basement burger-and-brew Georgetown U hangout immortalized in Exorcist III.... Tel 202/337–6668. 1226 36th Street, NW; Taxi zone 2A. $$

Tony Cheng's Mongolian Restaurant. Two ways to go here: With the Mongolian Fireboat you cook chicken, beef, and veggies at your own table in a pot of steaming broth; with the Mongolian Barbecue, you fill a bowl with meats, vegetables, spices, and oils from the buffet table and hand it to a chef. **Tony's Seafood Restaurant**, with lunchtime dim sum, is upstairs, but the pseudo-Mongolian formats are cheaper and more of a hoot.... Tel 202/842–8669. 619 H St., NW, Gallery Place–Chinatown Metro, Taxi zone 1C. DC, D not accepted. $$

Trumpets. Predominantly gay bar and restaurant, with loud music and gimmicky cooking. Low-fat dishes are designated by scissors; vegetarian ones with yin-yang symbols.... Tel 202/232–4141. 1633 Q St., NW, Dupont Circle Metro, Taxi zone 1B. $$$

Tunnicliff's. A little bit of New Orleans on Capitol Hill. The menu is eclectic American with Louisiana accents—crawfish salad on French bread, andouille po-boy, red beans and rice on Monday. Aim to sit on comfy furniture in the living room.... Tel 202/546–3663. 222 7th St., SE, Eastern Market Metro, Taxi zone 2D. $$$

Two Quail. In a Capitol Hill row house decorated with *Madame Sousatzka* abandon, this place serves a sweet little menu, with a handful of yummy things like corn bread and pecan-stuffed chicken, blue cheese and apple salad, tortellini primavera.... *Tel 202/543–8030. 320 Massachusetts Ave., NE, Union Station Metro, Taxi zone 2D. $$$*

Union Street Public House. This burly old saloon near the river in Alexandria's Old Town tourist quarter works on several levels: for snacks, sandwiches, full meals, desserts, or just a mug of their own beer in a barroom with street action view. The roomy upstairs dining room is best for families, but ground-floor raw bar has more waterfront soul.... *Tel 703/548–1785. 121 S. Union St., Alexandria, VA. $$*

Vidalia. Named after the sweet southern onion, this restaurant uses the South as a starting point for culinary explorations that go all over the map. A mandatory stop for serious foodies.... *Tel 202/659–1990. 1990 M St., NW, Dupont Circle or Farragut North Metros, Taxi zone 1B. Reservations recommended. $$$$*

Yenching Palace. Chinese food the way it was before we knew any better. This Cleveland Park spot is best known as a site of secret meetings that solved the Cuban Missile Crisis in 1962. Must have been written in the fortune cookies.... *Tel 202/262–8200. 3524 Connecticut Ave., NW, Cleveland Park Metro, Taxi zone 3B. $$*

Washington, D.C. Dining

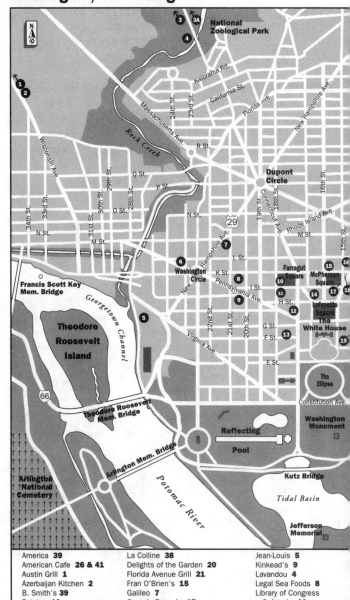

America **39**
American Cafe **26 & 41**
Austin Grill **1**
Azerbaijan Kitchen **2**
B. Smith's **39**
Balajee **10**
Ben's Chili Bowl **22**
Bombay Club **14**
Burma **33**
Checkers **43 & 48**
Coco Loco **30**

La Colline **38**
Delights of the Garden **20**
Florida Avenue Grill **21**
Fran O'Brien's **15**
Galileo **7**
Georgia Brown's **17**
Gerard's Place **18**
Go-Lo's **32**
Les Halles **27**
Hard Rock Cafe **35**
Hillwood Museum Cafe **3A**
Jaleo **34A**

Jean-Louis **5**
Kinkead's **9**
Lavandou **4**
Legal Sea Foods **8**
Library of Congress
  Cafeteria **44**
Maison Blanche **13**
Market Lunch **46**
Misha's Deli **47**
Monocle, The **40**
Morrison Clark Inn **23**

Adams-Morgan and Dupont Circle Dining

Asia Nora **19**	Mudd House **25**	Il Radicchio **15**
Bistro Twenty Fifteen **11**	Nora **8**	I Ricchi **20**
Gabriel **9**	Obelisk **12**	Saigon Gourmet **2**
Jin-ga **16**	The Palm **22**	Star of Siam **5 & 24**
Jockey Club **10**	Pan Asian Noodles	Straits of Malaya **6**
Las Cruces **7**	& Grill **13 & 26**	Tabard Inn **21**
Melrose **18**	Panevino **17**	Tom Tom **4**
Miss Saigon **3**	Pesce **15**	Trumpets **14**
Mrs. Simpson's **1**	Pizzeria Paradiso **12**	Vidalia **23**

Georgetown Dining

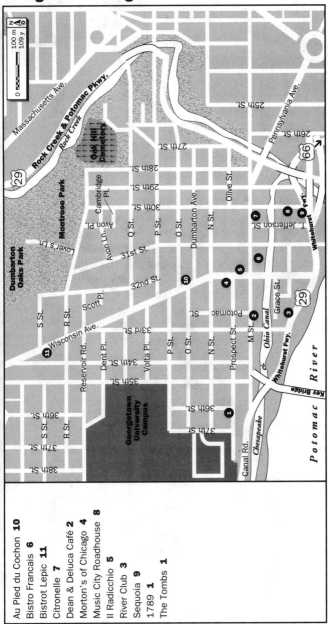

Au Pied du Cochon **10**

Bistro Francais **6**

Bistrot Lepic **11**

Citronelle **7**

Dean & Deluca Café **2**

Morton's of Chicago **4**

Music City Roadhouse **8**

Il Radicchio **5**

River Club **3**

Sequoia **9**

1789 **1**

The Tombs **1**

3 sions

Washington certainly lives up to its nickname, "Capital of the Free World"—almost everything worth doing here is free. Of course, everybody pays for Washington's attractions through their taxes. But since you have to pay whether you see them or not, come out and get your money's worth.

Getting Your Bearings

The U.S. Capitol is the focal point of Washington geography. North Capitol Street, East Capitol Street, South Capitol Street, and an invisible line in the middle of the Mall between the Capitol and the Potomac all theoretically converge under the Capitol and divide the city into quadrants. All D.C. addresses end with NW, NE, SE, or SW to indicate which quadrant. But the Capitol is not in the center of the city, so quadrants are not of equal size. The Northwest is by far the largest and most visited section; almost all hotels and restaurants, and most of the attractions, are here. Connecticut Avenue, the major north-south artery running through Northwest, is the street you'll return to over and over as you try to get around.

North-south numbered streets run in both directions parallel to North/South Capitol Street, and addresses on east-west streets correspond with them (i.e., addresses between 5th and 6th streets will be in the 500s). The much more colorfully designated east-west streets use letters or names in alphabetical order, with a few notable gaps. There's no J Street because (depending on whom you talk to) (a) city planners wanted to give the snub that keeps on snubbing to fractious first Supreme Court Chief Justice John Jay, or (b) the cursive letter "J" could too easily be misconstrued for the letter "I" in I Street (which to avoid confusion with 1st Street sometimes appears as Eye Street). There are no X, Y, or Z streets because... because... there just aren't.

The alphabetical streets immediately north of the Mall are simply letters. The next alphabet uses patriotic two-syllable names (Adams, Irving, Randolph); the third alphabet uses three-syllable names (Brandywine, Fessenden, Oliver), and the fourth alphabet, botanical names (Aspen, Juniper, lastly Verbena). The alphabet code actually helps you find your way around. If you know the name of the alphabetical street and the nearest numbered cross street, you should know about where you are.

Unfortunately, the elegant coherency of the D.C. grid is totally undone by the broad diagonals that slice through neighborhoods, twist around traffic circles, duck beneath underpasses, and flabbergast drivers. The diagonals are all named after states. Every state has a street. For the most part, streets named after northern states are located north of the Mall, southern states to the south, but there are many exceptions. **Pennsylvania Avenue** is the grand boulevard of the nation, connecting the White House and the Capitol; **Wisconsin Avenue** is the raucous main drag of Georgetown; **Massachusetts Avenue** between Dupont Circle and 33rd Street (where the Vice President's mansion sits on the grounds of the U. S. Naval Observatory) is also known as **Embassy Row; Connecticut Avenue** is so prestigious a business address that buildings around the corner and down the block somehow wangle to use it as their address.

Most of Washington's stellar attractions are on or near the **National Mall**, a quarter-mile-wide, three-mile-long expanse of green between the Potomac River and the U.S. Capitol (originally, the western half was *under* the Potomac). The term **downtown** is almost meaningless (though frequently heard) here. Most private businesses and hotels cluster in the wide diagonal swath bordered by Pennsylvania and Massachusetts avenues and running from 1st to 22nd streets, NW. Subsectors have distinct personalities: the courts and kindred institutions are located from 1st Street to 6th Street; the area west of Chinatown is dominated by the Washington Convention Center (H Street from 9th to 11th streets) and major convention hotels; associations and trade organizations occupy office buildings close to the White House (14th to 18th streets); K Street west of 16th Street and up along Connecticut Avenue is the district of lobbyists and lawyers.

Dupont Circle lies at the intersection of 19th and P streets and Connecticut, New Hampshire, and Massachusetts avenues, a mile northwest of the White House, though the

Scandal Sites

Tidal Basin Follies (October 7, 1964)—Independence Avenue at Kutz Bridge. When House Ways and Means Committee Chairman Wilbur Mills (D-AK) was stopped for speeding at 2am, his date for the evening, stripper Fanne Foxe, bolted out of the car and dove into the Tidal Basin. Ms. Foxe subsequently changed her stage sobriquet from "Argentine Firecracker" to "Tidal Basin Bombshell."
***Gary Hart's Lovenest** (May 1987)—517 6th Street, SE. Miami Herald reporters staked out home of presidential candidate Senator Gary Hart (D-CO) to catch him and model Donna Rice with their pants down. Their revelations torpedoed Hart's candidacy.*
***Vincent Foster Suicide** (July 22, 1993)—Fort Marcy Park, George Washington Parkway, Langley, Virginia. White House counsel Foster shot himself in roadside park near CIA headquarters.*

WASHINGTON, D.C. | DIVERSIONS

borders of the Dupont Circle neighborhood are limited only by real estate developers' audacity. **Georgetown** is located north of K Street and across Rock Creek from the rest of the city—the Metro doesn't even go there.

The Lowdown

Since you've been gone... If you haven't been to Washington lately, some pleasant surprises await you. You'll have to visit the new **White House Visitor Center** to pick up tickets for White House tours, but while you're there, the center tells you more about the White House than the tour itself. At the new **Korean War Veterans Memorial** (opened July 1995), a ghostly platoon climbs a treacherous slope opposite the Lincoln Memorial. Also opened in 1995, the **National Gallery of Caricature and Cartoon Art** occupies the old *Baltimore Sun* offices opposite the National Press Club. The **Kreeger Museum**, opened in June 1994, displays modern art in a 1967 Philip Johnson building, designed as a museum though the Kreeger family actually lived here for a while. There are plenty of Picassos, and the former dining room now serves nine Monets and a Renoir. And the West Wing of the old **National Gallery of Art** has a new Micro Gallery which, on computer monitors, displays many of the museum's holdings.

Postcard views... The west steps of the **U.S. Capitol** get a sweeping view of the National Mall with the Washington Monument in the background. Stand beside the **Reflecting Pool** on the Mall (at 3rd Street NW or SW) for a full frontal shot of the Capitol itself. Somewhat ironically, the best long-range view of Mall monuments and the august buildings of the federal government is from the porch of Arlington House, Robert E. Lee's home in **Arlington National Cemetery**. Nearby, you can see a striking alignment of the Capitol, Washington Monument, Lincoln Memorial, and the Iwo Jima Memorial from the slope behind the latter, officially named the **U.S. Marine Corps War Memorial**. The steps of the **Thomas Jefferson Memorial** offer a gorgeous view of the Tidal Basin (especially in cherry blossom time) and, in the distance, the White House. For an optical illusion that makes it look like the White House has a dome—the one on the Jefferson Memorial to be exact—stand in the middle of 16th Street beside **Meridian Hill Park** (bounded by 15th, 16th, W, and Euclid streets).

Monumental achievements... The **Washington Monument** is by law the tallest structure in the city, and the most distinctive element of the Washington skyline—but it's never had it easy. Construction of the 555-foot obelisk began in 1848 but wasn't completed until 1884, the 37-year gap caused first by a depletion of funds and then by the Civil War. By the time they got enough money to finish the project, the marble from the original quarry had been depleted, hence the two-tone effect you see today. Tickets run out quickly; if you get there too late, go instead to the Old Post Office tower, where the view's nearly as good and lines are usually nonexistent.

The **Lincoln Memorial**, a perfectly proportioned marble temple housing a pensive statue of Abraham Lincoln by Daniel Chester French, has, like Lincoln, attracted its share of potshots. First they came from Lincoln-haters, who stalled its opening until 1922, nearly threescore years after Lincoln's death. During World War II, a soldier on the roof of the Department of the Interior, about a half-mile away, accidentally shot off part of the marble roofline; most was repaired, but some damage is still visible over the Connecticut state seal above the front steps between the sixth and seventh columns. On the steps of this memorial, Marian Anderson sang on Easter Sunday 1939, when the Daughters of the American Revolution wouldn't let her sing in their Constitution Hall; on August 28, 1963, Dr. Martin Luther King Jr. delivered his "I Have A Dream" speech here (with an encore performance by Marian Anderson).

The **Thomas Jefferson Memorial**, a round-domed building ringed by 54 Ionic columns, mimics the design of Rome's Parthenon and Jefferson's home, Monticello, in Charlottesville, Virginia. Inside, a 19-foot-high statue of Jefferson clad in a fur-collared greatcoat—a gift from Polish Revolutionary War hero Thaddeus Kosciuszko—stares across the Tidal Basin at the White House. Dedicated in 1943—on the 200th anniversary of Jefferson's birth—it was initially an object of contempt. Art critics called the low circular structure "Jefferson's muffin," and early tree-huggers chained themselves to the cherry trees that had to be sacrificed to build the memorial.

Memorial moments... Initially rejected as too dark, depressing, abstract, and nontraditional, the **Vietnam Veterans Memorial**—two mirror-like black granite triangular walls wedged into the earth and engraved with the names of the 58,196 Americans who never returned from Vietnam—now draws around 1.5 million visitors every year, more than any of the other monuments, and many leave extraordinarily touching mementos: flowers, letters, photos, medals, flags. Opposite the Lincoln Memorial, a 24-hour vigil has become a flea market for The Wall T-shirts, MIA-POW bracelets, bumper stickers, books, and news about the plight of those still missing.

The **Korean War Veterans Memorial** honors (finally) the "silent generation" of soldiers who fought the "forgotten war" of 1951–53. Sitting on a patch of West Potomac Park off the right hand of the statue in the Lincoln Memorial, across the Reflecting Pond from the Vietnam Veterans Memorial, its focus is a ghostly platoon of 19 larger-than-life infantrymen on perpetual patrol in a triangular field of scrubby juniper. The Korean Memorial bears no names, but computers in an on-site kiosk can print out the biographies of (eventually) 50,000 casualties, including photographs when available. The **National Law Enforcement Officers Memorial** displays on low, marble oval walls the names of over 13,500 officers killed in the line of duty—beginning with U.S. Marshal Robert Forsyth, who was shot in 1794 while serving court papers in a civil suit.

Chances are that all those landlubbers idling on Pennsylvania Avenue across from the National Archives don't have a clue that the pavement beneath their feet is engraved with the world's largest grid map of the world, in two shades of granite. This is the outdoor section of the **U.S. Navy Memorial**, a 100-foot diameter plaza with 22 friezes, fountain pools "salted" by waters of the seven seas, and the *Lone Sailor* statue, a popular spot for candid poses.

Just north of Arlington Cemetery, in direct line with the Capitol, Washington Monument, and Lincoln Memorial, stands the **Marine Corps War Memorial**, much better known as the Iwo Jima Memorial. Six times life-size, the statue depicts six soldiers raising an American flag (it's never lowered) over the Japanese-held island of Iwo Jima on February 19, 1945, in one of the final assaults of World War II. Based on a Pulitzer Prize-winning photograph of the scene restaged the following day, the statue by Navy sculptor Felix W. de Weldon looks impressive enough as you drive by on George Washington Parkway. But it's worth a closer look to see the hyperdetailed faces modelled after the actual participants.

Round-the-block lines at the **U.S. Holocaust Memorial Museum** may lead you to believe this is a super-tough ticket, but relax, the lines are only for free tickets to the Permanent Exhibition. Anyone can enter the rest of the place, and there's plenty to see: the red-brick walls and gun-metal gray girders of its raw skylit interior; "Daniel's Story," for children over 8; the Wexner Learning Center, an interactive computer system for visitors to access documents, films, music on the Holocaust; the bi-level gift shop which focuses on Judaica and World War II; at least two temporary exhibits (one on the 1936 Olympics in Berlin is planned to coincide with the 1996 Olympics in Atlanta). But grim subject matter notwithstanding, the Permanent Exhibition (for visitors 11 and older) is a flat-out great museum experience, using video, photos, documents, replicas, and authentic artifacts to tell a story with a clear beginning, middle, and (somewhat happy) ending. It's hard for us to be irreverent about this place, but what's with its Museum Café? The matzo balls: nothing to write home about. For $7.50, the lox and bagels are not exactly what I'd call a bargain. And you call this service?

National treasures... At the **National Archives of the United States** visitors get up-close views of the original versions of America's Great Charters: the Declaration of Independence, the Constitution of the United States, the Bill of Rights. But they can't see the mechanism that each night lowers the documents 22 feet down into a 55-ton nuclear-bomb-proof concrete vault, built in 1952 so they wouldn't have to spirit off the priceless documents to Fort Knox whenever the U.S. got into some war. On display in the Archives' churchlike Rotunda, the parchment documents are barely legible under three panes of thick glass within bronze-framed helium-filled cases. The Archives' copy of the Magna Carta, England's 1215 rough draft of the U.S. Constitution, is on loan indefinitely from Ross Perot. The Archives' actually holds an impressive 7 million photos, 118,000 movie reels, 11 million maps, 170,000 sound recordings, and 285,000 artifacts, a tiny fraction of which is on display in the Circular Gallery behind the Rotunda.

And talk about vast holdings—the **Library of Congress**, which opened in 1800 as a one-room reference collection, has mushroomed into a 30 million-volume "library of last resort," owning a copy of nearly every book ever published in the United States. While absolutely no one—not even Congress members—can borrow books here, anyone above high school age who has a photo ID can prowl the reading rooms and summon books.

Anglophiles might nip across the street from the Library of Congress to the **Folger Shakespeare Library**, a private institution bankrolled by Standard Oil baron Henry Clay Folger, which has a good share of England's national treasures. Along with manuscripts, theatrical memorabilia, and (in storage) some of Queen Elizabeth I's corsets, it has by far the world's largest collection of Shakespeare first editions, including its most priceless item, a first edition of gory *Titus Andronicus*.

Where to see your tax $$$ at work... The U.S. **Capitol** (with an "o" because it refers to the very building) is open for business almost every day, and you can always view its museum rooms and architectural features. But the main reason to visit the Capitol is to see Congress in action (if that's the right word). Not much of substance occurs on Fridays; weekend sessions are rare but not entirely unknown. To enter either chamber, you need to obtain a gallery pass from your own senator or Congress member, but getting them is half the fun. First, determine your rep's office location (and name, if you don't know it) from information desks at the north and south ends of the first floor. Often more interesting than House or Senate sessions are committee hearings (locations and times listed in the *Post*'s "Today In Congress" box), which require no tickets but may have lines.

Another hit attraction is the **Bureau of Engraving and Printing**, a.k.a "The Mint," where most U.S. currency, postage stamps, bonds, and other securities have been produced since 1914. It's a cheerful place where tour guides wear bright red ties festooned with vivid greenbacks, they show a lighthearted introductory video entitled "The Buck Starts Here," and signs on the printing presses playfully taunt, "Have you ever been so close and yet so far away?"

Until 1934, the **Supreme Court** camped out in various chambers of the Capitol; Justice Louis Brandeis opposed the move because he thought "our little court-room kept us humble," and Justice Harlan Stone thought the new chamber's pink marble pillars and crimson curtains made the justices look like "nine black cockroaches." Visitors are welcome to hear oral arguments when court's in session (first Monday in October through June). Two lines form on the plaza: the line on the left for those who wish to hear an entire argument, the line on the right for those content with three-minute justice bites.

FBI Headquarters remains a super-popular attraction, its lines nearly as long as the ones outside the Hard Rock Cafe across the street. They sure don't line up to admire the building, a dun-colored block reputedly designed in "Penitentiary Moderne" style by former director and building namesake J. Edgar Hoover. They probably come to reassure themselves that the good guys are still on the case, and to see up-close-and-personal newsworthy items like assault rifles, pipe bombs, confiscated drugs, and posters of the ten most-wanted criminals. Tours end with a bang: a firearms demonstration by an agent—usually a pistol-packin' G-Mama—who shoots first and asks the audience for questions later.

You can visit the **Treasury Building** only on Saturday morning guided tours reserved in advance—weeks in advance during peak season. The Treasury Building is right across the alley from the White House—you may recognize the exterior from the back of $10 bills (the tour entrance is under the flag on the right side). The tour begins in a section built between 1836–42 by an architect who had the quaint notion that government offices in a democracy should all be the same size; how far this got is apparent in the opulent quarters of Salmon P. Chase (the Civil War Treasury Secretary who invented the IRS), under ceiling murals of blithe, chubby nymphs.

Where you can't see your tax $$$ at work... As arduous as it is to get in (see "Jumping the line," below), the **White House** tour is most famous for what it doesn't show you. You don't see Bill, Hillary, Chelsea, Socks, or even George Stephanopoulos, and you don't see where they live or work. You don't see the Oval Office, Rose Garden, Lincoln Bedroom, Roosevelt fireside, or anyplace else you might remember from history or the news. You don't even get a guided tour, just a chance to wander through a few dowdily furnished period rooms used for

DIVERSIONS | WASHINGTON, D.C.

official ceremonies, state dinners, and press conferences. Most people get through in under 20 minutes.

On the building tour of the **Pentagon**, headquarters of the Defense Department, there's no food, no gift shop, no bathroom stops, no serious attempt to show the building's unique attributes—five sides, five floors, five rings of offices, 17 miles of corridors—or the history made on its premises. The most interesting facet of the hour-long tour is that your guide, a uniformed member of one of the armed services, walks backward the entire time you're tramping around, as though to make sure no "tourists" slip off to steal military secrets. Tip: Arrive at the visitors lounge at the Metro entrance well ahead of time to get on the first-come tours. Kill time by checking out the jobs at the Defense Employment Information Center, a video job bank with free printouts; or get a military-style clip job in the Pentagon Barber Shop (open 0700–1600— that's 7am–4pm to you civilians).

The **Department of State** occupies a plain gray box; the drab gray corridors inside are even uglier. But tourists can't really see them anyway (state secrets, you know)— they'll only let you in on guided tours, and those only go to the eighth-floor Diplomatic Reception Rooms, where the secretary of state, his underlings, and overlings (president, vice president) entertain some 20 times a week.

You can't even go inside the block-square headquarters of the **Internal Revenue Service** (1111 Constitution Avenue, NW), but you can read the quote from Oliver Wendell Holmes above the main entrance: "Taxes are what we pay for a civilized society." Insert withering retort here: _____!

Having a ball on the Mall... Over the years, the Mall has been the site of open sewers, railway stations, wartime bivouacs, and postwar office buildings; today it serves as a combination city park, playing field, concert arena, and public meeting hall. The turreted and crenelated **Smithsonian Institution Building**—known as the Castle—contains no exhibits, only administrative offices, a subterranean crypt with Smithson's remains, and an information center. But stop by here (it opens at 9am, an hour before the museums) for brochures, illuminated maps, touch-screen information monitors in six languages, a 20-minute film overview of all the museums, even helpful human beings. Beside the Castle, the **Enid A. Haupt Garden** is one of the largest rooftop gardens in the world—though it looks like it's at ground level, it's technically on the roofs of the underground **Sackler Gallery** and **Museum of African Art** (more on those in a minute).

Officially, the Mall's attractions are the **Lincoln Memorial** and the **Washington Monument** (see "Monumental achievements," above), the **Vietnam Veterans Memorial** (see "Memorial moments," above), and the Smithsonian's many museums (see below).

Mall museums (art)...
The **National Gallery of Art** consists of two separate buildings popularly known as the West Wing and the East Wing, connected by a tunnel with an airport-style moving sidewalk. The three-block-wide West Wing opened in 1941 (on the site of the railroad station where President Garfield was shot) with a mere 121 paintings donated by former secretary of state Andrew Mellon. Old European masters—Raphael, Rembrandt, El Greco, and the only American-owned da Vinci (*Ginevra de Benci*)—fill small galleries on the west side of the building, but the thing to concentrate on is the American masters. The East Wing is newer (1978) and smaller and gets more attention, with its

Mr. Smithson's Neighborhood

The Smithsonian Institution was founded by James Macie—or so he was called at the time of his out-of-wedlock birth in London in 1765. No mere bastard, he was one of four illegitimate children of Hugh Smithson, the Duke of Northumberland, and Elizabeth Macie, a niece of the Duke of Somerset. A noted scientist, James Smithson was the first to isolate zinc carbonate, or smithsonite, and the first to analyze the chemical composition of a female human tear. No one knows for sure why Smithson left his half-million-dollar fortune "to found at Washington, under the name of the Smithsonian Institution, an establishment for the increase and diffusion of knowledge among men." He never visited the U.S. and (though D.C. tour guides say otherwise) wasn't a particular fan of the American form of government. In fact, when Smithson died in 1829, his primary heir was a nephew whose offspring would have inherited the estate, but the nephew died in 1835 without issue, legitimate or otherwise. Thus the Smithsonian was born—sort of.

sharply angled I.M. Pei-designed white marble walls—one 15-degree corner has been worn soft by the touch of tourists—and the blockbuster traveling exhibitions it frequently hosts. The permanent exhibit includes European moderns—with lots of familiar Picassos—on the upper level, and mainly wild-and-crazy Americans on the below-ground concourse level.

In its one-story Italian Renaissance-style building surrounding a courtyard, the **Freer Gallery of Art**, on the south side of the Mall, has the cool austerity of a monastery. The Freer has a split personality; part of it goes for modern American Art, or at least what was modern at the turn of the century, when Charles Lang Freer collected it. The lions's share of the gallery, though, is devoted to Asian art acquired by and after Freer. There's more Asian art next door, down in the subterranean **Arthur M. Sackler Gallery**, whose first thousand Asian art masterpieces were donated by physician/publisher Arthur M. Sackler. If you don't want to overdose on Asian art, though, opt for the Freer over the Sackler. Also underground, the three-story **National Museum of African Art** spotlights sub-Saharan household items, masks, textiles, and (don't tell the Republicans!) wildly well-endowed naked statues of warriors and maidens. Completing this south Mall museum row, the **Hirshhorn Museum and Sculpture Garden** looks the way a modern art museum ought to look: weird. A donut-shaped stilted bunker with one horizontal slit of windows, it looks like headgear for one of Homer Simpson's colleagues at the nuclear power plant. Circular galleries display modern and contemporary heavies.

Mall museums (artless)... The **National Air and Space Museum** has become the most popular museum in the world, its 8.5 million yearly visitors edging it ahead of the Louvre. From its ceiling dangle airborne treasures like the Wright Brothers' first manned plane, the 1903 *Flyer*; Charles Lindbergh's *Spirit of St. Louis*; and Amelia Earhart's snappy red Vega. With 200,000 square feet of exhibits in 27 galleries, Air and Space has no lines at the entrance, but long ones in several places. To see any of the space-oriented IMAX films in the Langley Theater, head to the box office for tickets as soon as you arrive (tickets are sold two weeks in advance, but you have to go in person, with cash, to the museum box office). Einstein Planetarium tickets aren't as hard to get.

With over 16 million artifacts of American political, social, and technological history, the **National Museum of American History** is really too much to swallow in one gulp. Five most gaped-at exhibits: Archie Bunker's chair from "All in the Family"; Judy Garland's ruby slippers from *The Wizard of Oz*; First Ladies' inaugural gowns; the tattered remnant of the 15-star flag that inspired Francis Scott Key to write "The Star Spangled Banner"; and the Fonz's leather jacket from "Happy Days."

The **National Museum of Natural History** is a museum of museums: long dim halls lined with dioramas and display cases, scant use of video, hardly any interactivity—and, consequently, a blessed absence of the crowds and lines that paralyze its neighbors. Its logo is the 13-foot-tall preserved African bull elephant dominating the entry rotunda, its nether parts delicately bowdlerized for the sake of the kiddies: no bull. The east side of the first floor is dinosaur country, and upstairs is the Hope Diamond, the world's largest—and most cursed—marquis diamond. (Marie Antoinette wore it around her neck, while she still had one). While you're here, you might as well peek into the ornate 1881 **Arts and Industries Building**, the site of President Garfield's inaugural ball, where a lot of hefty machinery is on display, then browse around the Victorian cast-iron-and-glass greenhouses at the **U.S. Botanic Garden**, at the foot of Capitol Hill, the oldest botanic garden in North America.

Dupont Circle... Six major thoroughfares converge at Dupont Circle, a mile northwest of the White House: Connecticut, Vermont, New Hampshire, and Massachusetts avenues, plus 19th and P streets. So do the most vital strains of Washington's urban culture and counterculture. The scrubby greensward of the circle itself is a popular gathering place for area residents: proto-yuppies, gay men and lesbians, the pierced and the tattooed. Like homing starlings, all the city's bicycle messengers beset one quadrant of the circle at sunset. Some 40 embassies and other residences of note are situated on Embassy Row, along or near Massachusetts Avenue northwest of Dupont Circle. (That's the high-rent Embassy Row; legations of international troublemakers like Nicaragua, Namibia, and

Rwanda are quartered on New Hampshire Avenue north-east of Dupont Circle).

Then there are Dupont Circle's bona fide house museums. **The Historical Society of Washington, D.C.** occupies the Heurich Mansion, former home of German-American brewmeister and real estate baron Christian Heurich. He lived to the ripe old age of 104 in this up-to-date—elevator, central vacuum system, burglar alarm—but over-the-top 1894 mansion. The historical society operates a library here, plus changing exhibits and lectures on Washington city history. **The Phillips Collection** could be the Cliffs Notes for Modern Art 101, displayed in a wonderful turn-of-the-century brownstone. The **Woodrow Wilson House** is, surprisingly, the only post-presidential home in town, since Wilson was the only president who stayed in Washington after leaving office (and the only one who's still here: he's buried on the grounds of the National Cathedral).

Places to dawdle... You could have a pretty good time in Washington without ever leaving **Union Station**, an architecturally distinguished, historically significant structure with over 100 shops (see Shopping), more than 40 places to eat, and a nine-screen cinema complex. Located in what had been a sleazy neighborhood of hookers and thieves known as Swampoodle, Union Station opened in 1908, designed by Chicago architect Daniel H. Burnham to ape the dimensions and grandiosity of ancient Rome. The triple-arched main entrance copies the Arch of Constantine; the gilded Main Hall re-creates the central hall of the Baths of Diocletian. Note the 96-foot barrel-vaulted ceiling, two bubbling fountains, and statues (by Augustus Saint-Gaudens) of 36 Roman legionnaires at attention on a surrounding balcony. The soldiers were sculpted nude but, following a public outcry, shields were placed in strategic locations. Stand off to the side below any of the statues, crane your neck upward, and you can still glimpse the glory that was Rome.

The **Pavilion at the Old Post Office Building** is the oldest building within the Federal Triangle, the compound of seven government-is-awesome-style buildings on a plot bordered by Pennsylvania Avenue, Constitution Avenue, and 15th Street (the others were all built during the 1930s). When it opened in 1899, the post office was considered a Romanesque eyesore—which one senator described as "a cross between a cathedral and a cotton mill." Somehow it dodged the wrecking ball long enough to evolve from monstrosity to national treasure, and in 1983 it was turned into postal service offices, with the skylit Victorian-era courtyard where postal clerks once lost your mail turned into a 10-story atrium pavilion of shops, pushcarts, and fast-food stalls.

The two-block-square **Department of the Interior Building** has less to offer than Union Station or the Old Post Office, but it does have its charms. One is that it's a warm/cool/dry place close to the open-air monuments (Washington, Lincoln, Vietnam, Korea) on the west end of the Mall. Another is an almost total absence of tourists. The Interior Museum (tel 202/208–4743, open weekdays 8–4) is an utterly noninteractive display of photographs and dioramas about Interior Department activities, which mainly involve responsibility for natural resources, national parks, mines, Native Americans, and America's remaining trust territories. The museum is less interesting than the 1936 building itself, a New Deal project displaying 1930s realism-style frescoes and statues of Indian life, national parks, public works projects, and westward exploration.

Artful, converted mansions... Built in 1798, **The Octagon** actually has only six sides, plus a rounded front entrance pavilion that somebody decided to count as another two. The American Institute of Architects acquired it in 1902 and made it its national headquarters; when the AIA relocated into newer quarters next door, the Octagon House became a museum displaying period furniture owned by its various occupants and temporary exhibits related to architecture. After the British burned the White House in 1814, it was the temporary Executive Mansion for President James Madison and his wife, Dolley. The underground passages to the Potomac and the White House, two blocks east, are walled up, but Dolley's ghost may still party hearty at midnight, allegedly with the shade of Aaron Burr among her guests. Also near the White House, the **Renwick Gallery** is a Smithsonian branch in an 1859 mansion by James Renwick, who also designed the Smithsonian Castle. It has two circa-1860s period rooms, while its modern galleries display made-by-Americans jewelry, pottery, and furniture.

Opened in 1921, the **Phillips Collection** sprang out of the private collection of Jones & Laughlin Steel Company scion Duncan Phillips, whose four-story turn-of-the-century brownstone near Dupont Circle feels less like a public museum than a gallery in an elegant private home. An eclectic array of modern furniture—from barrel chairs to fifties rumpus room divans—is strategically at hand, accompanying an impressive survey of late-19th- and 20th-century art. A 41-room Georgian mansion and 25 acres of formal gardens beside Rock Creek Park, **Hillwood Museum and Gardens** was the home of heiress and art collector Mrs. Marjorie Merriweather Post, of the Post Toasties fortune. Of her four husbands, number three was Joseph E. Davies, the ambassador to the Soviet Union, and that marriage turned her on to the Russian art that would become her life's passion. A bracing Royalist antidote to all the damned democracy on the Mall, Hillwood displays the most extensive collection of Russian decorative art outside Russia: 90 pieces by Fabergé, including two of the world's 56 imperial Easter eggs; gold and silver chalices galore; silver *kovshi* (beer ladles); scores of icons, and an if-fixtures-could-talk chandelier from Catherine's boudoir.

The **Kreeger Museum** on Foxhall Road—a two-lane blacktop that rolls through an improbably rustic D.C. neighborhood of diplomatic estates, minutes north of Georgetown—was built in 1967 by prominent architect Philip Johnson. Though art collectors David Lloyd Kreeger, chairman of GEICO insurance, and his wife, Carmen, lived there for a while, it was always meant eventually to be a museum. Comprised of 22-foot-square travertine modules, the Kreeger displays the fruits of their over 30 years of collecting: distinguished works by modern American and European masters (Picasso, Van Gogh, Cézanne, Monet, Chagall, Gorky, Stella); a room devoted to the Washington Color School; a stunning sculpture terrace; and some unusual paintings like a trite Venetian canal scene by Renoir, and *Mill on the River* by Mondrian, which actually looks like a mill on the river.

Where bureaucrats roamed... Can your stamps pass the "lickometer test"? Find out at the delightful **National Postal Museum**, the U.S. Postal Service's entertaining effort to gain some public respect. Opened in 1993 in the basement of the opulent former Washington City Post Office, the compact museum mingles serious postal history and rare stamps with oddities and amazing facts.

Enter the 1887 block-wide, red-brick **National Building Museum** structure (originally the Pension Building) and you get a big surprise: it's hollow inside. The Great Hall—316 by 116 feet and up to 159 feet high—is the largest interior space in the city, with a central fountain and eight floor-to-ceiling Corinthian columns that look like they're straight out of a C.B. DeMille epic. (They're actually made of plastered and painted brick, not marble.) It was designed by Montgomery C. Meigs, an army general inspired by Italian Renaissance palazzi to build a structure with an inner courtyard large enough (it was said) to contain his ego.

Two outstanding museums, the **National Museum of American Art** and **National Portrait Gallery**, occupy the Old Patent Office Building, a pillared Greek Revival structure that was the largest building in the country when it opened in 1867. The lion's share of it goes to the National Museum of American Art, which is not quite as boisterous inside as the rip-snorting, six-shooter-waving fiberglass-epoxy cowboy on a bucking steed (*Vaquero* by Luis Alfonso Jiménez Jr.) on its front steps. The artists in the Western Art collection outdid Disney's *Pocahontas* in idealizing Native Americans, with pictures and nude statues of svelte, buns-of-steel maidens and iron-pumping warriors. You'll see familiar faces at the **National Portrait Gallery**, from formal paintings of the Founding Fathers to a day-glo self-portrait by Billy Dee Williams. The top floor is a stunner: it's the gaudy American Victorian Renaissance-style Great Hall, which reminds you of the building's Patent Office past, with intricate models of 19th-century inventions. Once the largest room in America, it was the scene of a food riot at a party celebrating Lincoln's second inauguration. Tip: Show up between 10 and 3 and request a docent for a customized tour. No charge—this is Washington!

Historic houses... The most amazing thing about **Ford's Theatre**, where Lincoln was assassinated by John Wilkes Booth in 1865, is that it's still around at all. Following the assassination, angry mobs wanted to torch the two-year-old theater. The federal government took it over; it housed the Army Medical Museum, stored War Department records, and didn't get back into show business until 1968, when it reopened with everything restored but the original cane-backed chairs. The reproductions in the State Box where Lincoln sat, exactly re-create the crime scene. A Lincoln Museum in the basement exhibits memorabilia, including the murder weapon used by Booth and the very clothes Lincoln was wearing that night. **Petersen House**, directly across 10th Street, is the boardinghouse where the unconscious Lincoln was carried after the shooting and where he died the next morning at 7:22am. (It was April 15, now a day of reckoning for all.) The furniture's not original, but the back bedroom where Lincoln succumbed displays his bloodstained pillow cases.

War of 1812 hero Commodore Stephen Decatur is far less known than Lincoln, of course, but Federal-style **Decatur House** is worth a visit even if you don't care who lived there. When it was built in 1818, it was the first private house on Lafayette Square, opposite the White House. Furnishings and memorabilia inside date from the Decatur era and later.

Not for women only... The palatial 1907 building housing the **National Museum of Women in the Arts** has always had a place for women in the arts: it used to be the Town Theater, a popular burlesque house. Since 1987, though, it has housed the only American museum to showcase female artists exclusively. The **Daughters of the American Revolution Headquarters**, an entire block of prime real estate three blocks from the White House, offers a rare close–up view of patrician America. Within the complex, DAR Constitution Hall is most famous for a concert that never happened: when management canceled a gig for African American contralto Marian Anderson scheduled for Easter 1939, First Lady Eleanor Roosevelt instead arranged a free concert, with the Lincoln Memorial as a bandstand. The complex's eastern wing, Continental Hall, houses the DAR a Museum and library. You can tour the small gallery of traditionally "female" decorative arts (clothing and household items) unattended—enter the door marked 1776 D Street—but a real-live Daughter has to guide you through the 33 period rooms, decorated by state DAR chapters.

Wildlife... The **National Zoological Park** proves that bad things do happen to nice zoos. First it was Ling-Ling and

Hsing-Hsing, the adorable but somnolent giant pandas donated to the zoo by the People's Republic of China in 1972, who couldn't produce the next generation of pandas. (Ling-Ling, the female, died in 1992, her frozen eggs awaiting a more virile mate, but Hsing-Hsing endures and dines publicly at 11 and 3 daily.) Then, in March 1995, a mentally disturbed woman who wandered into the lion's den early one morning during closing hours became breakfast for a couple of cats named Tana and Asha. Amazingly, though the woman was a native of Little Rock, Tana and Asha were never implicated in White-water. What sets the National Zoo apart from the competition are a free-ranging primate pen called Gibbon Ridge, a Byzantine-style Reptile House that the American Institute of Architects voted the most outstanding brick building in the eastern United States, and a new exhibit, Amazonia, that replicates a South American rain forest.

The **U.S. Botanic Garden** provides a little spot of sanity at the foot of Capitol Hill; take a look (maybe a last look) at the endangered species of plants near the entrance, which were confiscated by Customs and sent to the Botanic Garden for protection. Housed in the basement of the Department of Commerce, the cool, dark **National Aquarium** has been around forever—well, since 1873, at least—and displays 1,700 species in 80 old-style tanks. None of the frisky, friendly sea mammals, but kids can handle some aquatic denizens in the Touch Tank. It's best to come around 2 o'clock for the feedings: piranhas on Tuesday, Thursday, Sunday; sharks on Monday, Wednesday, and Saturday.

Sea and space explorers... The U.S. Navy's first onshore facility, **Washington Navy Yard** opened in 1800 along the north bank of the Anacostia River from what is now 1st to 11th streets, SE. Here a vast former gun factory has been turned into the **Navy Museum**, with exhibits on every war the U.S. has ever fought, including obscurities like the Quasi War with France (1798–1801). Highlights include a replica of the gun deck of the frigate *Constitution* ("Old Ironsides") and climb–on WW II anti-aircraft guns and space capsules. All this is significantly more interesting than the **Marine Corps Museum**, also in the Navy Yard, a dry march through official Corps history that only a militarist could love. Traipsing through the USS *Barry*, a destroyer in service from 1956 to 1982, requires the adroitness of a mountain goat, but offers insight on how cramped life could be on the bounding main.

Infinitely more interesting, the glass-walled visitor center of the **National Aeronautics and Space Administration (NASA) Goddard Space Flight Center** looks like a car showroom filled with all the snazzy new models. Get behind the wheel of a full-scale mock-up Gemini spacecraft. Hop aboard the padded chair where astronauts were strapped for anywhere from five hours to 14 days (and wonder how they went to the bathroom).

Art off the mall... The **Corcoran Gallery of Art** has something from most every period of art history. Founded in 1869, the Corcoran vies with New York's Metropolitan and Boston's Museum of Fine Arts for the title of oldest nationwide. Based on the collection of William Wilson Corcoran, businessman and cofounder of Riggs Bank, it has evolved into a more-or-less chronological survey of American art history, with a few European trimmings. Other Washington museums clearly have declared their majors. **The Phillips Collection** hangs all the brand–name moderns in seemingly disorganized profusion. Stellar attractions: Renoir's *The Luncheon of the Boating Party* and Daumier's *The Uprising*. Washington's newest art gallery, the **Kreeger Museum**, also focuses on the moderns, particularly the European Impressionists. The **National Museum of American Art** houses a strong collection of art on American themes that dates back to 1829. Like its London namesake, the **National Portrait Gallery** displays paintings, photographs, sculpture, engravings, and sketches of celebs and VIPs from all walks of American life. The **National Museum of Women in the Arts** is the only major museum in the world that exclusively displays the works of women artists. The **Renwick Gallery** exhibits 20th-century American crafts in a 19th-century mansion across the street from the White House. **Hillwood Museum**, the Rock Creek Park mansion owned by Marjorie Merriweather Post, has stuffed 18th- and 19th-century French period rooms with Russian and French decorative art and furniture. More humbly, the **National Gallery of Caricature and Cartoon Art** exhibits its serious attempts at humor in a downtown storefront.

Museums that won't bore the kids... If you've come with children, just about all of the **National Air and Space Museum** is mandatory—make a beeline for IMAX show tickets as soon as you enter the building. Lines also form to touch the moon rock, to walk through *Skylab*, and to fiddle with "Where Next, Columbus?," an interactive exploration of future space travel. The **National Geographic Society Explorer's Hall** is nearly as hands-on but not nearly as crowded. Its interactive exhibit Geographica features cyberscopes (super microscopes) trained on minerals and plants, a tornado you can touch, and grab-them-yourself holograms of strange animals; the heart of Geographica is the Earth Station One amphitheater, a simulated orbital flight focused on the 11-foot globe that serves as the society's logo. Children will like a lot of the **National Museum of American History**, but especially the Hands-On History Room, where they *do* historical things like tap out Morse code telegrams, pick cotton, ride high-wheeler bikes, don 18th-century waistcoats or corsets. Dinosaurs who would eat Barney for lunch (and nibble Baby Bop and B.J. for dessert) roam half a floor of the **National Museum of Natural History**.

High tech and low tech meet hands-on at the all-interactive **Capital Children's Museum**, in a sprawling, somewhat ramshackle former convent a few dicey blocks beyond walking distance from Union Station (take a cab). The skylit entryway features the Nek Chand Sculpture Garden, with its hundred or so people and creatures made out of junk. Defiantly unslick and fun for fun's sake, it's suitable for kids from the time they start walking until they're hooked on MTV.

Forget the **White House**—the lines are too long. But the **National Zoo** is a universal kid-pleaser, and the **FBI Building** has agents shooting tommy guns, wanted posters, and authentic illicit drugs: what's not to like? Kids *love* the **Bureau of Engraving and Printing** (let them come up with the "free samples" line on their own). They'll appreciate the pomp and precision of the changing of the guard at the Tomb of the Unknowns at **Arlington National Cemetery**. The **U.S. Holocaust Memorial Museum** has "Daniel's Story," an exhibit for children over eight, which follows one Jewish boy into and out of the Holocaust. Exhibits at the **National Postal Museum** are fun enough to keep kids' attention, especially the machines that custom-design free souvenir postcards.

Celebrity cemeteries... **Arlington National Cemetery** contains the graves of over 225,000 service people and their dependents on 612 rolling acres beside the Potomac River, across Memorial Bridge from the Lincoln Memorial. Two presidents are buried here (Kennedy and Taft), many famous warriors (General Philip Sheridan, Admiral Richard E. Byrd, General Omar Bradley, General George Marshall), plus many ex-soldiers more celebrated for achievements in other arenas: heavyweight champion Joe Louis, civil rights leader Medgar Evers, mystery writers Mary Roberts Rinehart and Dashiell Hammett. Though there is a Tourmobile, the most gratifying way to experience Arlington is to wander among the unsung memorials and graves of fairly notable Americans buried here. Plain black marble stones and an eternal flame mark the Kennedy Gravesite, and just to the south, Robert Kennedy rests beneath a plain white cross. Self-guided tours are offered of Arlington House, Lee's pillared mansion (Pierre L'Enfant, designer of the city of Washington, is buried outside the front door). At the Tomb of the Unknowns, containing one soldier each from World Wars I and II, Korea, and Vietnam, a robotic changing of the guard takes place on the half-hour from April to September, on the hour the rest of the year. Nearby, in an unexceptional grave, lies Audie Murphy, America's most decorated World War II soldier—and least talented postwar movie star. Sorry, but the creepy memorial to the space shuttle *Challenger* crew looks more like a poster for *Night of the Living Dead* than a tribute to tragic heroes.

The difference between spit-and-polish Arlington Cemetery and the gently dilapidated **Congressional Cemetery** bespeaks the difference between the legislative branch and the military. Congressional Cemetery today is about as popular as the Congress. Founded in 1807 on a 30-acre slope beside the Anacostia River at the southeast end of the Capitol Hill neighborhood, it houses graves of over 150 U.S. senators and representatives. Notable graves include Vice President Elbridge Gerry, a Declaration of Independence signer whose political machinations inspired the term "gerrymander"; Civil War photographer Matthew Brady; "March King" John Philip Sousa, with a bar of "Stars and Stripes Forever" engraved on his tomb; and J. Edgar Hoover, who was given an unobstructed view of D.C. City Jail next door. It's a safe haven in an iffy part of town unless you're afraid of dogs: members of a dog-owners group each pay the cemetery administration $100 a year to let their pooches run free.

Only two celebrities in **St. Mary's Church Cemetery** in the suburb of Rockville, Maryland: F. Scott and Zelda Fitzgerald. Why Rockville? Because Francis Scott Key Fitzgerald was descended from the same old Maryland family that produced the composer of "The Star Spangled Banner," and he wished to be buried among his Maryland ancestors. When he died in 1940, though, the bishop of Baltimore barred him from Catholic St. Mary's Cemetery because he wrote dirty books and never received last rites. So he was buried in the Rockville Union Cemetery, where Zelda joined him in 1948. In 1975, the church relented and let the Fitzgeralds' daughter, Scottie, transfer her parents' remains to St. Mary's; Scottie joined her parents there in 1986.

Reverent guide to Washington... Washington may be the only city in the world that doesn't bill itself "City of Churches," but it does have a number of important and unusual religious institutions. **Washington National Cathedral** has the highest profile in a city of high profiles; its 301-foot central tower isn't as tall as the Washington Monument, but its setting atop the tallest hill on the northwest side makes it visible from almost everywhere. Officially named the Cathedral of Saint Peter and Saint Paul, it is the world's sixth-largest cathedral, and the seat of the bishop of the Episcopal diocese. Teddy Roosevelt laid the foundation stone in 1907, but work wasn't completed until 1990. Martin Luther King Jr. delivered his last sermon here on March 31, 1968, a few days before his assassination. The tomb of the only president buried in D.C., Woodrow Wilson, is near the Space Window embedded with a shard of moon rock from the Apollo XI moon landing in 1969.

Situated beyond the bunkers across Lafayette Square, **St. John's Church** bills itself the "Church of Presidents," since every presidential fanny since James Madison's in 1815 has occupied Pew 54—at least once. Its stained-glass windows honor various statesmen. The **New York Avenue Presbyterian Church** is called "Lincoln's

Church" because during the Civil War Old Abe sneaked over from the White House, three blocks away, for Wednesday night services. The current nouveau Federal-style structure, built in 1951, displays Lincoln's pew and his original manuscript of a proposal to abolish slavery. The Clintons worship regularly at the **Foundry United Methodist Church**, a 180-year-old mixed-race, -class, and -sexual preference activist congregation a mile north of the White House. No, the President hasn't waffled off from the Baptists, but Hillary and Chelsea are real Methodists. (Bob and Liddy Dole used to attend until conservative columnists complained about Foundry's theologically and politically liberal sermons.)

The **Metropolitan African Methodist Episcopal (A.M.E.) Church** is the Cathedral of African Methodism, a religion founded in 1787 when black congregants refused to put up with segregated seating arrangements in a Philadelphia Methodist Episcopal Church. Since then, this downtown church has sheltered slaves escaping on the Underground Railroad, served as a pulpit for Frederick Douglass, Eleanor Roosevelt, Martin Luther King Jr., and Jesse Jackson, and invariably played a leading role in African American activism. Instead of the relatively sedate 11am Sunday service, opt for the more exuberant rhythm 'n' repentance at 8am.

Northeast Washington has a virtual Catholic Bible Belt—Catholic University, Trinity College, and the **National Shrine of the Immaculate Conception**, the largest Catholic church in the United States, its blue-and-gold neo-Byzantine onion dome a prominent feature of the Washington away-from-the-Mall skyline. Its crypt gallery displays the coronation crown of Pope Paul VI, and mosaic altars in 32 chapels interpret Marianism, worship of the Virgin Mary, who by papal decree is the patron saint of America. Also in the area, the 100-year-old sandstone **Franciscan Monastery**, in a quiet residential neighborhood, is dedicated to training priests and brothers for service in the Holy Land. It's sort of a Taste of the Holy Land theme park—the main church, patterned after Istanbul's Hagia Sophia, displays a replica tomb of Christ, while underneath, a spooky rendering of the Roman Catacombs is occupied by the actual hands and feet (attached to replicated body) of St. Innocent, a seven-year-old martyr who died around 200 A.D.

Jumping the line... The **White House** leads the list of Washington attractions where entry may require advance planning, not to mention a touch of chicanery. Nowadays, instead of lining up outside the White House gates, you line up outside the new White House Visitor Center in the Great Hall—formerly the patent research library—at the north end of the Department of Commerce building. (This applies only during the busy March–September season; the rest of the year tickets are unnecessary.) To make sure you get a ticket that day, be in line by the time doors open at 8am, by which time lines are already serpentining along the E Street sidewalk; the line closes when all tickets are gone, usually by 9:30. (Kiosks at both ends of the block dispense tasty walking breakfasts.) Approximately 4,500 free same-day tickets are distributed—up to six per person, so only one in a party has to stand in line. Tickets bear a tour number and (estimated) time of departure, every ten minutes between 10am and noon (and never on a Sunday, or a Monday). You may have up to three hours to wait until your time comes. Best nearby places to kill the time: the National Museum of American History, Old Post Office Building. But linger at the Visitor Center itself to enjoy its videos and displays of White House lore, gift shop, and washroom, especially if it's cold or wet or hot outside. Ten minutes before your designated tour time, meet at the bleachers in the northeast corner of the Ellipse (15th and E streets). Tours often run late; your ticket will admit you to later tours (higher numbers) that day, but not earlier ones. Once your number comes up, your group of about 200 is herded two blocks to the White House entrance for metal-detector inspections and entry to what the guides claim is "the only residence of a head of state regularly open to visitors." There are easier ways to gain entry: either write to your congressperson in advance (see You Probably Didn't Know), or buy a ticket for about $10 from a scalper whose minions waited in line for the six freebies (if you wait in the line, you'll know who they are). Scalpers can usually be found in the blocked-off street east between the White House and Treasury Building.

Visiting the **Bureau of Engraving and Printing** also requires advance planning during the March–September peak season. If your Congress member hasn't arranged to get you on the tour, plan to arrive *very* early at the kiosk on the 15th Street side of the building to pick up a ticket for a timed tour that day. From October–February, enter on 14th Street. A new ticketing system has reduced lines for the **Washington Monument** from up to three hours down to about 15 minutes; after the wait you ascend via elevator to a cramped observation deck, where you elbow your way to prison-cell-sized windows for a view that may or may not make it all worthwhile. There is a better way, though, if you have the leg strength. Weekend guided "walk-down tours" begin on the observation deck and proceed down 897 steps past 193 memorial stones donated by various governments, societies, and individuals. When it's over you can take the elevator right back to the top. To get on the tour, show up at least 15 minutes ahead of time (9:45 for the 10am tour, or 1:45 for the 2pm) and check in with one of the rangers on duty, either at the entrance or roaming around the perimeter. If you're among the first 25 or so, you're in.

Only the Permanent Exhibition of the **U.S. Holocaust Memorial Museum** requires line-waiting. Free tickets (up to four per person) are issued, good for admission that day only at specific times every 15 minutes from 10 to 3:45. Lines begin forming by 8 but move quickly when the museum opens at 10. All tickets are usually distributed by noon, but even during peak periods (April, May) you're virtually certain to get a ticket if you're in line by 10.

Waiting in line for up to two hours for guided tours of the **U.S. Capitol** is the biggest waste of time in town. The guided tours are brief and perfunctory at best, and besides, unlike at the White House or the FBI building or the Mint, you can just walk into the Capitol on your own. Just pass through security under the east steps or at either the north or south ends of the building, snag a free copy of *The United States Capitol: A Self-Guided Tour*, and you can wander around all day just like you owned the place. (Which, technically, you do.)

The Index

Arlington National Cemetery. America's most famous military cemetery. No cars allowed; on-site Tourmobile stops at Kennedy Gravesite, Arlington House (Robert E. Lee's home), Tomb of the Unknowns. No food sold on premises.... *Tel 703/607–8052. Virginia side of Memorial Bridge opposite Lincoln Memorial, Arlington Cemetery Metro. Open 8–7 Apr–Sept, 8–5 rest of year. Tourmobile fare charged, paid hourly parking.*

Arthur M. Sackler Gallery. Underground gallery with overview of Eastern art, from tip of Mediterranean to Japan, since 3000 B.C. Museum shop.... *Tel 202/357–3200, TDD 202/786–2374. 12th St. and Independence Ave., SW, Smithsonian Metro, Taxi zone 1D. Open daily 10–5:30 (except Christmas).*

Arts and Industries Building. An exhibit of 19th-century mechanical marvels and industrial ingenuity. Discovery Theater presents live shows for kids (see Entertainment).... *Tel 202/357–2700, Discovery Theater 202/357–1500 (voice or TDD). 900 Jefferson Dr., SW, Smithsonian Metro, Taxi zone 1D. Open daily 10–5:30 (except Christmas).*

Bureau of Engraving and Printing. Cheerful yet tightly secure crowd pleaser reveals some stages in the printing of currency. Often hard to get into, congressional intercession recommended.... *Tel 202/874–3188. Entrance at 14th and C streets, SW, ticket kiosk (Mar–Sept only) 15th and C streets, NW, Smithsonian Metro, Taxi zone 1A. Tours every 15 minutes, weekdays only 9–2 (additional tours may be added during peak seasons); visitors center open weekdays 8:30–3:30.*

Capital Children's Museum. Hands-on fun for kids—interactive exhibits, frequent puppet shows, live performances, arts and crafts activities, special events. No food concessions;

paltry gift shop.... *Tel 202/675–4149. 800 Third St., NE, Union Station Metro (car or cabs recommended), Taxi zone 2C. Open daily 10–5 (except New Year's Day, Easter, Thanksgiving, Christmas). Admission charged (children under age two free).*

Congressional Cemetery. Semiofficial burial ground for congress members and others. Beside Anacostia River and D.C. City Jail.... *Tel 202/543–0539. 1801 E St., SE (take Independence Ave. east, south on 18th St., SE, to E St.), Potomac Avenue Metro, Taxi zone 2D (car or cab advised). Gates open daily dawn–dusk.*

Corcoran Museum of Art. Washington's first art museum features coherent chronological display of American art. Many lectures, seminars, courses, performances. Gift shop, sit-down cafe.... *Tel 202/638–1439 (recording), 202/638–3211. 500 17th St., NW, Farragut West Metro, Taxi zone 1A. Open daily (except Tue) 10–5, open Thur until 9. Closed New Year's Day, Christmas. Admission charged.*

DAR Headquarters. Complex of DAR offices, museum, genealogical library. Gift shop.... *Tel 202/879–3241. Enter 1776 D St., NW, Farragut West Metro, Taxi zone 1A. Open Mon–Fri 8:30–4, Sun 1–5; guided tours Mon–Fri 10–3, Sun 1–5. Admission charged to library.*

Decatur House. Home of early naval hero Commodore Stephen Decatur. Museum shop.... *Tel 202/842–0920. 748 Jackson Pl., NW, Farragut West Metro, Taxi zone 1A. Open Tue–Fri 10–3, weekends noon–4 (except New Year's Day, Thanksgiving, Christmas), tours every half–hour. Admission charged.*

Department of the Interior. An old-fashioned museum of departmental achievements, in building laden with public art. Cafeteria, Indian crafts shop, National Park Service information office, "topo" map outlet.... *Tel 202/208–3100. Enter C or E St., between 18th and 19th streets, NW, Farragut West Metro, Taxi zone 1A. Open weekdays 7:30–5.*

Department of State. Visitors can tour only Diplomatic Reception Rooms. Advance reservations required. No strollers, no food, no restrooms after tour begins.... *Tel 202/647–3241, fax 202/736–4232, TDD 202/736–*

4474. 23rd St. between C and D streets, NW, Foggy Bottom Metro, Taxi zone 2A. Guided tours only, weekdays 9:30, 10:30, 2:45 (arrive 20 minutes early for security check).

FBI Headquarters. Hideous building, frequently long lines, but some fascinating displays focused on the Federal Bureau of Investigation's crime-fighting mission. Congress member can set up VIP tour.... Tel 202/324–4000. 9th St. and Pennsylvania Ave., NW, tour entrance on E St.; Federal Triangle, Archives, or Gallery Place Metros, Taxi zone 1D. Tours weekdays 8:45–4:15 (except federal holidays).

Folger Shakespeare Library. Impressive collection of British historical documents. Regular series of concerts, plays, readings.... Tel 202/544–7077. 2nd and E. Capitol streets, SE, Capitol South Metro, Taxi zone 2D. Open Mon–Sat 10–4, tours at 11. Admission charged for evening events.

Foundry United Methodist Church. Activist urban melting pot congregation a mile from the White House.... Tel 202/332–4010. 16th and P streets, NW, Dupont Circle Metro, Taxi zone 1B. Services Sun 9:30, 11.

Ford's Theatre/Petersen House. Scene of assassination, once again a working theater, with a basement museum of Lincolniana and 19th-century theater. Not really much to see in the nearby boarding house where Lincoln died (516 10th St.), but it doesn't take long.... Tel 202/426–6924, TDD 202/426–1749, tel 202/347–4833 (box office information). 511 10th St., NW; Metro Center, Gallery Place–Chinatown, or Federal Triangle Metros, Taxi zone 1D. Museum/theater/house open daily 9–5 (except Christmas). Theater closed to visitors during matinees and rehearsals.

Franciscan Monastery. Serene edge-of-D.C. setting for full-scale re-creations of top Holy Land shrines. Well-stocked religious gift shop; snack bar.... Tel 202/526–6800. 14th and Quincy streets, NE, Brookland–CUA Metro, Taxi zone 3D. Mass Sun 7, 8:30, 10:30, noon, 4:30 (Spanish), Mon–Sat 6, 7, 8am, Sat also 5pm. Grounds open daily 9–5, hourly tours except Sun am.

Freer Gallery of Art. Turn-of-the-century American art and ancient treasures from Asia. Gallery shop.... Tel 202/357–4880, 202/357–3200 (taped info), TDD 202/786–2374.

12th St. and Independence Ave., SW, Smithsonian Metro, Taxi zone 1D. Open daily 10–5:30 (except Christmas).

Hillwood Museum and Gardens. Imperial Russian and 18th-century French art crammed into Rock Creek Park mansion of Marjorie Merriweather Post. Two-hour guided house tours. Museum shop; cafe with Russian specialties.... *Tel 202/686–5807. 4155 Linnean Ave., NW, Van Ness–UDC Metro, Taxi zone 3B. Open Tue–Sat 11–3 (except February and national holidays); house tours at 9, 10:30, noon, 1:30, 3. Advance reservations required for house tours and access to grounds. Admission charged.*

Hirshhorn Museum and Sculpture Garden. Modern and contemporary work on the Mall. Museum shop.... *Tel 202/357–2700. 7th St. and Independence Ave., SW, Smithsonian Metro, Taxi zone 1D. Open daily 10–5:30 (except Christmas).*

Historical Society of Washington, D.C., at the Heurich Mansion. Tours of brewmeister's 1894 Dupont Circle abode. Library and displays on local history.... *Tel 202/785–2068. 1307 New Hampshire Ave., NW, Dupont Circle Metro, Taxi zone 1B. Guided house tours Wed–Sat on the hour, noon–3. Admission charged.*

Iwo Jima Memorial. See **U.S. Marine Corps War Memorial**.

Korean War Veterans Memorial. Memorial honors 62,000 American casualties (54,000 dead, 8,000 missing) of Korean War.... *Tel 202/208–3561. On Mall off Independence Ave., southeast of Lincoln Memorial, Foggy Bottom–GWU Metro, Taxi zone 2E. Memorial always open; information kiosk open 8am–midnight.*

Kreeger Museum. Private modern art collection in contemporary-style house museum amid Foxhall Road mansions.... *Tel 202/337–3050. 2401 Foxhall Rd., NW (M St. west, right on MacArthur Blvd., right on Foxhall Rd.), Taxi zone 3A. Guided tours only Tue–Sat 10:30, 1:30. Closed Aug. Reservations required. Admission charged.*

Library of Congress. Guided tours of Jefferson Building, a stunning temple of learning; temporary exhibits and permanent galleries in Madison Building; Reading Room open to all. Cafeteria, museum shop... *Tel 202/707–8000, TDD 202/707–6200. Enter Madison Building, First St. and Independence Ave., SE, Capitol South Metro, Taxi zone 1D. Madison Gallery and exhibits open weekdays 8:30am–9:30pm, Sat 8:30–6; other exhibition areas open weekdays 8:30–5. Guided tours weekdays 10:30, 11:30, 1:30, 3:30; tickets available at Information Desk on first-come basis.*

Lincoln Memorial. Classic Greek temple housing statue of sitting Lincoln. Extensive exterior renovation in progress. Tiny bookstore.... *Tel 202/425–6895. West end of Mall (23rd St.), Foggy Bottom–GWU Metro, Taxi zone 2E. Open 24 hours; rangers on duty 8am–midnight (except Christmas).*

Metropolitan African Methodist Episcopal (A.M.E.) Church. Historic, socially active cathedral for African Methodism, around the block from the *Washington Post....* *Tel 202/331–1426. 1518 M St., NW, McPherson Square, or Farragut North Metros, Taxi zone 1B. Open Mon–Sat 10–6. Services Sun 8, 11; Wed noon.*

NASA Goddard Space Flight Center. First U.S. all-space scientific lab, in Maryland beyond the Beltway. Visitor center with climb-in spacecraft, interactive displays; 90-minute tours of less security-sensitive facilities. Gift shop.... *Tel 301/286–8981, TDD 301/286–8103. Soil Conservation Rd., Greenbelt, MD (Baltimore-Washington Parkway to Greenbelt Rd.–MD Rte. 193). Open daily 10–4 (except New Year's Day, Christmas, Thanksgiving). Tours Mon–Sat 11:30 and 2:30.*

National Air and Space Museum. Aviation's sacred relics, interactive exhibits, and compelling prognostications of what's going to happen next. Two attractive but overpriced restaurants; two museum shops, one devoted to space.... *Tel 202/357–1686, TDD 202/357–1729; Langley Theater and Einstein Planetarium, tel 202/357–1686. 6th St. and Independence Ave., SE, L'Enfant Plaza Metro, Taxi zone 1D. IMAX Langley Theater, Einstein Planetarium charge admission.*

National Aquarium. The oldest aquarium in the country, founded in 1873, and it really looks its age. Cafeteria and gift shop.... *Tel 202/482–2825. Department of Commerce Building, 14th St. and Constitution Ave., NW (enter on 14th St.), Federal Triangle Metro, Taxi zone 1A. Open daily 9–5 (except Christmas). Admission charged.*

National Archives. Reverent display of major historical documents, temporary theme exhibits from Archives' vast holdings. One-hour guided tours (advance reservations required) of the stacks, preservation labs, and model of the bombproof vault. Museum shop.... *Tel 202/501–5000 (recorded information), 202/501–5205 (tour reservations). Constitution Ave. and 7th St., NW, Archives Metro, Taxi zone 1D. Exhibition Hall open daily 10am–9pm April 1–Labor Day; 10–5:30 Labor Day–March. Guided tours 10:15, 1:15.*

National Building Museum. Exhibits on building design and the City of Washington are overshadowed by the building itself, the former Pension Building, and its immense Great Hall. Gift shop features architecture books and cunning gadgets.... *Tel 202/272–2448. 401 F St., NW, Judiciary Square Metro, Taxi zone 1D. Open Mon–Sat 10–4, Sun noon–4 (except New Year's Day, Thanksgiving, Christmas). Guided tours Mon–Fri 12:30, Sat–Sun 12:30, 1:30.*

National Gallery of Art. The West Wing has classic European and American work, East Wing concentrates on 20th-century art, with frequent gallery talks, art films, movie classics; call for schedule. Terrace Cafe overlooking East Wing central court is delightful; also cafeteria and espresso bar. Three shops.... *Tel 202/737–4215, TDD 202/842–6176. Constitution Ave. between 3rd and 7th streets, NW, Archives–Navy Memorial Metro, Taxi zone 1D. Open Mon–Sat 10–5, Sun 11–6 (except New Year's Day and Christmas).*

National Gallery of Caricature and Cartoon Art. New museum exhibits caricatures, editorial cartoons, comics, animation cels, etc.... *Tel 202/638–6411. 1317 F St., NW, Metro Center Metro, Taxi zone 1A. Open Tue–Sat 11–4.*

National Geographic Society Explorers Hall. Interactive exhibits on earth and space sciences on ground floor of National Geographic Headquarters. Planetarium of Washington night sky. Frequent guest lectures. Gift shop features maps, globes.... *Tel 202/857–7689. 1145 17th St., NW, Farragut North Metro, Taxi zone 1B. Open Mon–Sat 9–5, Sun 10–5 (except Christmas).*

National Law Enforcement Officers Memorial. Engraved with names of 13,500 officers killed in line of duty since 1794.... *Tel 202/737–3400. E St. between 4th and 5th* *streets, NW (Visitors Center at 605 E St.), Judiciary Square Metro, Taxi zone 1D. Memorial open 24 hours; Visitors Center open weekdays 9–5, Sat 10–5, Sun noon–5.*

National Museum of African Art. African art, consisting mostly of items from daily life and religious articles, displayed in underground museum and research center.... *Tel 202/357–4600. 950 Independence Ave., SW, Smithsonian Metro, Taxi zone 1D. Open daily 10–5:30 (except Christmas).*

National Museum of American Art/National Portrait Gallery. A two–fer in 1866 Old Patent Building. NMAA, the oldest federal art collection, chronologizes the gamut of American art; NPA displays paintings and photographs of notable Americans (and others). Gift shops in both museums; Patent Pending cafeteria (see Dining).... *Tel 202/357–2700, TDD 202/357–1729. Enter on 8th or 9th streets between F and G streets, NW, Gallery Place–Chinatown Metro, Taxi zone 1D. Open daily 10–5:30 (except Christmas). NMAA guided tours weekdays at noon, weekends at 2. NPA guided tours 11:15 or upon request.*

National Museum of American History. Vast collection mingles serious history and technology with light cultural stuff. Vast ground-floor museum store; cafeteria and restaurant.... *Tel 202/357–1481, TDD 202/357–1563. 12th–14th streets and Constitution Ave., NW, Federal Triangle or Smithsonian Metros, Taxi zone 1A. Open daily 10–5:30 (except Christmas).*

National Museum of Natural History. Big Mall museum, top exhibits are dinosaurs and diamonds. Four appealing gift shops; cafeteria and restaurant.... *Tel 202/357–2747. 9th–11th streets and Constitution Ave., NW; Federal Triangle, Smithsonian, or Archives Metros, Taxi zone 1A. Open daily 10–5:30 (except Christmas).*

National Museum of Women in the Arts. America's only woman-artist-only gallery. Ambitious series of musical programs and lectures. Shop features women-made books, posters, cards, jewelry; Mezzanine Cafe serves light fare.... *Tel 202/783–5000. 1250 New York Ave., NW, Metro Center Metro, Taxi zone 1B. Open Mon–Sat 10–5, Sun noon–5 (except New Year's Day, Thanksgiving, Christmas). Admission charged.*

National Portrait Gallery. See **National Museum of American Art**.

National Postal Museum. Fun exhibits on postal history, in basement of former Washington City Post Office beside architectural twin Union Station. Two gift shops, plus real post office across hall.... *Tel 202/357–2700, TDD 202/ 357–1729. First St. and Massachusetts Ave., NE, Union Station Metro. Open daily 10–5:30 (except Christmas).*

National Shrine of the Immaculate Conception. Largest Roman Catholic church in America, home office of Marianism, the veneration of the Virgin Mary.... *Tel 202/526–8300. 4th St. and Michigan Ave., NE, Brookland–CUA Metro, Taxi zone 2B. Open daily 7–7 March–Nov, 7–6 Dec–Feb. Guided tours Mon–Sat 9–3, Sun 1:30–4. Sat vigil 5:15pm; Sun Mass 7:30, 9, 10:30, noon, 1:30, 4:30; weekday Mass 7, 7:30, 8, 8:30, 12:10, 5:15.*

National Zoological Park. Rock Creek Park home for 3,000 animals. Several gift shops, snack bars.... *Tel 202/673– 4800 (recording), 202/673–4955, TDD 202/673–4823. 3001 Connecticut Ave., NW, or Harvard St. off Beach Dr., Woodley Park–Zoo Metro, Taxi zone 2B. Grounds open daily 8–8 May–mid-Sept, 8–6 rest of year; most buildings open 9–4:30. Paid hourly parking.*

New York Avenue Presbyterian Church. Lincoln's church during the Civil War, three blocks from White House.... *Tel 202/393–3700. 1313 New York Ave., NW, Metro Center or McPherson Square Metros, Taxi zone 1A. Open Tue–Fri 9–5; services Sun 8:45, 11am.*

The Octagon. Architectural exhibits and period rooms in Federal-style six-sided 1798 house.... *Tel 202/638–3105. 18th St. and New York Ave., NW, Farragut West Metro, Taxi zone 1A. Open Tue–Fri 10–4, Sat–Sun 1–4. Admission charged.*

Pavilion at Old Post Office Building. Reappraised 1899 monstrosity with atrium food court, shops, free entertainment; views from top of Old Post Office Tower.... *Pavilion tel 202/ 289–4224, tower tel 202/523–5691, TDD 202/523–5694. Pennsylvania Ave. and 12th St., NW, Federal Triangle Metro, Taxi zone 1D. Shops open Mon–Sat 10–8. Tower tours daily 8am–11pm mid-Apr–mid-Sept, 10–5:45 mid-Sept–mid-Apr.*

The Pentagon. Disappointingly perfunctory tour of the headquarters of the world's most powerful military force.... *Tel
703/695–1776. I-395 and Jefferson Davis Hwy., Arlington,
VA, Pentagon Metro. Guided tours weekdays on half-hour,
9:30–3:30 May–Oct; on the hour 9–3 Nov–Apr. Photo ID
required for those over 16.*

Petersen House. See **Ford's Theatre.**

Phillips Collection. Modern art museum in a Dupont Circle
brownstone mansion. Museum shop; cozy basement
cafe.... *Tel 202/387–2151. 1600 21st St., NW (at Massachusetts Avenue), Dupont Circle Metro, Taxi zone 2A. Open
Tues–Sat 10–5, Sun noon–7. Admission charged.*

Renwick Gallery of National Museum of American Art.
Smithsonian collection of fine American crafts and design.
Museum shop features crafts, books on crafts.... *Tel 202/357–
2700. 17th St. and Pennsylvania Ave., NW, Farragut West
Metro, Taxi zone 1A. Open daily 10–5:30 (except Christmas).*

Sackler Gallery. See **Arthur M. Sackler Gallery.**

St. John's Church. Episcopal parish across Lafayette Square
from White House, built in 1815.... *Tel 202/347–8766.
1525 H St., NW; McPherson Square, Farragut West, or
Farragut North Metros, Taxi zone 1B. Open daily 8–4 (except
federal holidays and during services). Services Sun 8, 9, 11,
weekdays 12:10pm.*

St. Mary's Church Cemetery. Much–visited Roman Catholic
reburial site of F. Scott and Zelda Fitzgerald.... *Tel 301/424–
5550. Veirs Mill Rd. and MD Rte. 355, Rockville, MD
(Capital Beltway to I-270 north, east on MD Rte. 28 to MD
Rte. 355), Rockville Metro.*

Smithsonian Institution Building (The Castle). Information
center for all things Smithsonian.... *Tel 202/357–2700
(general Smithsonian information), 202/357–2020 (Dial-A-
Museum recording), TDD 202/357–1729. 1000 Jefferson
Dr., SW, Smithsonian Metro, Taxi zone 1D. Open daily
9–5:30 (except Christmas).*

Supreme Court. Witness justice in action when court is in session, hear lectures on the judicial system in the courtroom

WASHINGTON, D.C. | DIVERSIONS

when it's not. Gift shop; outstanding cafeteria.... *Tel 202/479–3000. East Capitol and 1st streets, NE, Union Station or Capitol South Metros, Taxi zone 1D. Open weekdays 9–4:30, lectures (when Court not in session) 9:30–3:30. Court in session first Mon of Oct through June (approximate), Mon, Tue, Wed 10–3 (approximate) with hour recess at noon.*

Thomas Jefferson Memorial. Bronze statue of third president, in round domed structure amid Tidal Basin cherry trees. Gift shop beside Jefferson statue; bookstore in base.... *Tel 202/426–6822. South side of Tidal Basin, Smithsonian or L'Enfant Plaza Metros, Taxi zone 2E. Open 8am–midnight.*

Treasury Building. Guided tours, Saturday morning only, of 19th-century offices of people who keep their eye on the nation's till. Advance reservations required, as far in advance as possible.... *Tel 202/622–0896, TDD 202/622–0692. Enter 15th St. between F and G streets, NW, Metro Center or McPherson Square Metros, Taxi zone 1A. Guided tours only, Sat 10, 10:20, 10:40, 11; photo ID required.*

Union Station. Magnificent restored neoclassical transportation hub, with over 40 places to eat, 100 shops, 9 movie screens. Also a liquor store, post office, phoneboard with free calls to low-priced hotels and B&Bs (Gate G), Traveler's Aid desk (Gate L, open 9:30–5:30, tel 202/546–3120).... *Tel 202/371–9441. 1st St. and Massachusetts Ave., NE, Union Station Metro, Taxi zone 1D.*

U.S. Botanic Garden. At foot of Capitol Hill, greenhouses and garden with four yearly flower shows.... *Tel 202/255–8333 (general information), 202/225–7099 (special events). 1st St. and Independence Ave., SE, Federal Center SW Metro, Taxi zone 1D. Open 9–5.*

U.S. Capitol. Extraordinary architecture, grand statuary, art galleries and period rooms, and, in the Senate and House of Representatives, the greatest shows on earth. Tickets from Congress members required for entry to Senate and House galleries. Gift shop, numerous restaurants and cafeterias.... *Tel 202/225–6827 (recording and information on Congressional offices), TDD 202/224–4049. East end of Mall, Union Station (Senate side) or Capitol South (House side) Metros, Taxi zone 1D. Open daily 9–4:30 (except New Year's Day,*

Thanksgiving, Christmas); Rotunda, Statuary Hall open until 8pm in summer. Guided tours every 15 minutes from 9–3:45.

U.S. Holocaust Memorial Museum. Grim subject matter—the millions of victims of Nazis from 1933–1945—presented effectively and objectively in stark, stunning building. Tickets required only for Permanent Exhibition. Museum shop, cafeteria.... *Tel 202/488–0400, TDD 202/488–0406; Ticket-Master (for advance tickets), tel 800/551–7328, 202/432–7328. 100 Raoul Wallenberg Pl. (15th St.), enter on 14th or 15th streets, Smithsonian Metro, Taxi zone 1A. Open daily 10–5:30 (except Yom Kippur and Christmas). Service charge for advance tickets to Permanent Exhibition.*

U.S. Marine Corps War Memorial (Iwo Jima Memorial). Inspirational larger– (and realer–) than–life sculpture of WW II's Iwo Jima flag–raising by five Marines and one Navy hospital corpsman.... *Tel 703/285–2598. North of Arlington Cemetery, U.S. 50 and Mead Dr., Arlington, VA, Rosslyn Metro. Always open.*

U.S. Navy Memorial & Naval Heritage Center. Outdoor plaza with Navy friezes, masts, fountains; indoor visitor center with 70mm movie *At Sea* (admission charged) and interactive exhibits.... *Tel 202/737–2300; event hotline ext. 768. 701 Pennsylvania Ave., NW, Archives–Navy Memorial Metro, Taxi zone 1D. Visitor center open Mon–Sat 9:30–5, Sun noon–5.*

Vietnam Veterans Memorial. Black granite wall bearing names of 58,196 casualties is the most visited monument in the city.... *Tel 202/634–1568. On the Mall, 21st St. and Constitution Ave., Foggy Bottom–GWU Metro, Taxi zone 2E. Memorial always open; information kiosk open daily 8am–midnight.*

Washington Monument. When opened in 1884, the 555-foot memorial to the first U.S. president was the tallest structure in the world; now, by law, it's the tallest in D.C. Free tickets (six per person) distributed on first–come basis at kiosk beside Monument on 15th Street between Independence and Constitution avenues, starting 8:30am, or reserve tickets in advance through TicketMaster (tel 800/505–5040; 301/350–8830 for recorded info). Museum shop on grounds.... *Tel 202/426–6841. On Mall off 15th St., NW,*

Smithsonian Metro, Taxi zone 1A. Open daily (except Christmas) 9–5 Sept–March, 8am–midnight Apr–Aug.

Washington National Cathedral. World's sixth largest cathedral and seat of Episcopal diocese, but open to many faiths. Highlights include specialized chapels and commemorative bays off nave. Cathedral Museum Shop and snack bar in lower-level crypt.... *Tel 202/537–6200, TDD 202/537–6211. Massachusetts and Wisconsin avenues, NW, Taxi zone 3B. Services Mon–Sat 7:30am, noon, 4pm; Sun at 8, 9, 10am, in summer also 11am, 4, and 6:30pm. Open to visitors Mon–Sat 10–4:30, Sun 12:30–4:30; guided tours Mon–Sat 10–3:15, Sun 12:30–2:45, (except Christmas, Palm Sunday, and during services). Suggested donation.*

Washington Navy Yard. Oldest U.S. Navy facility has Navy and Marine museums plus destroyer USS *Barry*. Navy Yard safe, but surrounding area scary; drive or cab. McDonald's restaurant on base.... *Navy Yard entrance, 9th and M streets, SE, Navy Yard Metro, Taxi zone 2D.* **Navy Museum**, *Bldg. 76, tel 202/433–2651. Open Mon–Fri 9–4 (until 5 in summer), weekends 10–5 (except New Year's Day, Thanksgiving, Christmas).* **Marine Corps Museum**, *Bldg. 58, tel 202/433–3534. Open Mon–Sat 10–4 (Fri until 8pm May 1–Labor Day), Sun noon–5 (except New Year's Day, Christmas).* **USS *Barry***, *guided tours daily 10–5 Mar–Oct, 10–4 rest of year (except Thanksgiving, Christmas).*

White House. The presidential home and office, hard to get into and frankly not worth the trouble. Write your congressperson for free tickets or be prepared to stand in line. New visitor center nearby (1450 Pennsylvania Ave.) has videos, exhibits, museum shop.... *Tel 202/456–7041, TDD 202/456–2121; White House Visitors Events Line, tel 202/456–2200. 1600 Pennsylvania Ave., NW; McPherson Square, Federal Triangle, or Metro Center Metros, Taxi zone 1A. Self-guided tours 10am–noon Tue–Sat. Visitor center open daily 8–5, 7–7 Memorial Day–Labor Day.*

Woodrow Wilson House. Authentically furnished 1915 town house where ex-president Wilson lived from 1920–24.... *Tel 202/387–4062. 2340 S St., NW, Dupont Circle Metro, Taxi zone 2A. Open Tues–Sun 10–4 (except New Year's Day, Thanksgiving, Christmas). Admission charged.*

Dupont Circle Diversions

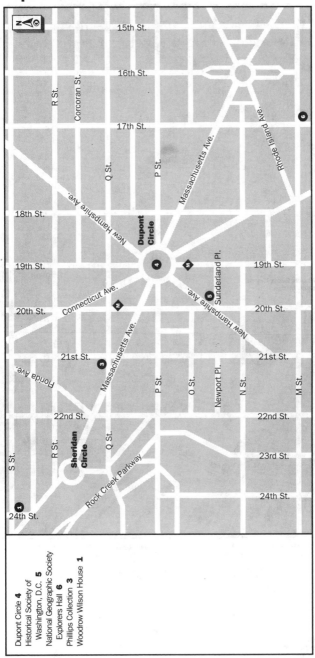

Map legend:

Dupont Circle **4**
Historical Society of
Washington, D.C. **5**
National Geographic Society
Explorers Hall **6**
Phillips Collection **3**
Woodrow Wilson House **1**

Washington, D.C. Diversions

National Zoological Park

getting

4

outside

Washington needs
lots of recreational
spaces, partly
because Washing-
ton workers get so
much free time
(which we tax-

payers pay for, of course.) Federal workers receive three-day weekends for *every* federal holiday—including the Martin Luther King Jr., Columbus Day, and Veterans Day holidays that go largely uncelebrated elsewhere. To keep up with Uncle Sam, most of the city's other employers also shut down.

Also, the weather makes it possible (if not necessarily pleasurable) to play outside almost all of the year. Even December, January, and February are relatively mild months; snow is rare and temperatures seldom dip below the thirties. Locals probably spend more time indoors during July and August, to escape the oppressive muggy heat. Cherry blossoms—and humans—start to emerge around the middle of March. Outdoor cafes leave their furniture outside until Thanksgiving.

As you'd expect for a government company town, Washington makes a federal case out of outdoor recreation. Rock Creek Park, one of the largest urban parks in the country, is run by the National Park Service. The Department of Agriculture takes care of the vast National Arboretum. The pathways traversing the National Mall are popular running trails—in the morning, evening, and around lunchtime. The Mall, "America's front lawn," is also the best place in town to pick up a game of something a bit more physical than hardball politics.

The Lowdown

The world of Rock Creek Park... Extending from the mouth of Rock Creek at the Potomac beside Georgetown, all the way across the Maryland border, **Rock Creek Park** takes up 1,754 acres of midcity real estate, nearly five percent of the city. That makes it more than twice the size of New York's Central Park. The park is shaped like an IV bag—the narrow southern tip limited to a strip of land on either side of the creek, widening to over a mile wide above the National Zoo. Rock Creek Park also serves as something of a socio-political barrier: West of the park, running to the Potomac and the Maryland border, are the affluent, mostly white neighborhoods of Northwest Washington. The homes to the immediate east of the park are equally grand, but things fall off quickly a few blocks away.

Congress purchased the land for the park in 1890, and President Teddy Roosevelt, the great outdoorsman, used the place for vigorous hikes. Even today, winding

Rock Creek Parkway, Beach Drive, and their tributary byways look as remote as the country roads of West Virginia. High-traffic jogging and bike paths run the length of the park, with particularly heavy use south of Calvert Street; the action goes farther north on weekends, when cars are banned from Beach Drive between Broad Branch Road and the Maryland frontier, and cyclists and rollerbladers take over. If you drive on Beach Drive on weekdays, you too can participate in one of D.C.'s favorite outdoor sports: playing chicken with spandex-suited cyclists, who are ferociously determined not to yield one inch of pavement to your vehicle. But be warned: there's about a 75 percent chance that that bike rider you're about to slam into is a lawyer.

All that's free, of course, but Rock Creek Park also has recreational facilities you can pay for. The 18-hole **Rock Creek Golf Course** (tel 202/882-7332; 16th and Rittenhouse streets, NW) is well maintained and reasonably challenging. **Rock Creek Park Horse Center** (tel 202/362-0117; Military and Glover roads, NW) runs escorted rides on bridle paths in the rugged north end of the park. Inexpensive **tennis courts** are located at 16th and Kennedy streets, NW, and off Park Road near Beach Drive; reservations are recommended (tel 202/722-5949).

The park has a few minor attractions, worth visiting only if you're here already. **Pierce Mill** (tel/TDD 202/

Tidal Bin Basics

*The steps of the Jefferson Memorial end at the Tidal Basin, a Potomac River lagoon designed (unsuccessfully) to control floods. It's now ringed with 1,300 cherry trees, a 1909 gift from the Empire of Japan; the first ones all died from an infection, but Japan sent another batch in 1912. The annual **Cherry Blossom Festival** in late March–early April—timing depends on when those unpredictable trees blossom—features a parade on Constitution Avenue, the crowning of Cherry Blossom Princesses, a Japanese Lantern-Lighting Ceremony, a ball, and a marathon race (for ticket information, call 202/646-0366). The path encircling the Tidal Basin is a popular runners' course. **Paddle boats** are rented mid-March–September (tel 202/479-2426). The **Annual Floral Library** on the north end near Kutz Bridge displays nearly 100 annual flowers and plants; cross Kutz Bridge to the 300-year-old **Japanese Stone Lantern**, a 1954 gift from the governor of Tokyo.*

GETTING OUTSIDE — WASHINGTON, D.C.

426–6908; Tilden St. near Beach Dr.; open Wed–Sun 8–4:30) is an 1820 grist mill that was used until 1958 to grind flour and corn for federal cafeterias. Adjacent to it, the **Rock Creek Gallery** (tel 202/244–2482; open Thu–Sun 11–4:30) is a barely restored barn used for temporary exhibits of local artists. The **Carter Barron Amphitheater** (tel 202/393–3939; 16th St. and Colorado Ave.) holds free performances of Shakespeare plays in June and classical or jazz concerts (some free, some not) throughout the summer. If you've got kids along, head for the **Rock Creek Nature Center** (tel 202/426–6829; Glover Rd. near Military Rd., open Wed–Sun 9–5), where they can investigate a working beehive, watch true-life adventure films, take nature hikes, and visit a small planetarium. You may be mystified by the crummy little hovel known as **Joaquin Miller Cabin** (Beach Dr. just north of Military Rd. overpass): Miller, the late 19th-century "Poet of the Sierras" and a notorious eccentric, lived here while he was job-seeking in Washington. The only reason to come here is for shackside poetry readings (tel 202/726–0971) Tuesday evenings in June and July, with everybody invited to a reception at somebody's house afterwards.

Tranquil spots above the fray... Buried in the foot of Capitol Hill just northwest of the Senate chamber is a secluded **grotto** where Indians and early travelers refreshed themselves from the flowing spring waters (and where many a legislator has repaired to contemplate the fractiousness of peers). The triangular park opposite the U.S. Botanic Garden (intersection of 1st St., Independence Ave., and Canal St., Federal Center Southwest Metro) focuses on **Bartholdi Fountain**, a massive illuminated Victorian masterpiece/monstrosity designed in 1878 by Statue of Liberty sculptor Frederic Bartholdi. A favorite spot for brown-bagging bureaucrats, shady **Pershing Park** offers picnic tables, cafe chairs, waterfalls, and a below-street-level setting to deaden the traffic noise across the street from the White House Visitor Center (15th St. and Pennsylvania Ave., Metro Center Metro). If you eat here, use street vendors rather than the lousy park cafe. The serene **sculpture garden** between the Museum of Modern Art of Latin America (open Tue–Sat 10–5) and the Organization of American States building (between 17th and 18th streets and Constitution Ave., NW, Farragut West Metro) really makes you feel transported to Latin America—come here to find one hundred years of solitude (or at least 100 minutes of solitude). The garden's centerpiece is a large pool guarded by the sculpture of a fierce Aztec warrior; a succinct tropical rain forest within the OAS features the Peace Tree, a 1910 grafting of a fig and rubber tree. To get away from the Georgetown bustle, duck into the two-level Jefferson Court of the **Foundry Building** (K St. between Thomas Jefferson and 30th streets), a secluded, quiet outdoor place to sit, with a couple of pretty fountains. In Georgetown's northern reaches, stroll down **Lover's Lane**, a real street (though closed to vehicular traffic) that winds past Dumbarton Gardens down to Rock Creek (R St. near 31st St.). The folks who repair here are not exactly what Jesse Helms would call lovers—it's a popular gay trysting spot. Jesse might approve, however, of the **Kahlil Gibran Memorial Garden** (Massachusetts Ave. at 31st St., Woodley Park–Zoo Metro), beside the South African embassy, with its stone walkways, footbridges, bubbly fountain, and granite benches inscribed with Gibran's mushy words of wisdom and love.

Parks with a past... Neighborhood residents cast out the drug dealers and brought good people back to **Meridian Hill Park** (tel 202/387–8128; between 15th, 16th, W, and Euclid streets, U Street Metro), the city's first formal park, a mere mile and a half north of the White House. It's called Meridian Hill because Jefferson thought the center of the world would rightly pass through the White House and up along 16th Street; this name prevailed over its black-power-era nickname, Malcolm X Park. The park's central feature is a classic Italian "water chain" cascading down a 90-foot slope, made to look even longer by some optical gerrymandering—the bottom pool is twice as big as the top one. The statue of Jeanne d'Arc—Washington's only equestrienne sculpture—was designed for but never delivered to its intended site at the French Embassy. Tip: looking south from the middle of 16th Street beside the park, it seems there's a dome on the White House. (It's really the dome of the Jefferson Memorial poking up behind it.) Jefferson Memorial architect John Russell Pope arranged the illusion as payback for the rejection of

Jefferson's design of a "President's House" with a Roman-style dome. Definitely off the beaten path, **Fort Leslie J. McNair** (tel 202/475-1782; enter at 4th and P streets, SW, Waterfront Metro) is the patch of green at the confluence of the Potomac and Anacostia Rivers about a mile south of the Capitol. The first U.S. Penitentiary (1826) was on this site; here four conspirators in the Lincoln assassination were tried, imprisoned, and hanged before a standing-room-only throng on July 9, 1865. Today, much of it serves as campus for the National Defense University, which teaches the art of war to senior military strategists. The grounds surrounding the Beaux Arts-style main building are a golf course where—with a goofy touch of military class—half-buried bowling pins serve as tee markers. You can't get in without a photo ID, and most buildings are closed to the public.

Urban wilderness... **Theodore Roosevelt Island** (tel 703/285-2598; north of Theodore Roosevelt Bridge [I-66, US-50]) is a swatch of wilderness in the Potomac, nestled between Kennedy Center and the Rosslyn section of Arlington, Virginia; most of the reason it's so unspoiled is that it's so damn hard to get to. Drive north on the George Washington Memorial Parkway to the island's parking lot, get out and cross a wooden footbridge over the Potomac; you can also walk here from Rosslyn, taking Key Bridge or the Theodore Roosevelt Bridge and then taking a footbridge over the parkway. The easiest way to get here, actually, is to canoe from the Thompson Boat Center (see "Boats and Bikes", below). Hikers, bikers, and runners are welcome on three main trails—Woods Trail, Upland Trail, Swamp Trail—but emphatically unwelcome on "social trails" (unofficial shortcuts) lest they do further damage to the fragile vegetation. The most unnatural thing about the island is the monument to TR at its center, a vast stone plaza surrounded by a moat that suggests the altar of some strange woodland cult. At its center stands a 17-foot bronze statue of TR flanked by granite tablets inscribed with his pronouncements on The State, Manhood, Nature ("Conservation means development as much as it does protection"), and Youth ("I want to see you game boys").

Just above Georgetown, off Canal Road, **Glover Archbold Park** is 183 acres of paths rarely taken across the bed of meager Foundry Creek. An untrammeled patch of green called **Whitehaven Park** connects it to **Battery Kemble Park** (Chain Bridge Rd. and MacArthur Blvd.), a preserved Civil War cannon battery that has evolved into a weirdly jungle-like bamboo forest filled with wooden footbridges across a rushing brook.

Garden spots... The **U.S. National Arboretum** (tel 202/ 475–4815; 3501 New York Ave., NE, Taxi zone 3D; open Mon–Fri 8–5, Sat–Sun 10–5, admission free) is hard to get to—the Metro doesn't come close—but well worth the drive through a few blocks of urban hell. You'll need a car, anyway, to explore the nine miles of road through the 444-acre research facility and living museum, but the most important attractions are close to the information center/gift shop. The **National Bonsai and Penjing Museum** (open 10–2:30) is an austere Asian–style setting for every imaginable kind of container-grown miniature shrub (Bonsai is the Japanese technique, Penjing Chinese), including one 350-year-old white pine. The **National Herb Garden** has a historic rose garden (blooms mostly May to early June) and 10 specialty gardens of herbs used for dyes, medicines, fragrances, etc. The most striking feature of the arboretum, however, is completely nonorganic: a grove of 22 Corinthian columns transplanted to the arb after the U.S. Capitol was renovated. Standing apart on a green hilltop, they eerily suggest the ruins of a lost civilization.

People who live in Washington always talk about going to the **Kenilworth Aquatic Gardens** (tel 202/426– 6905; open 7–4:15; guided walks summer weekends, admission free), but few actually get around to it. It's strange and wonderful, a whole national park devoted exclusively to waterplants, blooming in an otherwise verboten section of Northeast Washington. Twelve acres of reclaimed Anacostia River marshland have been turned into 44 display ponds surrounded by grassy dikes, like an inside-out Venice. Early morning is the best time to see flora that change with the season: hardy lilies in June, Asian lotuses in July, tropical lilies in August and September. The rest of the year the place is strictly for the birds—and frogs and turtles. To get here (and it ain't easy), take East Capitol Avenue east to Kenilworth Avenue/D.C. Rte. 295, exit on Eastern Avenue, and follow signs to parking lot.

WASHINGTON, D.C. | GETTING OUTSIDE

No caveats are needed for the neighborhood surrounding **Dumbarton Oaks and Gardens** (31st and R streets, NW, Taxi zone 2A): it hugs the northern fringe of Georgetown among the town houses of the rich and politically connected. The 1944 conference that set up the United Nations was held here, when it was a private estate; today, it's a house museum and a Harvard-owned research center for Byzantine and pre-Columbian history (1703 32nd St., NW; open Tue–Sun 2–5, contribution suggested). Inside, there's a small collection of pre-Columbian and Byzantine art, as well as a music room that Igor Stravinsky liked enough to compose *The Dumbarton Oaks Concerto* in its honor. The terraced 10-acre gardens (tel 202/342–3200, recording at 202/338–8278 tells what's currently in bloom), built by former Ambassador Robert Woods Bliss and wife Mildred during the 1920s, incorporate elements of formal French, Italian, and English garden design.

Out and about... You become another tourist's wackiest Washington memory when you waddle down the street in **DC Ducks** (tel 202/966–DUCK) tour vehicles. Ducks—converted 30-passenger 13-ton DUKW amphibious vehicles used for World War II Allied invasions—offer standard Mall tours broken up with a half-hour dip in the Potomac. Ducks put in at the old Pentagon marina, paddle downstream (beneath a creaky 14th Street railroad bridge that hasn't been repaired since it was struck by lightning in 1961), and emerge beside National Airport. The 90-minute tours leave a nest at 1323 Pennsylvania Ave., NW, between the J.W. Marriott Hotel and the National Theater. Duck season runs from April through October.

Another goofy only-for-tourists hoot, **Potomac Pedicabs** (tel 202/332–1732) are modern-day rickshaws that use 23-speed mountain bikes to pull two-passenger carriages around the greater downtown area, Georgetown to Capitol Hill. "The only transportation service that can still take you in front of the White House," it bases rates according to the distance and steepness of the route, and temperature (but not supposedly on customer girth). Hail one down or call for pick-up; rides hire out for about $30/hour.

From April through October you can cruise the Georgetown section of the C&O Canal on 90-foot mule-drawn **canal boats**. Boatmen clad in 19th-century garb provide running commentary, spin yarns, croon chanteys. Tickets for the 90-minute cruises are sold at the Georgetown Ranger Station/Visitor Center (tel 202/653–5190; 1057 Thomas Jefferson St., NW, Foggy Bottom–GWU Metro, Taxi zone 2A).

Happy trails for you... Washington has loads of scenic running/jogging trails in historically significant locales; trouble is, unless you can persuade the president to lend you a Secret Service agent or two, none are particularly safe by night. You should be okay if you stick with the crowds on two popular circuits: **The Ellipse** (0.6 miles/1km), just south of the White House; and the much longer path (1.8 miles/3km) encircling the **Tidal Basin**. During the daytime, join the packs of Georgetown yuppies trotting along the fashionable trails in **Rock Creek Park**, as far north as the Duke Ellington Memorial Bridge (beyond is literally a Zoo). Reach them from any of the streets that overpass or intersect Rock Creek Parkway: Virginia, Pennsylvania, Massachusetts, and Connecticut avenues; K, M, P, Q, and Calvert streets. The stretch beside Rock Creek Parkway from the Potomac to Connecticut Avenue is the safest and most popular section. The **C&O Canal Towpath** begins behind the Four Seasons Hotel in Georgetown (29th and M streets, NW) and runs beside the Potomac for 184 miles, all the way to Cumberland, Maryland; most runners turn back at the Georgetown Reservoir, a couple miles from the start. The longest run is the **Mount Vernon Trail**, which runs along the Potomac in Virginia. The 17-mile stretch goes from Theodore Roosevelt Island, through the Lyndon Baines Johnson Memorial Grove, beside National Airport, along the streets of Old Town Alexandria, all the way to George Washington's estate at Mount Vernon.

Orienteering... For this Nordic sport that combines the skills of treasure hunting, road running, and Boy Scout map-reading, the **Quantico Orienteering Club** (tel 703/528–4636) holds meets in a Capital region woodland every other weekend from September through June.

Boats and bikes... Situated on a spit of land where Rock Creek flows into the Potomac, the **Thompson Boat Center** (tel 202/333–9543; off Rock Creek Pkwy. and

Virginia Ave., NW; open mid-March through mid-November) rents canoes, kayaks, rowboats, and sculls for cruises on the Potomac between Key Bridge and Memorial Bridge, including Theodore Roosevelt Island. It also rents mountain and cruiser bikes for spins along the Potomac or up through Rock Creek Park. **Fletcher's Boathouse** (tel 202/244–0461; Reservoir and Canal roads, NW) rents bikes and boats and canoes along the C&O Canal Towpath beside the Potomac River. **City Bikes**, which is "next to Ben and Jerry's" (tel 202/265–1564; 2501 Champlain St., NW, Woodley Park–Zoo Metro) in Adams-Morgan, is just off the great Rock Creek bike paths. If you want some exercise but are too lazy to pick up a bike yourself, let **United Tel Inc.** (tel 202/289–4411, 1110 6th St., NW, Mount Vernon Square–UDC Metro) deliver 10- to 18-speed street and mountain bikes to your hotel; weekend, weekly, overnight rates available.

Kayak-lty-yak... The Potomac upstream from D.C. is primo whitewater kayaking country. The U.S. National team trains at **Lock 6** on the Little Falls section of the river (Clara Barton Pkwy. and Valley Rd., Glen Echo, Maryland). The stream at **Anglers Inn** (10801 MacArthur Blvd., Potomac, Maryland) ranges from Class 1 to 4 depending on location and river level. The closest place to rent kayaks is **Spring River** (tel 301/881–5694; 5606 Randolph Rd., just east of MD Rte. 355, Rockville, MD). Call the U.S. Geological Survey River Line (tel 703/260–0305) for recorded information on river conditions.

Par for the course... Our great golfing presidents—Ike, Jerry Ford, and Bill Clinton—have all been more likely to play on exclusive country club courses, but D.C. does offer a few public golf courses for the masses. Most scenic (and crowded) is the **East Potomac Golf Course** (tel 202/554–7660; East Potomac Park, Taxi zone 3H) just south of the Jefferson Memorial in East Potomac Park, on a patch of swampland reclaimed by Army engineers to protect the Washington Channel harbor. It has one 18- and two nine-hole courses, plus miniature golf. Good monument views—you may be able to line up a shot with the dome of the Capitol. There's also the 18-hole **Rock**

Creek Golf Course (see Rock Creek Park above) and **Langston Golf Course** (tel 202/397–8638, 26th St. and Benning Rd., NE, Taxi zone 3E), which has 18 holes and a driving range along the Anacostia River just south of the U.S. National Arboretum.

Good skates... Rollerblading is so popular that many plazas, parks, and memorials have posted signs specifically banning it. But you can still merrily roll along the pathways on the Mall, the bike paths in Rock Creek, along the Potomac, and, most popularly, the closed-to-traffic section of Pennsylvania Avenue in front of the White House. Rent blades at **City Bikes** (tel 202/265–1564; 2501 Champlain St., NW, Woodley Park–Zoo Metro, Taxi zone 2B).

Weather permitting—which it usually isn't—ice skating takes place on the **C&O Canal** near 30th and M streets above Georgetown; call 301/299–3613 for weather conditions. Other picturesque outdoor rinks with skate rentals include **Pershing Park** (tel 202/737–6938; 14th St. and Pennsylvania Ave., NW, Metro Center Metro, Taxi zone 1A) opposite the White House Visitor Center, and the **Sculpture Garden Ice Rink** (tel 202/371–5342; 7th St. and Independence Ave., NW, Archives–Navy Memorial Metro, Taxi zone 1D) on the Mall opposite the National Archives.

Mall crawl... To fall into casual pick-up games, there's no place better than the National Mall. The midsection between Independence and Constitution avenues from 3rd to 14th streets teems with weekend **volleyball** and **touch football** games. Open **softball** games, and scheduled softball grudge matches between politicians' staffs and agency personnel, also crop up in the middle of the Mall and—except on Sundays from May to October, when ponies fill the field—on the Polo Grounds northwest of the Tidal Basin. **Soccer** and ultimate **frisbee** are ferociously played on the field south of the Lincoln Memorial reflecting pool and on the Ellipse.

Go fly a kite... The hillside below the **Washington Monument** is a treeless slope with prevailing breezes favored by kite-flyers; it's the site of the Smithsonian Kite Festival the last weekend in March.

5

ping

Those who go to
Washington for
the shopping
would be—like
Bogie going to
Casablanca for
the waters—

"misinformed." You can buy anything you want in Washington, even if it requires trekking to a mall far from the Mall. But there's nothing unique here, or irresistibly cheap, so don't bother bringing an empty suitcase.

What to Buy

Books, magazines, reports, treatises, manuals: Washingtonians are readers, with plenty of busy bookstores and newsstands to support their habit. There are bookstores devoted to gay/lesbian, feminist, African American, or New Age concerns, and bookstores operated by government and quasi-governmental agencies, as well as the kind of ultraspecialized stores that cognoscenti the world over know. Naturally, Washington is a major stop on the authors' tour circuit and many signings/readings/lectures, most of them free, take place daily. The weekly *Washington City Paper* lists them in the "Reading/Literature" area of its Events section, and bookstores usually place day-of ads in the morning papers.

The business of Washington is politics, and the most locally relevant gift items are politically oriented souvenirs and memorabilia sold in museum gift shops and specialty stores. Clintoniana and "property of White House"-type items are in long supply, as are historic photos, videos, fine china, and commemorative coins. Biggest sellers are the cheapies: mugs, T-shirts, key chains, hats, and, of course, buttons and bumper stickers tinged with every color on the political spectrum.

Target Zones

Back in the 1950s, a shopper could obtain a Washington Shopping Plate with which to charge purchases at seven fine **downtown** department stores: Hecht's, Jelleff's, Garfinckel's, Lansburgh's, Raleigh's, S. Kann, and Woodward & Lothrop (Woodie's). Today, the Hecht's charge card would suffice—the rest have all ascended to department store heaven. (Woodie's was last to bite the dust, in mid-1995.) Downtown D.C. does have the Shops at National Place, with its 50 or so shops, stores, boutiques, and pushcarts; you'll find souvenir and novelty shops in the Old Post Office Pavilion, and a few chic establishments around Connecticut and K. Where do you go for serious shopping now? The nearest major suburban mall is **Fashion Centre at Pentagon City**, directly across an interstate highway from the Pentagon in Arlington, Virginia. It's largely blamed for performing the coup de grace on D.C.'s downtown shopping district; maybe so—it's right on top of the Metro

Blue and Yellow lines, only a 14-minute ride from Metro Center. The anchor department stores are class-act Nordstrom (tel 703/415–1121) and Macy's (tel 703/418–4488); and the gap between D.C. sales tax (5.75 percent) and Virginia's (4.5 percent) represents a de facto 1.25 percent rebate. The **Chevy Chase Shopping District** straddles the D.C.-Maryland border with two small malls and some unattached upscale department stores. Other fashionable malls are located beyond the Capital Beltway: Tysons Corner Center and Tysons II Galleria in **Tysons Corner**, Virginia; Montgomery Mall in **Bethesda**, Maryland; White Flint Mall in **Rockville**, Maryland. The oldest part of the city, **Georgetown** boasts the densest concentration of antiques shops: around 30 near the pivotal intersection of Wisconsin and M streets, plus another 20 art galleries. Georgetown also boasts (or at least acknowledges) its allure for the young and the restless with stores selling biker boots, vintage comic books, and erotic clothing. Georgetown Park, a four-story mall encrusted with Victorian glitz, is the spot for high-fashion recreational shopping. Drop by its ground-level concierge office to pick up free directories to neighborhood antiques shops, galleries, and other points of interest. In **Old Town Alexandria**, buildings of about the same vintage as Georgetown house a

Get Yer D.C. Souvenirs Right Here!

Pencil of Justice. "With liberty and justice for all" motto and erasers as gavels (Supreme Court gift shop, 61¢). *Elvis Meets Nixon Note Pad.* Edge of pad depicts 12/21/70 encounter when Tricky Dick gave The King a special Narcotics Agent Badge (National Archives gift shop, $8.95). *Hope Diamond baby bib.* Drawing of gem captioned "Precious!" (Museum of Natural History gift shop, $5.50). *Postal Teddies.* Teddy bears of various sizes, genders, possibly even sexual persuasions, dressed as U.S. Postal Service workers (Post Impressions store, Union Station or Old Post Office Building, $19.95–$57.95). *Rock Collection Pencil.* Pencil shaft contains pebbles from around the world (Arts & Industry Building gift shop, $2.95). *IRS Christmas Tree Ornament.* Gold-wash etching of 1913 Tax Form 1040 with greeting "Eighty Years of Income Tax, Many Happy Returns" (Treasury Building gift table, $11). *Zoo Doo.* Odor-free compost mixture of National Zoo herbivore droppings (zebra, elephants) mixed with grass clippings and wood, aged for a year (National Zoo parking lots, $3 for 5-pound bucket, $6 for 40-pound bag, pick-up truckloads by arrangement).

similar assemblage of galleries, antiques shops, and one-of-a-kind boutiques. For something completely different, there's **Takoma Park**, Maryland. Born in 1884 as a "railroad suburb" of Washington and long dominated by the Seventh Day Adventists (whose world headquarters used to be here), it has evolved into a multiracial, nuclear-free bastion of 1960s hippiedom, sometimes called the "People's Republic of Takoma Park," where folks periodically attempt to ban gas lawn mowers as excessive polluters and let non-U.S.-citizens vote in local elections. A funky collection of stores ranges around the Carroll Avenue shopping district, a short walk from the Takoma station on the Metrorail Red Line, and the area's best farmers' market germinates on a closed downtown street on Sundays (Saturday is the Adventists' day of rest) from March through Thanksgiving.

Bargain Hunting

Most stores charge full price but the sidewalks of D.C. are another story. No matter the season or weather, downtown sidewalks are thronged with stalls selling souvenir T-shirts and caps, jewelry, sunglasses, and African-style clothing. Best deals are eminently wearable "all-silk" men's ties at the going rate of $4 apiece, three for $10. Street vendors are also conveniently on hand for weather-induced impulse buys of umbrellas, hats, scarves, and gloves.

The sidewalks of D.C. are also an open market, a *wide*-open market, for counterfeits: unreal Rolex, pirated Power Rangers, virtual Vuitton. Can't make it to the multiplex for that new action flick? Buy the video version (shot by a hand-held camera smuggled into a movie theater) for $10 on the street. With an estimated 2,000 street vendors in D.C., contraband is exchanged freely, thanks to lenient laws, lax enforcement of those lenient laws, and a vast market of tourists in high-spending mode passing through every day.

For legal discounts on authentic goods, Washingtonians must pilgrimage to **Potomac Mills** (tel 800/VA–MILLS, 703/643–1770, Exit 156, I-95), a "super-regional" outlet and off-price mall of over 220 stores in Dale City, Virginia, some 20 miles southwest of downtown D.C. Stores here include IKEA, the massive Swedish home furnishings store; Waccamaw Pottery; and outlet stores for Nordstrom, Sak's Fifth Avenue, Barney's New York, JCPenney, Marshall's, Syms, Spiegel, and Macy's. They're all on one floor, and it's a mile-and-a-half walk from one end to the other. The Potomac Mills mall is only the hub of a rapidly multiplying colony of mini-malls and free-standing category killers—Wal-Mart and Sam's Club, Home Depot, and the 180,000-square-foot Incredible Universe, one of the world's largest electronics and appliance stores.

Hours of Business
Most stores in D.C. are open daily except Sunday from 10am to 6pm. Georgetown shops keep later hours (usually until 9pm) nightly, and others may stay open until 9 on Thursday night. Mall stores in D.C. and environs are usually open 10am–9pm Monday–Saturday, noon–6pm Sunday.

Sales Tax
The District of Columbia charges 5.75 percent; Maryland, 5 percent; and Virginia, 4.5 percent.

The Lowdown

Books for special interest groups... Browse for touchy-feely, one-hand-clapping fare at **Yes!** in Georgetown. **The Health Source Bookstore** is an internationally known source for books and videos on illness and wellness (they even transmit healing messages via the Internet, at http://www.appi.org/healthsource). **Vertigo Books** is a Dupont Circle hive for activists, with a focus on international politics, African American studies, and cutting-edge fiction. Also near Dupont Circle, **Lambda Rising** claims to stock virtually every gay/lesbian book in and out of print, and functions as more than just a bookstore for the gay/lesbian community; and **Lammas** serves all feminists, gay or straight. **Cheshire Cat** is a cuddly, children's bookstore in Chevy Chase, D.C., carrying both books for kids and how-to manuals for parental units. **The Map Store** is cartography heaven, containing topographic, nautical, decorative, and road maps, plus travel guides and gadgets. The brighter and more expensive **Rand McNally** is a virtual travel superstore, brimming with maps, guidebooks, videos, games, and cunning items to lighten your travel load. **Backstage** is a Dupont Circle specialty bookstore for works on the theater and film, with a dramatic collection of scripts.

Books for policy wonks... Downtown, at 50-year-old **Sidney Kramer Books**, politics junkies get their fixes of everything weighty in the areas of political science, foreign affairs, military history, government, and business. **Reiter's** is an earnest nerdatorium that stocks over 50,000 scientific and technical titles—computers, medicine, law, science—plus tomes on business and philosophy. Need to keep up with the latest news from home? No matter where home is, you should be able to find your native newspaper or magazine at the **Newsroom**, near Dupont Circle and Embassy Row, or else try Farragut Square's **News World**, though there is precious little space for browsing in peace here. Bureaucrats, scholars, and people who *really* have trouble falling asleep at night will want to peruse the official tomes at the **U.S. Government Bookstore**—an indispensable outlet for impact studies, workplace manuals, statistical compilations, task force findings, technical reports, plus general interest material on health and leisure activities. Looking for a copy of *Rural Realignment in South Saharan Africa?* You'll find it, along with hundreds of other reports and technical documents in many tongues, at the **World Bank Bookstore**.

Political connections... Totally nonpartisan **Political Americana** sells collectibles and souvenirs: books and tapes, presidential china and linen, bumper stickers, mugs, T-shirts, life-size Bill and Hillary cut-outs, and campaign buttons for every pol who ever dreamed of tossing a hat into the ring. **Capitol Coin & Stamp Company** is a numismatic shop with serious political collectibles—presidential campaign memorabilia is a specialty. Serious doesn't necessarily mean dull, though—it carries a line of inflammatory bumper stickers and campaign buttons, proclaiming rancorous political sentiments that can be a bit hard to stomach. The liberal left lives in the heart of the K Street Corridor at the **NOW Store**, a politically correct (and proud of it!) shop operated by the National Organization for Women. Whatever the liberal cause—pro-feminist, anti-gun, pro-kid, you'll find T-shirts, buttons, mugs, cards, books, and bumper stickers pushing it here. Watergate would never have happened if the Plumbers had visited the **Counter Spy Shop**, the place to go for phone scramblers, night vision systems, telephonic lie detectors, bulletproof clothing, phone tap and room bug detectors, hidden video systems, and everything else you need to find out or keep secrets.

Historical interest... The **Old Print Gallery** in George-town sells pieces of history in the form of the area's largest selection of antique prints and maps. Views of Washington as a provincial country town, images of historical events, and sweeping cosmopolitan vistas help to adjust your perspective on D.C. **The Artist's Proof**, which has three stores around town, handles old photos of city scenes and celebrities from various walks of life. **Blue & Gray Books and Prints** in Old Town Alexandria carries a balanced stock of Union and Confederate gear—not only rare books and prints, but also swords, flags, buckles, and bullets used by both sides in the War Between the States. The **Collector's Armoury** in Old Town Alexandria sells nothing but "fakes," i.e., nonlethal "museum–quality reproductions" of historic weapons—firearms, swords, medieval armor—but their phonies have been convincing enough to fool you in the movies for over 25 years. If you want the real thing, however, you'll have to wheel on over to **Old Town Armory**, also in Alexandria, a second-floor walk-up stocked with guns, ammo, and die-hard NRA leaflets. What they can ship back home—forget cash 'n' carry—depends on the firearm and the laws of your state.

The British are coming... In cramped Old Town digs, the **British Connection** is a closet-sized purveyor of British food and beverages, in the back of the Tea Cosy english tea room. Expats migrate here for a taste of home cooking, with trifle, blancmange, orange barley water, imported-from-England Heinz Baked Beans, and nearly 20 brands of British beer. Also in Old Town, the **Scottish Merchant** pays tribute to the town's Scottish merchant namesake, John Alexander, displaying kilts and other garments plaid, Scottish music, even golf balls from St. Andrews.

Hippie-dippy-dom... Head to the People's Republic of Takoma Park for out-of-the-mainstream items. **Insights Galleria** boasts "One-stop shopping for all your meta-physical needs!": quartz clusters, *feng shui* items, fetishes, energy grids, singing bowls—and a free crystal with every purchase. **House of Musical Traditions**, a nationally known empire of unpluggedness (folk, ethnic, blues, jazz), sells musical instruments from around the world, new and used CDs and tapes, books, and sheet music. Got a yen for a Tibetan "tiger" rug? Try **dzi, the Tibetan Collection**, which specializes in sweaters, pillows, hats, rugs, books, and other Richard Gere gear from Tibet. In Georgetown, browse for books and tapes on yoga, Eastern religion, psychology and Jungian studies, and kindred body/mind/spirit concerns at **Yes!** bookstore. **Earth Friendly**, in the Shops at National Place, has a decidedly green bent.

Crafty design... **Finewares** in Takoma Park carries handmade-in-America craft items—pottery, clothes, toys, much jewelry—about a third of it by local artisans, and all of it made by Americans (and a couple of honorary Americans who live in Canada). **Blackberry**, at Pentagon City, sells *objets* with an African American slant, as does Union Station's **Aurea**, along with pre-Columbian and Native American wearable art. Also in the East Hall at Union Station, **Appalachian Spring** sells crafts not just from the Appalachians, but from all over the U.S. **The Russian Store**, in the Shops at National Place, features crafts and clothes straight from the dacha.

Incredible edibles... **Dean & Deluca**, an outpost of New York's fancy-schmancy gourmet foodery, sits across from the Georgetown Park mall in the historic Markethouse structure. If you can't wait to eat the goodies you've bought, you can sit down in the attached cafe. If it's English cookery you crave (there's no accounting for taste), shop for authentic imported-from-the-U.K. comestibles at the **British Connection**, tucked away behind a tea shop in Old Town Alexandria. Nearby, **John Crouch Tobacconist** features a walk-in cooler lined with mostly imported stogies to remind us that Alexandria's founder, a Scottish merchant named John Alexander, purchased the future town site for "six thousand pounds of Tobacco and Cask."

Kid stuff... The Georgetown Park mall has Washington's only outlet of **FAO Schwarz**, a great upscale toy store except for the mind-numbing "Welcome to our world of toys…" jingle played ad nauseam; more earnest parents will make a beeline for **Learningsmith**, which has a great stock of computer games, crafts, puzzles, videos, and other toys that are actually fun *and* educational. **Why Not** is an outstanding full-service children's store (toys, books, music, clothes) opposite the Visitors Center in Old Town Alexandria; there's a cool play area downstairs and stuff for older children upstairs. Buy the classic French clothing at **Jacadi** in Pentagon City to make sure your kids dress better than you do. **Cheshire Cat** specializes in children's books, with frequent author signings and entertainment. Older kids may get a kick out of **Juggling Capitol**, in the Old Post Office Pavilion, which sells all sorts of equipment for jugglers; they offer free lessons when you buy their devil sticks and diabolos. **Magic Masters**, in the Shops at National Place, supplies aspiring magicians.

The Index

Appalachian Spring. Good buys on tasteful American crafts.... *Tel 202/682–0505. Union Station, 1st St. and Massachusetts Ave., NE, Union Station Metro, Taxi zone 1D.*

Arise. See **dzi, the Tibet Collection**.

The Artist's Proof. Photos of the way things used to be—and not just in Washington.... *Tel 202/298–0446. Georgetown Park, 3222 M St., NW, Taxi zone 2A. Tel 202/408–9830. Union Station, 1st St. and Massachusetts Ave., NE, Union Station Metro, Taxi zone 1D. Tel 202/393–4922. 529 14th St., NW, Metro Center Metro, Taxi zone 1A.*

Aurea. Museum-quality pre-Columbian, Native American, and African American wearable art.... *Tel 202/371–0640. Union Station, 1st St. and Massachusetts Ave., NE, Union Station Metro, Taxi zone 1D.*

Backstage. Bookstore spotlighting theater and film, with a dramatic collection of scripts.... *Tel 202/775–1488. 21st and P streets, NW, Dupont Circle Metro, Taxi zone 1B.*

Blackberry. Items of African American interest and origin.... *Tel 703/418–1506. Fashion Centre at Pentagon City, 1100 S. Hayes St., Arlington, VA, Pentagon City Metro.*

Blue & Gray Books and Prints. Civil War books and collectibles.... *Tel 703/739–9849. 210 King St., 2nd floor, Alexandria, VA. Opens at noon.*

British Connection. Minuscule Alexandria Old Town shop behind dowdy English tea room sells foodstuffs imported from U.K.... *Tel 703/836–8181. 119 S. Royal St., Alexandria, VA.*

Capitol Coin & Stamp Company. For stamps, coins, campaign memorabilia.... *Tel 202/296–0400. 17th and L streets, NW, Farragut North Metro, Taxi zone 1B. Closed Sun.*

Cheshire Cat. Children's bookstore in Chevy Chase section of D.C.... *Tel 202/244–3956. 5512 Connecticut Ave., NW, Taxi zone 4B.*

Collector's Armoury. Replicas of historic weapons, made as movie props.... *Tel 703/549–3808. 101 N. Union St., Alexandria, VA.*

Counter Spy Shop. Espionage gimmicks and gadgets.... *Tel 202/887–1717. 1027 Connecticut Ave., NW, Farragut North Metro, Taxi zone 1B. Closed weekends.*

Dean & DeLuca. Fabulous food and kitchenware, across the alley from the Georgetown Park mall.... *Tel 202/342–2500. 3276 M St., NW, Taxi zone 2A.*

dzi, the Tibet Collection. For Tibetan crafts and books. The other half of the store, Arise, sells Asian antique and new furniture, art, and textiles. Within D.C. at Takoma Park, MD border.... *Tel 202/882–0008 (dzi), 202/291–0770 (Arise). 6925 Willow St., NW, Takoma Metro, Taxi zone 4C.*

Earth Friendly. For lovers of the environment.... *Tel 202/639–0720. Shops at National Place, 13th and F streets, NW, Metro Center Metro, Taxi zone 1A.*

FAO Schwarz. The big kahuna, toy-wise.... *Tel 202/342–2285. Georgetown Park, 3222 M St., NW, Taxi zone 2A.*

Finewares. Compact two-story Takoma Park shop sells only handmade crafts, made only by Americans.... *Tel 301/270–3138. 7042 Carroll Ave., Takoma Park, MD, Takoma Metro. Closed Mon.*

Health Source Bookstore. World-class specialist in books on medicine, health, wellness.... *Tel 202/789–7303, 800/713–7122 (outside D.C.). 1404 K St., NW, McPherson Square Metro, Taxi zone 1B.*

Hecht's. The last remaining full-service department store in downtown Washington—or anywhere in D.C. for that matter. Convenient location on top of Metro Center Metrorail station and good selection in all categories, but little you can't buy back home or pay less for elsewhere.... *Tel 202/628–6661. 12th and G streets, NW, Metro Center Metro, Taxi zone 1A. Additional locations.*

House of Musical Traditions. Nationally known folk and jazz music store for albums, books, instruments, sheet music, lessons. Runs a Monday Night Concert Series.... *Tel 301/270–9090, 800/450–3794. 7040 Carroll Ave., Takoma Park, MD, Takoma Metro. Closed Mon.*

Insights Galleria. Crystals and other metaphysical paraphernalia.... *Tel 301/270–8210. 7014 Westmoreland Ave., Takoma Park, MD, Takoma Metro.*

Jacadi. Classic French clothing for kids, infant to age 12.... *Tel 703/415–0055. Fashion Centre at Pentagon City, 1100 S. Hayes St., Arlington, VA, Pentagon City Metro.*

Juggling Capitol. For juggling gear.... *Tel 202/789–1799. Old Post Office Pavilion, 11th St. and Pennsylvania Ave., NW, Federal Triangle Metro, Taxi zone 1D.*

John Crouch Tobacconist/The Scottish Merchant. Two historically relevant shops in one Old Town Alexandria cubbyhole. The Scottish Merchant sells kilts and Scottish gift items; the tobacconist sells, well, tobacco.... *Tel 703/548–2900 (Tobacconist), 703/739–2302 (Merchant). 215 King St., Alexandria, VA.*

Lambda Rising. Bookstore and cultural center for gay men and lesbians.... *Tel 202/462–6969. 1625 Connecticut Ave., NW, Dupont Circle Metro, Taxi zone 1B.*

Lammas Women's Books & More. Off-Dupont Circle shop and gathering place for feminists.... *Tel 202/775–8218. 1426 21st St., NW, Dupont Circle Metro, Taxi zone 1B.*

Learningsmith. A palatably educational store for children.... *Tel 202/337–0800. Georgetown Park, 3222 M St., NW, Taxi zone 2A.*

Magic Masters. A tricky store staffed by master magicians.... *Tel 202/628–0779. Shops at National Place, 13th and F streets, NW, Metro Center Metro, Taxi zone 1A.*

The Map Store. For maps and travel gadgets.... *Tel 202/ 628–2608. Farragut Sq., 1636 I St., NW, Farragut West or Farragut North Metros, Taxi zone 1B.*

News World. Vast selection of magazines and out-of-town/out-of-country papers.... *Tel 202/872–0190. K St. and Connecticut Ave., NW, Farragut North or Farragut West Metros, Taxi zone 1B.*

Newsroom. Dailies from most U.S. cities and international capitals, plus magazines from all over the world.... *Tel 202/332–1489. 1753 Connecticut Ave., NW, Dupont Circle Metro, Taxi zone 1B.*

NOW Store. The National Organization for Women runs this unapologetic emporium for political correctness.... *Tel 202/ 467–6980. 1615 K St., NW, Farragut North Metro, Taxi zone 1B. Closed weekends.*

Old Print Gallery. Georgetown shop has area's largest selection of antique prints and maps.... *Tel 202/965–1818. 1220 31st St., NW, Taxi zone 2A. Closed Sun.*

Old Town Armory. Large selection of handguns, rifles, ammo, and holsters amid bombardment of NRA (National Rifle Association) propaganda.... *Tel 703/548–2005. 215 King St., Alexandria, VA.*

Political Americana. A host of souvenirs and collectibles, all dutifully inscribed with depictions of popular (and lunatic fringe) politicians and ideologies. Convenient locations in Union Station and near White House.... *Tel 202/547–1871, 15th and G streets, NW, Metro Center Metro, Taxi zone 1A. Tel 202/547–1685, Union Station, First St. and Massachusetts Ave., NE, Union Station Metro, Taxi zone 1D.*

Rand McNally Map & Travel Store. Maps of everything under the sun, with travel guides to match.... *Tel 202/223–6751.*

1201 Connecticut Ave., NW, Farragut North Metro, Taxi zone 1B. Additional locations.

Reiter's Books. Well-stocked store for technical and professional books.... *Tel 202/223–3327. 2021 K St., NW, Farragut West Metro, Taxi zone 1B.*

The Russian Store. All-Russian crafts and clothing.... *Tel 202/737–8030. Shops at National Place, 13th and F streets, NW, Metro Center Metro, Taxi zone 1A.*

The Scottish Merchant. See **John Crouch Tobacconist**.

Sidney Kramer Books. Long-established bookshop for politics junkies.... *Tel 202/293–2685. International Square, 1825 I St., NW, Farragut West Metro, Taxi zone 1B.*

U.S. Capitol Historical Society. Souvenirs of Washington.... *Tel 202/898–0972. Union Station, 1st St. and Massachusetts Ave., NE, Union Station Metro, Taxi zone 1D.*

U.S. Government Bookstore. Policy wonk playpens, chock full of unreadable government publications.... *Tel 202/512–0132. 710 N. Capitol St., NW, Union Station Metro, Taxi zone 1D. Tel 202/653–5075, 1510 H St., NW, McPherson Square Metro, Taxi zone 1A.*

Vertigo Books. Bookshop that functions as a cultural center for political progressives and African Americans. Frequent author appearances.... *Tel 202/429–9272. 1337 Connecticut Ave., NW, Dupont Circle Metro, Taxi zone 1B.*

Why Not. Charming Old Town Alexandria all-purpose kids emporium offers an "outrageously expensive to really reasonable" selection of toys, books, clothing (mostly all-cotton), games, and music.... *Tel 703/548–4420. 200 King St., Alexandria, VA.*

World Bank Bookstore. Reports and technical tomes in many tongues.... *Tel 202/473–2941. 18th St. and Pennsylvania Ave., NW, Farragut West Metro, Taxi zone 1A. Closed weekends.*

Yes! The question, O Great Carnak: What Georgetown store materializes Washington's best mind/spirit/body books?.... *Tel 202/338–7874. 1035 31st St., NW, Taxi zone 2A.*

nigh

tlife

6

Given D.C.'s drab
bureaucrat image,
its wild-and-
crazy nightlife
scene comes as a
total surprise. It
makes sense,

though, when you think about it, considering the profusion of colleges, hordes of young singles a long way from home, an energetic urban black community, and a steady stream of worldly visitors in the Washington metroplex. Olympian drinking is in, abetted by seductive happy-hour specials, all-you-can-drink nights, circulating shooters and Jell–O shots within clubs, and chartered bus pub crawls between them. Pool halls—excuse me, billiard cafes—are as big here as elsewhere. Washingtonians love to dance, too, and are willing to stay out most of the night to do it right.

The Lay of the Land

The nightlife scene is concentrated in geographic, demographic, and psychographic clusters. Geographically, **Georgetown** has the largest and densest concentration of restaurants, bars, and clubs. But you don't find many locals there (unless you consider college kids locals) because, as Yogi Berra once said about someplace else, "Nobody goes there anymore: it's too crowded." Georgetown's hub is the intersection of Wisconsin Avenue and M Street; even at night, you can safely walk on Wisconsin Avenue from K Street up to about Q Street, or on M Street from 28th Street (Rock Creek Park) to the Key Bridge at 34th Street. Georgetown side streets are safe, too, and much prettier to look at. **Dupont Circle** is less singlemindedly hedonistic; clubs and restaurants line K Street through the circle all the way up to the Washington Hilton at T Street. The Dupont Circle area is also more gay-oriented, especially on P Street between the Circle and 25th Street, and 17th Street between P and R. Part of this area thinks it's hot enough to claim a trend-o-name: BeDuCi (below Dupont Circle). Most **Adams-Morgan** action takes place on 18th Street between U Street and Columbia Road, with a lively offshoot south on Columbia Road to Belmont Road. You can get anything you want in Adams-Morgan—all kinds of restaurants, jazz and blues clubs, dance palaces, cheap saloons—except a place to park; take a cab.

A number of hot spots, from glamorous discos to twisted hell-holes of progressive sound, exist in decaying older buildings **downtown** almost in the shadow of the FBI Building. The bars of **Capitol Hill**, both around Union Station and along Pennsylvania Avenue, SE, are mainly neighborhood hangouts that will sometimes bring in a band. Cutting-edge clubs, theaters, and restaurants can still pay the rent in the dicey **U Street** area around the intersection of 14th and U streets, NW. Evocative of Manhattan's East Village, it's an area on the edge in more ways than one.

Sources

Besides the publications listed in the Entertainment chapter, check out *Scene*, "DC's Alternative Free Weekly Entertainment Guide," which runs a Dance Club Calendar listing live bands, DJs, cover charges, age restrictions, and drink specials each night. It comes out every Friday. While the *Washington Blade* aspires to serious journalism on gay concerns, *m/w* just wants to have fun, with a map—entitled "Here, there, and queer in DC"—of bars, clubs, restaurants, and other businesses (Baltimore, too). The freebie appears Thursdays in businesses around Dupont Circle, particularly P Street and 17th Street. Find out where to hear the blues in the night by calling the **D.C. Blues Society** (tel 202/828–3028), which sponsors jams and concerts to preserve the pure form.

Liquor Laws and Drinking Hours

The drinking age is 21, and most clubs that serve alcohol won't let anyone under 21

Go-Go: D.C. Roots Music

Go-go is a 25-year-old forerunner to hip-hop that can be heard only in Washington, D.C. and some nearby Maryland suburbs. Go-go resembles hip-hop in many ways, but it features more heavily African accented call-and-response between musicians and audience. Go-go never really hit it big, partly because recordings never catch the spontaneity and ultra-intense audience involvement—you really have to be there (and if you are, there's a fair chance you'll be swept into the audience-participation violence that has unfortunately become associated with go-go performances). Go-go goes on somewhere in the Washington area most weekend nights, but you might have to do a little detective work to find it. The most accessible place, despite its distance from any Metro stop, is the Ibex Club (tel 202/726–1800, 5832 Georgia Ave., NW, Taxi zone 3C), which presents at least one go-go band a week. Check out the Washington City Paper's listings under "Clubs: Go-go/Hip-hop." Bands to look for: Rare Essence, Backyard Band, Junkyard Band, Northeast Rockers. Just remember that you won't hear go-go in the safe parts of town.

through the door. Some clubs admit 18-, 19-, and 20-year-olds on a non-alcohol-drinking basis, distinguishing them from drinkers with hand stamps or wristbands. Some bars only admit 18- to 20-year-olds on certain nights (usually weeknights) or before certain hours; call to find out before you go, since doorpersons are not into discussing the matter. If you're 21, bring a picture ID to prove it, because Washington is fierce about checking.

Virtually every place stays open until at least 2am. Most clubs with live music and a major dance scene stay open until 3am, at least on weekends. A handful of dance clubs can stay open until 4am, but that's the absolute legal limit, people, go home!

Tickets

The places we call "concert clubs," below, would have you believe that their bands are so hot, their dance floors so crowded, that you had better buy tickets in advance through **TicketMaster** (tel 202/432–SEAT, 800/551–7328) or **Protix** (tel 703/218–6500). The clubs may or may not have the best bands money can buy, but calling TicketMaster or going to one of their outlets can spare you anxiety and line time, a convenience for which they slap on a hefty service charge. Another advantage: TicketMaster lets you charge tickets, while some concert clubs demand hard cash at the door. Black Cat, Capitol Ballroom, Bayou, Kilimanjaro (see below) use TicketMaster, while the 9:30 Club uses Protix.

The Lowdown

Special places after dark... The **Mall** is ideal for strolls after dark: the sights are unforgettable, the crowds have vanished, all that's left are a few tourists and a dozen kinds of cops. All monuments are accessible 24 hours a day, with National Park Service guards around usually until midnight. Climb the **Lincoln Memorial** steps and look east across the Washington Monument to the glowing Capitol dome: it's very reassuring. Ascending the **Washington Monument** is even better at night, when the city below (and, presumably, the country it rules) looks as if everything's going according to plan. The **Vietnam Veterans Memorial** seems to have been designed for nocturnal visitations—even at night, you'll never be alone. Or you can walk around the **White House**, peer into the windows; you might catch a glimpse of the president and his family, but don't hold your breath.

For undergrads/recent grads... College students seem drawn to places where older folks fear to tread (maybe that's why they go there). Kids amplify the meganoise and freak murals—Siamese twins, headless females—at **15 Minutes**. This off–K–street place must pass out a map and drink tickets with college diplomas, because every recent grad seems to wind up here sometime during an evening on the town. The **Insect Club** is infested with kids who have just found (or just gave up trying to find) their first jobs. Bug dishes have been exterminated from the menu, but the three-story Penn Quarter hive still teems with plastic spider webs, fake ant farms, and creepy-crawly sculptures. Closer to Dupont Circle, **Planet Fred** has thrift-shop Star Trek scenery, lots of goofy promotions, and a celestial variety of rock and world music, live and on CD. When that palls, the youthful offenders are close enough to stagger over to the nonstop keg party at the **Big Hunt**, with 27 brews on tap in seasonal rotation. Also in the Dupont Circle nabe, the **Brickskeller's** allure is simply hundreds of different types of beer in funny bottles and cans. You'll spot as many different college sweatshirts worn here as there are beers.

Hillie haunts... Hillies are mostly young, low-paid Capitol Hill staffers—informal mingling with other congressional staff is an implicit part of their job descriptions, and indeed their entire social life. The youngest and lowliest (mostly male) Hillies congregate at **Tune Inn**, a charmless Capitol Hill dive—no microbrews, no happy hour, just big cheap drinks and trophy decor (animal trophies, bowling trophies, etc.). Just down 1st Street, **Bullfeathers** offers nonpartisan hospitality for midlevel aides, and sometimes their bosses. Unaccompanied females won't get hassled here—not even if they're congresswomen. On the (north) Senate side, **Tiber Creek** attracts the young and hungry with free buffets and happy-hour specials; it serves huge, bulbous yard and half-yard glasses of draft beer, with rounded bottoms cradled in wooden racks. Tiber Creek also serves as a shrine to the long-gone Washington Senators ("Washington: first in war, first in peace, last in the American League"), with a remarkable mezzanine-level mural of Griffith Stadium.

    Tavern on the Hill is popular with Hillies and bureaucrats probably because no one else can find them there—it's just a few steps off Pennsylvania Avenue, but in a little old building concealed by a vast parking structure on one side and the Department of Labor on two others. Congressional staffers of a conservative bent can't resist the deliriously overdone southern-fried style of the **Dixie Grill**, happily placed next door to the "House Where Lincoln Died." **The Dubliner** has this Irish thing going where everybody's as good (and drunk) as everybody else and, at least early in the evening, college kids can bend elbows with the politically mighty. Regulars insist that the Guinness tapped in the back bar tastes better than the Guinness up front (cleaner pipes, maybe). The bars at **The Monocle** and **La Colline** (see Dining) are good places to see which lobbyist is wining-and-dining which legislator. The main floor of three-story **Jenkins Hill**—the name recalls the original name of Capitol Hill—is a neighborhood hangout in a neighborhood of Hillies, and a 24-hour restaurant on Friday and Saturday. Downstairs, the dismal Underground has blues or rock bands and dancing; upstairs, it's a sports bar with pool tables and a jukebox.

Diplomatic immunity... Washington has a large population of resident and visiting foreigners who are accustomed to staying out late (why is it that people of other nationalities seem to recede into couch-potatoohood later in life than Americans do?). **Cities,** in Adams-Morgan, not too far from the Kalorama neighborhood where many live, is a favorite rendezvous. Its gimmick is to shut down periodically and redecorate according to a new theme city—Hong Kong, Rome, Istanbul, New Orleans, who knows what's next—with cuisine and drinks menu to match. Those who think they might really have a crack at ambassador drink at the **Fairfax Bar**, a discreet wood-paneled hideout in the Ritz-Carlton Hotel on Embassy Row. The **Marquis de Rochambeau** simulates Paris the way it ought to have been—two floors of glittery music and dancing (international sounds, jazz, and blues below; pop music with a Latin beat above). Live acts range from Piafesque *chanteuses* to bongo drum jams; outrageous prices for drinks and traditional Parisian bistro fare complete the illusion. For dancing, cosmopolites enjoy the noise and flash and flagrant class distinctions at downtown's **Club Zei**, a New York warehouse-club wannabe. While a younger crowd throngs the thousand-square-foot floor here for dance-and-decadence, folks in the old, richer, international set pay $500/year for access to Zei Privé, a surrealistic third-floor aerie. A mainly black audience—African Americans and African Africans—comes to **Kilimanjaro** to shake it up to hot world-beat music from Africa and the Caribbean. Located in a completely unexotic white-brick shell at the southern tip of Adams-Morgan, the interior plays up the jungle motif with plastic fronds and taut zebra skins.

Pickup spots... If you're young and have steel-plated eardrums, try your luck downtown at the **Insect Club** and **15 Minutes**. Young people with jobs in the city—professional and otherwise—take their chances at **The Cellar**, a vast subterranean disco between Dupont Circle and Foggy Bottom that's a major meat market for (pre-*Pulp Fiction*) Travoltas and their big-hair female counterparts. Then it's on to **Rumors**, a foliage-filled downtown establishment where under-40 professionals and college kids with decent clothes come late to connect, when all else fails. Down a back alley off Wisconsin Avenue in Georgetown, recent post-grads and those with their college years far behind them try to score at **Champions** sports bar, where there's even more action on the various floors than on the sports-tuned TVs.

A mature, affluent, and well-dressed crowd hooks up at the **Fifth Column**, a converted bank that welcomes late-night trendies who wish they could live in a bank. Teller service for drinks includes "smart" drinks that allegedly improve memory, though you may want to feign amnesia when you wake up in some stranger's bed the next morning. A dressy young African American crowd goes to **The Ritz**, directly opposite the visitor's entrance to the FBI Building, where they can listen to live jazz, then dance until 4am to rap, hip-hop, and funk. Each of the five floors' decor matches the music. For gay males, the sex nexus is **JR.'s**, one large room with one long bar that stays lively from cocktail hour until very late. It's knee-deep in stand-and-model attitude: money and status are aphrodisiacs here.

The **Capitol City Brewing Company** attracts downtown professionals from the five o'clock whistle onward, though it's often infiltrated with out-of-towners from the convention center nearby. If you're rich and beyond your first youth, the **Yacht Club** in Bethesda has a skipper on board—DJ/yenta Tommy Curtis—who will personally introduce you to Mr. or Ms. Right. (He's mixed dance music and patrons to the tune of about a marriage-a-month for the last eight years.) Not for singles only—about a third of the crowd are on dates or, as Tommy puts it, "dating your wife." In Georgetown, below collegetown Georgetown, the art deco-style **River Club** brings well-heeled over-40's together for pricey cocktails and touch dancing.

Where to order a martini... At the **Town & Country Lounge,** a venerable power center in the Renaissance Mayflower, order one from Sam, who's been mixing (shaking?) them there for over 20 years. Reportedly, martini and manhattan orders here rose with the onset of the Republican Congress, while draft beer went flat. Your drink will be as austere and dry as the patrician atmosphere of the clubby **Fairfax Bar** in the Ritz-Carlton, where the new rich meet the still rich. The **Washington Grill Bar** in the Sheraton Centre is a fine place for a thoughtful drink, the kind of big-city hotel bar capable of referring to its bartender as a "mixologist"—it serves 70-plus brands of single-malt scotch, the best collection in town. Well-off **River Club** patrons drink martinis at night while they bemoan the demise of the three-martini lunch; this is one club where a lady in her forties is considered a sweet young thing. Slinky, cat-suited blonds mix the drinks in the pseudobrothel confines of the **Marquis de Rochambeau,** an overwrought, frou frou-laden Georgetown cabaret aimed at flamboyant fantasy seekers of a certain age and younger. The 36 vodkas served at **State of the Union,** the grungy Russian restaurant and acid jazz bar on U street, come from as far away as Australia and as near home as the five varieties doctored with added flavors on the premises. Patrons include the head-shaven and the pierced, along with more conventional types aged from late twenties to early forties, but it's still a hip, offbeat place to know about, with nary a tourist, yuppie, or Republican in sight.

Concert clubs... A tough, punk crowd of bikers and head-bangers prowls **Black Cat,** a swaggering big newcomer in an unobtrusive 14th-and-U area warehouse. The bill here spotlights cult bands that usually have "death" or "black" or "war" in their names. The name of Washington's oldest established alternative music club, **9:30 club,** refers to its old address on F Street in the grubby heart of downtown. On New Year's Day 1996, however, it moved into a revamped former concert hall in a raffish neighborhood near the U Street nightlife zone, thus gaining more space, no columns, real food, and blessed relief from That Smell. Even so, few patrons over 35 can handle the noise level and crowds at what's still the city's top showcase for national talent. Opened in 1995 (with the Ramones), **Capitol Ballroom**—a converted boiler factory in the scary environs of the Washington Navy Yard—makes a niche for groups too big for clubs like 9:30 or the Black Cat but not up to filling big halls or arenas. It draws a young punky crowd, with some acts inspiring mosh-pit groping. **Bayou**, a big, ugly 400-seat concert space under the freeway at the Georgetown waterfront, presents pop, rock, reggae, and zydeco bands. The Grateful Dead knockoff group The Next Step is a Monday fixture here. Also check out what's on at **Kilimanjaro**, the world-music dance hall in Adams-Morgan, and Alexandria's folkie/blues/new-grass palace, **The Birchmere**, which often does sell out.

Painting the town pink... Not all that long ago, the Washington gay scene consisted of lurking around Lafayette Square and stealing off to do it on the Mall. Now the picture is appreciably more diverse, with *m/w*, the first word on such matters, listing 26 gay/lesbian bars/clubs and 14 gay-oriented restaurants. P Street west of Dupont Circle is the easiest place to find gay nightlife, but 17th Street between P and R streets has more style. The men of **JR.'s** (the reigning presence on 17th Street) project billows of A-List/B-List Washington attitude, but everybody winds up there at some time during the night. Bar specials accompany ceremonial screening of choice TV shows, lately "Melrose Place" and "Absolutely Fabulous." One flight below 17th Street, a low-ceilinged basement creates intimacy for the slightly older clientele of **Trumpets**. The decor, which features trumpets and other postmodern forms of twisted tubing, and a wall of video screens where hits keep on happening, stirs up the dancers. **The Circle**, a newcomer just off Dupont Circle, attracts a wider range of ages and, unlike other establishments, enjoys a conspicuous presence of lesbians and blacks. Its three levels offer several options: bright terrace lounge (with outdoor seating when at all possible); noisy, jammed dance floor; or quiet basement bar with pool table. A mostly young, casually dressed, all-female crowd comes mainly to dance at **Hung Jury**, Washington's first and only all-women's bar and one of the oldest lesbian bars in America. It's only open on weekends, when a movie screen showing old film clips enlivens high-energy disco dance music. Gay men own, operate, and dominate **Tracks**, Washington's biggest and best gay ballroom, but everyone else goes there too—everyone but homophobes, who are explicitly warned off by a sign posted at the door. The 20,000-square-foot indoor-outdoor disco is big enough for a volleyball court and the city's wildest dance floor.

Local hangouts... Sometimes you've gotta go "where everybody knows your na-ay-ame...." In Adams-Morgan that place is **Dan's Cafe**: with just a bar, stools, and well-worn pool table, it's a narrow, smoke-filled holdover from the days before Adams-Morgan even needed to be gentrified. With brick walls, a fireplace, and tables close enough to eavesdrop, **Polly's Cafe** set up shop near 14th and U long before the onslaught of chic, and will probably hang in there after the rest are gone. Two choices near Dupont Circle: so much as utter "BeDuCi" at **Mr. Eagan's** and you could be in for a fat lip. No obnoxious yuppie scene, just low prices for six draft beers, 25 brands in bottles, and eccentric bar-food menu items like shepherd's pie and steak-and-kidney pie. **Timberlake's** preserves the essence of the ancient (circa 1980) fern bar, but north of Dupont Circle this is as down-to-earth as it gets. Popular with people that even Newt Gingrich would concede were "normal Americans," it's a comfortable place for unaccompanied women. You can see the Capitol dome from the sidewalk in front of the Hillie hangout **Tune Inn**, but inside it could be any beer joint south of the Mason-Dixon line.

99 bottles of beer... Like the rest of the country, Washington has discovered Beer. **Capitol City Brewing Company**, opposite the Convention Center, was D.C.'s first legal brew pub since Prohibition; large, bright, clean, and yuppified, it supplements a rotating selection of a half-dozen of its own brews with a large selection of imports and microbrews. **Brickskeller**, by contrast, is a dingy basement near Dupont Circle with the world's largest selection of beer—over 550 brands at this point, and not one of them on draft. Prices range from $2.65 for American megabrews to $67.50 for a 3-liter bottle of Duvel from Belgium. Nonpurists might sample a "Beer-Tail," like the American Colonist's Whistle Belly Vengeance (beer, rum, molasses), or chew on one of the buffalo dishes. With 27 domestic and imported varieties, **The Big Hunt**, south of Dupont Circle, is the post-grad frat-rat place for draft beer within D.C.; entertainment consists of a couple of pool tables and a 100-CD jukebox with tunes even early baby boomers would play. Out in Arlington, **Bardo Rodeo**, which claims to be the largest brew pub *in the entire Western Hemisphere*, serves its own draft brews and about 25 others inside and beside a vast, graffiti-encrusted former Olds showroom. Go Thursdays for a free brewery tour and bargain rates on freshly made beer.

Coffee, tea, and whatever... SoHo Tea & Coffee is your clean, well-lighted (but alcohol-free) place off Dupont Circle that sometimes provides light entertainment and is almost always open. Big windows, bright artwork, and coffee concoctions attract nearby office workers and students with their notebook computers during the day, and quite a different breed of hombre at night. Also near Dupont Circle, **Food for Thought** should be an old beatnik coffeehouse, with its folk music and blues and poetry, but it has a full bar, vegetarian food, and really is more into tea. For serious coffee go to **Sirius Coffee** (bet they haven't heard that one before!), near the University of the District of Columbia, where beans are roasted on the premises and drinks are concocted to order. Want to stay up for the rest of the century? Order a Two Black Eyes: a double espresso with a regular cup of coffee chaser.

Billiard cafes... Washington's gotten caught up in the trend to yuppify nasty pool halls into charming "billiard cafes" with microbrewery beers, tables for nonsmokers, and women customers. Unlike old pool halls, these places are serious about those "No Gambling" signs. The reborn **Georgetown Billiards** now serves microbrews and sandwiches, offers happy-hour specials from a beer/wine only bar, and has a hot CD jukebox. The joint likes students from the local colleges so much, it lets them play for half price on certain nights. Caveman-themed **Bedrock Billiards** in Adams-Morgan keeps players on their games by delivering capuccino to their tables (along with microbrews, wine, and snacks). The well-dressed crowd—up to their mid-forties, with equal numbers of male and female players—can also play darts, video games, and electronic poker. Pool is a sidelight at **Bardo Rodeo**, the vast brew pub in Arlington, but it still has something like 30 tables on two levels, and it's wildly popular with under-35 suburbanites.

All that jazz (and blues)... Blues Alley in Georgetown really is off an alley, but the emphasis is more jazz than blues—it presents the biggest jazz stars outside the concert halls, for the biggest prices in town (and buying off your minimum with their Creole-style dinners is not such a great idea). For lesser names but smoke-filled jazz room ambience, hit **One Step Down** in Foggy Bottom. Even musicians feel at ease here, sitting on defrocked church pews and in diner-style booths (with table-top jukeboxes to play jazz classics during breaks). **Cafe Lautrec** in Adams-Morgan is a worn-down French bistro with some kind of live American jazz going every night. An older neighborhood crowd enjoys its Left Bank cafe ambience along with classic bistro cuisine. **Takoma Station** is a low-key neighborhood jazz bar out in Maryland, where yuppies and buppies listen closely to top local players. Southern-style cuisine is served; they play that reggae music for a younger crowd on Sundays. On U Street, the Russian restaurant **State of the Union**, which features busts of Lenin and dingy Russian chandeliers, fills the night with acid jazz, which may be a little too close to progressive rock for some sensibilities. **Madam's Organ** in Adams-Morgan (get the anagram?) fancies itself to be a low-down rhythm-and-blues joint, but don't count on anything except a wondrous strange experience. The entrance is painted purple; the walls, fingernail-polish red. And redheads *always* pay half price for Rolling Rock and rail drinks because the owner's a carrot-top and because they fit in so well with the color scheme. Live electric and acoustic rhythm and blues most nights, DJ Stella Neptune's "Nutt Bustin Funk" dance sets on Saturdays.

Sounds of the suburbs... Three music clubs in the suburbs are worth the trek. Fleetwood Mac's Mick Fleetwood's **Fleetwood's** (got all that?) brings top national blues and jazz musicians to a hot new club in Old Town Alexandria. An eclectic crowd gathers on Fleetwood's gorgeous terrace overlooking the Potomac, with patio seating in summer. **The Birchmere** in the Alexandria hinterland is a no-frills space with national and regional acoustic and electric, folk, country, and new-grass talent: Jerry Jeff Walker, Tom Paxton, Christine Lavin, the Nitty Gritty Band. There's a wide range of ages, but everyone dresses jeans-casual. **Tornado Alley** in Wheaton, Maryland, is the seemingly unlikely convergence of musical pipelines that begin in Chicago, Louisiana, and Austin. The southern roadhouse decor of this former wholesale carpeting outlet looks as authentic as the music sounds; there's a big dance floor for Western swing, cajun, rockabilly stompin'. Any kind of clothes will do; Western gear won't look out of place. It's beyond the Beltway but only a block from a Metro station.

Dance fever... The Saturday Night Fever never broke at **The Cellar**, a huge disco that has the city's only illuminated dance floor. It's uncool enough to play songs you've actually heard before (top 40, progressive rock, even flatout disco), occasionally even songs that people over 25 have heard before. Europeans and Americans who can keep up with them flock to **Club Zei**, a loud multilevel state-of-the-disco club off its own downtown alley. The joint overflows with techno excess: a three-story, 32-screen "video wall"; XYLO Turbine lighting software preprogrammed to coordinate lighting sequences with music; and a 32,000-watt sound system that generates 32 decibels of sound, some of which resembles music. Occupying a former bank downtown, the **Fifth Column** regards itself as a dance club, art gallery, and (for its eclectic clothes-horse crowd), fashion show. Five floors of disco feature different music styles—from taut techno/industrial rock to acid jazz to reggae—and there's a conversation pit in the basement. African American professionals, not all of them young, can choose among five dance floors and five styles of dance at **The Ritz**. The international set shakes and bakes to live world-beat music at **Kilimanjaro** in Adams-Morgan. **Tracks** is a gay-owned, hangar-sized Studio 54 for the nineties, on the wrong side of the tracks in a deplorable neighborhood near the Washington Navy Yard; it welcomes everyone to dance till they *shvitz*.

Formats change nightly, with Thursday's "College Night" predominantly hetero. If you think social dancing means writhing among a crush of other sweaty bodies, the **9:30 Club** downtown, Adams-Morgan's **Madam's Organ**, and the **Capitol Ballroom** way the hell out by the Navy Yard (TAKE A TAXI) are the places to go. But card-carrying adults can still touch-dance to live big bands and a Latin beat at the chic art deco **River Club** in Georgetown. The happy hoofers at **Chelsea's**, also in Georgetown, know that hot salsa isn't only for tacos and that merengue is more than a pie.

The big game... Champions in Georgetown is Washington's oldest established memorabilia-encrusted sports bar: if you're not rooting for the Redskins or Hoyas it's best to keep it to yourself. **Grand Slam** in the Grand Hyatt, across from the Washington Convention Center, attracts a transient and therefore somewhat more ecumenical clientele—there's great fervor for ACC (Atlantic Coast Conference) basketball action, with a decided Duke-ward slant. **Senators**, a new contender in the Holiday Inn on the Hill, spent a star quarterback's ransom to cover every visible surface with caps, yearbooks, photos, uniforms, documents, and trinkets recalling the late, lamented Washington Senators, who decamped for Minnesota in 1960, re-formed, and turned into the Texas Rangers in 1972.

XXX-rated... Washington gives you everything you want in a strip show—and less. Certainly less than the live sex shows in lewd places like New York, San Francisco, and Paris. The tamer forms of voyeurism can be indulged in places that seldom have cover charges or minimums, though they charge dearly for drinks. The "exotic dancers" at 25-year-old **Archibald's** don't take it all off but, come on, it's only three blocks from the White House. Wide-screen satellite TVs add sports action, if you need it. The **Royal Palace**, off Dupont Circle, gives its audience of free-spending hearty partyers a more provocative breed of entertainment: two floors of dirty dancers close enough to touch (but only with rolled-up currency). **Good Guys**, in upper Georgetown, is kind of a neighborhood strip joint with gorgeously athletic female dancers who form an entirely different neighborhood.

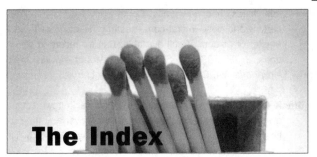

The Index

Archibald's. Strong point of this girlie joint is convenience for downtown businessmen and tourists: it's near the corner of 15th and K streets, within the same pleasure dome as the Comedy Cafe and Fanatics sports bar. Open for lunch daily (except Sunday, when it opens at 7pm). Call to find out who's "up" today.... *Tel 202/737–2662. 1520 K St., NW, McPherson Square Metro, Taxi zone 1A.*

Bardo Rodeo. Vast brew pub in former Olds showroom serves a dozen types of American- and Euro-style homebrews plus 20 drafts from other brewers. Outdoor beer garden and plenty of pool tables up and down.... *Tel 703/527–9399. 2000 Wilson Blvd., Arlington, VA, Court House Metro.*

The Bayou. Large Georgetown concert space features national headliners, with local talent opening up. Normally age 18 entry but all ages admitted to some shows. Tickets available from TicketMaster or at door.... *Tel 202/333–2897. Wisconsin Ave. and K St., NW, Foggy Bottom–GWU Metro, Taxi zone 2A. Cover charge.*

Bedrock Billiards. Flintstones cave motif dominates yuppie Adams-Morgan pool hall. Hourly rates of $4 to $15 determined by day, hour, number of players.... *Tel 202/667–7665. 1841 Columbia Rd., NW, Woodley Park–Zoo Metro, Taxi zone 2B.*

The Big Hunt. Hunt ends here if your quarry is draft beer. Animal House atmosphere.... *Tel 202/785–2333. 1345 Connecticut Ave., NW, Dupont Circle Metro, Taxi zone 1B.*

The Birchmere. Where have all the folkies gone? Gone to the Birchmere, every one—a wide-open joint in a non-Old Town Alexandria strip mall, that presents top national names in folk, blues, and new-grass. Come early for close-in free parking and close-in first-come seating. Tickets from Ticket-Master or at door, if still available. Call for recorded directions.... *Tel 703/549–5919. 3901 Mount Vernon Ave., Alexandria, VA. Closed Sun–Mon. Cover charge.*

Black Cat. The largest alternative rock space in town, plays everything *but* rap and heavy metal. No cover any time to hear jukebox oldies in smoky Red Room bar. Tickets available from TicketMaster, box office, and door.... *Tel 202/ 667–7960. 1831 14th St., NW, U Street–Cardozo Metro, Taxi zone 1B. Cover charge.*

Blues Alley. Biggest names in jazz in exposed brick Georgetown showroom. High cover charge plus hefty minimums run off the kids.... *Tel 202/337–4141. 1073 Wisconsin Ave., NW (enter through alley south of M St.), Foggy Bottom–GWU Metro, Taxi zone 2A. Cover charge and minimum.*

Brickskeller. College crowd and slightly older beer fiends descend to brick-lined catacombs for some 550+ beers, most of them in bottles, a few in cans, no draft.... *Tel 202/ 293–1885. 1523 22nd St., NW, Dupont Circle Metro, Taxi zone 1B.*

Bullfeathers. Friendly Victorian-style tavern two blocks south of the House office buildings, a hangout for Hillies somewhat above the lowest rung on the totem pole. Live music Saturday night, and Sunday brunch.... *Tel 202/543–5005. 410 S. 1st St., SE, Capitol South Metro, Taxi zone 1D.*

Cafe Lautrec. Casual *boite* on the Adams-Morgan strip, where there's some form of live jazz—contemporary, classic, Brazilian-accented—every night, bar-top tap dancing on weekends.... *Tel 202/265–6436. 2431 18th St., NW, Woodley Park–Zoo Metro, Taxi zone 2B. Minimum charged.*

Capitol Ballroom. Big alternative rock venue near Navy Yard. Half Street Club hosts weekend dancing next door. All ages admitted and shows *try* to end in time for patrons to catch the last Metro out of Dodge. Tickets from Ticket Master or at door.... *Tel 703/549–7625. 1015 Half St., SE, Navy Yard Metro, Taxi zone 2E (taxis recommended). Open for shows only. Cover charge.*

Capitol City Brewing Company. Converted warehouse comes alive after 5 with downtown workers and out-of-towners attending conventions across the street. Monthly brewmaster's schedule appears in *Washington City Paper* ad.... *Tel 202/628–2222. 11th and H streets, NW, Metro Center Metro, Taxi zone 1C.*

The Cellar. Huge disco and massive low-rent singles scene. Sunday all-the-beer/drinks-you-can-drink special, $5 for women, $10 for guys; 18-to-20s admitted Thursday.... *Tel 202/457–8182. 2100 M St., NW, Foggy Bottom–GWU or Dupont Circle Metros, Taxi zone 1B. Closed Mon–Wed. Cover charge.*

Champions. Huge, frequently jam-packed sports bar, and a gold-medal pickup joint, especially on weekends.... *Tel 202/965–4005. 1206 Wisconsin Ave., NW (go down alley on west side of Wisconsin), Foggy Bottom–GWU Metro, Taxi zone 2A.*

Chelsea's. Most nights the swanky Georgetown supper club hosts Latin bands and an older international crowd on a roomy dance floor. Persian sounds flow Wednesday and Sunday, and on Saturday it's the showcase for the Capitol Steps comedy satire troupe.... *Tel 202/298–8222. 1055 Thomas Jefferson St., NW, Foggy Bottom–GWU Metro, Taxi zone 2A. Cover charge some nights.*

The Circle. Tri-level gay establishment hosts a casual melting pot of gay populism—male patrons through their forties, both white and black, as well as lesbians (especially on Wednesday's Ladies' Night).... *Tel 202/462–5575. 1629 Connecticut Ave., NW, Dupont Circle Metro, Taxi zone 1B.*

Cities. Adams-Morgan wine bar hangout with international flair. Upstairs dance club Thursday through Saturday.... *Tel 202/ 328–7194. 2424 18th St., NW, Woodley Park–Zoo Metro, Taxi zone 2B. Minimum for dance club only.*

Club Zei. Big downtown high-tech dance club. Over-18s admitted except Fri, Sat.... *Tel 202/842–2445. 1415 ZEI Alley, NW (south of I St. between 14th and 15th streets), McPherson Square Metro, Taxi zone 1B. Closed Sun, Tue. Cover charge.*

Dan's Cafe. Pool table, half-dozen beers, it's an old guys' bar with a strange retro attraction for the young.... *Tel 202/ 265–9241. 2315 18th St., NW, Woodley Park–Zoo Metro, Taxi zone 2B.*

Dixie Grill. Faux redneck hangout for southern congressional staffers and other transplants.... *Tel 202/628–4800. 518 10th St., NW; Metro Center, Gallery Place–Chinatown, or Federal Triangle Metros, Taxi zone 1D.*

The Dubliner. Lively hangout for middle-management Hillies; occasionally their bosses and lobbyists drop over from the Powerscourt restaurant in the attached Phoenix Park Hotel. Irish menu, nightly live Irish music.... *Tel 202/737–3773. 520 N. Capitol St., NW, Union Station Metro, Taxi zone 1D.*

Fairfax Bar. Tucked into the back of the Ritz-Carlton, a calm gathering place for old money, old power, and ambitious youngsters who want it. Afternoon tea and unobtrusive piano bar most evenings.... *Tel 202/293–2100. Ritz-Carlton Hotel, 2100 Massachusetts Ave., NW, Dupont Circle Metro, Taxi zone 1B.*

15 Minutes Club. Rothschild's Cafeteria by day, it converts by night to a warren of chambers of loud live and recorded alternative roots music. If you can't figure out what the name means, don't go, you won't like it. Kids 18 to 20 sometimes admitted.... *Tel 202/408–1855. 1030 15th St., NW, McPherson Square Metro, Taxi zone 1B.*

Fifth Column. Trendy nightspot in a converted bank, fashionably attired weekend crowds.... *Tel 202/393–3632. 915 F St., NW, Metro Center or Gallery Place Metros, Taxi zone 1D. Closed Sun. Cover charge.*

Food for Thought. A hippie/beatnik presence creates virtual coffeehouse with menu of vegetarian dishes, a full bar, and tea by the pitcher. Live music nightly (except Tuesday), mostly acoustic folk, bluegrass, jazz, with D.C. Blues Society programs the first Sunday of the month.... *Tel 202/ 797–1095. 1738 Connecticut Ave., NW, Dupont Circle Metro, Taxi zone 1B.*

Fleetwood's. Owner Mick Fleetwood of Fleetwood Mac made his fortune in rock, but always had his heart in the blues.

Opened in Old Town Alexandria in 1994, this club features top blues artists (plus crossovers like Maria Muldaur. Popular gospel brunch Sundays.... *Tel 703/548–6425. 44 Canal Center Plaza, Alexandria, VA. Cover charge.*

Georgetown Billiards. Most players in this pool-hall-turned-billiards cafe are eds and coeds from local colleges. Some 20 tables rent for a flat $10 hourly rate.... *Tel 202/965–7665. 3251 Prospect St., NW, Foggy Bottom Metro, Taxi zone 2A.*

Good Guys. Three dance floors, endless waves of pulsating rock, and troupes of strippers draw customers here, slightly off the beaten tourist path. Popular lunch spot for upper Georgetown neighborhood businessmen.... *Tel 202/333–8128. 2311 Wisconsin Ave., NW, Taxi zone 2A.*

Grand Slam. A sports bar for grown-ups, across from the convention center. Daily specials, microbrews, free popcorn munchies.... *Tel 202/582–1234. Grand Hyatt Washington at Washington Center, 1000 H St., NW, Metro Center Metro, Taxi zone 1D.*

Hung Jury. Long-running lesbian dance bar. Over-18s admitted with ID; if they're men, must have female escorts.... *Tel 202/379–3212 (info line), 202/785–8181. 1819 H St., NW, Farragut West Metro, Taxi zone 1B. Open Fri, Sat only. Cover charge.*

Insect Club. A posture of outrageousness attracts young dancers for music as grungy as the bug-themed décor. Long lines for alternative dance/all-you-can-drink party on Thursday and all-female DJ/dance crew on Wednesday's Valley of the Dolls Night.... *Tel 202/347–8884. 625 E St., NW, Gallery Place or Judiciary Square Metros, Taxi zone 1D. Cover charge at times.*

JR.'s. Popular yuppie gay bar, good for meeting and greeting.... *Tel 202/328–0090. 1519 17th St., NW, Dupont Circle Metro, Taxi zone 1B.*

Jenkins Hill. Tripartite Capitol Hill establishment—some parts branch out into live music and sports bar territory, but the main floor accommodates drinking and talk.... *Tel 202/544–4066. 319 Pennsylvania Ave., SE, Capitol South Metro, Taxi zone 2D. Cover charge for downstairs Underground.*

Kilimanjaro. Adams-Morgan world-beat music hall attracts a cosmopolitan Third World crowd (translation: they wear neat clothing and have courtly manners).... *Tel 202/328–3838. 1724 California St., NW, Taxi zone 2B. Closed Mon-Tue. Cover charge.*

Madam's Organ. They play the blues but mostly they just play at this "neighborhood joint" on the southern cusp of Adams-Morgan. Casual urban crowd, mostly under 40.... *Tel 202/667–5370. 18th St. and Florida Ave., NW, Taxi zone 1B. Cover charge weekends only.*

Marquis de Rochambeau. Sultry French decadence, music, and dancing in Georgetown late into the night.... *Tel 202/333–0393. 3108 M St., NW, Foggy Bottom–GWU Metro, Taxi zone 2A. Cover Thurs–Sat.*

Mr. Eagan's. Time and the rising tide of Dupont Circle real estate values have left Mr. Eagan's largely unscathed—still a comfortable neighborhood bar for a thirtyish crowd that appreciates the anti-scene scene.... *Tel 202/331–9768. 1343 Connecticut Ave., NW, Dupont Circle Metro, Taxi zone 1B.*

9:30 Club. Long-running alternative music club, recently relocated. No cover in downstairs bar. Advance tickets now available from Protix, or at door (cash only).... *Tel 202/393–0930. 815 V St., NW, U Street–Cardozo Metro, Taxi zone 2B. Cover charge.*

One Step Down. The jazz talent at this Foggy Bottom club is a step or two down from nearby Blues Alley—but so are the prices. National acts play weekends, locals the rest of week.... *Tel 202/331–8863. 2517 Pennsylvania Ave., NW, Foggy Bottom–GWU Metro, Taxi zone 2A. Cover charge and minimum.*

Planet Fred. Long, narrow, grubby Connecticut Avenue space brightened by day-glo planets and the glow of lava lamps. Specials include hot bingo games, free salsa dance lessons on floor embedded with fossils.... *Tel 202/466–2336. 1221 Connecticut Ave., NW, Dupont Circle or Farragut North Metros, Taxi zone 1B. Cover charge some nights.*

Polly's Cafe. No live music, no scene, just a cozy neighborhood tavern in the 14th-and-U area. Outdoor tables; three draft beers and a beer-of-the-month; margaritas, mimosas, and Bloody Marys by the pitcher.... *Tel 202/232–2710. 1355 U St., NW, U Street–Cardozo Metro, Taxi zone 1B.*

River Club. Deco-style Georgetown dance and supper club; DJs, live Brazilian bands, and on Thursday the Doc Scantlin big band. Valet parking available, and if you can afford the prices here you can afford to pay for it.... *Tel 202/333–8118. 3223 K St., NW, Taxi zone 2A. Cover charge.*

The Ritz. Mostly buppies in this African American-owned five-clubs-in-one establishment. Long lines after midnight on weekends.... *Tel 202/638–2582. 919 E St., NW, Metro Center or Gallery Place Metros, Taxi zone 1D. Cover charge.*

Royal Palace. Ample north-of-Dupont Circle establishment is probably least-restrained Washington strip joint.... *Tel 202/462–2623. 1805 Connecticut Ave., NW, Dupont Circle Metro, Taxi zone 1B.*

Rumors. Singles bar, DJs spin dance music and current hits Tuesday through Sunday. Different meal or drink deals each night.... *Tel 202/466–7378. 19th and M streets, NW, Farragut West or Dupont Circle Metros, Taxi zone 1B. Cover charge.*

Senators. Spiffy hotel sports bar displays memorabilia of erstwhile Washington Senators baseball team, as well as other baseball teams, and other sports. Drink specials and 19 TVs-worth of games.... *Tel 202/347–7678. Holiday Inn on the Hill, 415 New Jersey Ave., NW, Union Station Metro, Taxi zone 1D.*

Sirius Coffee Company. Tiny University of District of Columbia campus hangout also serves microbrews and live music outside during summer.... *Tel 202/364–2600. 4250 Connecticut Ave., NW, Van Ness–UDC Metro, Taxi zone 3B.*

SoHo Tea & Coffee. Last stop (geographically and schedule-wise) on the P Street gay strip. Live music some nights, some outdoor seating, long hours.... *Tel 202/463–7646. 22nd and P streets, NW, Dupont Circle Metro, Taxi zone 1B. Open 6:30am–4am Sun–Wed, 24 hours Thur–Sat.*

State of the Union. Soviet Union, that is. The hammer-and-sickle dominates the decor; menu touts Russian specialties;

bar pours 36 vodkas. However, the music is mostly all-American acid jazz—live or recorded—with dollops of semi-danceable Latin music, funk, and hip-hop. Open-air dance floor. All you can drink (vodka, beer) Sunday brunch.... *Tel 202/588–8810. 1357 U St., NW, U Street–Cardozo Metro, Taxi zone 1B. Cover charge for live music, DJs.*

Takoma Station Tavern. Buppies and yuppies mingle in casual neighborhood jazz joint opposite Takoma Metro station. Crowd of well-dressed adults come to really listen to local pros.... *Tel 202/829–1999. 6914 4th St., NW, Takoma Metro, Taxi zone 4C. Minimum charged.*

Tavern on the Hill. Good plain place where Hillies and other bureaucrats meet to deliberate on important matters like softball games and TV game shows. Live music Fridays.... *Tel 202/639–0441. 233 2nd St., NW, Judiciary Square Metro, Taxi zone 1D.*

Tiber Creek Pub. A happy-hour hot spot where hotel guests mingle with lower-echelon Capitol Hill staffers.... *Tel 202/638–0900. Bellevue Hotel, 15 E St., NW, Union Station Metro, Taxi zone 1D.*

Timberlake's. North Dupont Circle pub and restaurant where a long bar and low-impact music enable locals of all ages to chat each other up.... *Tel 202/483–2266. 1726 Connecticut Ave., NW, Dupont Circle Metro, Taxi zone 1B.*

Tornado Alley. A back street in Wheaton, a middle-class multiethnic suburb at the end of the Metro Red line, has one of the top places in the area for "roots" music, mainly rooted in Louisiana, Chicago, and Austin.... *Tel 301/929–0795. 11319 Elkin St., Wheaton, MD, Wheaton Metro. Closed Sun. Cover charge.*

Town & Country Lounge. Lobbyists, lawyers, and legislators hatch plots in the Renaissance Mayflower's off-lobby cocktail lounge. Major weeknight action, when the piano bar is in session, but weekends are fairly dead.... *Tel 202/347–3000. Renaissance Mayflower Hotel, 1127 Connecticut Ave., NW, Farragut North Metro, Taxi zone 1B.*

Tracks. Located in a tough neighborhood near the Washington Navy Yard, Tracks welcomes men/women, gay/straight,

black/white/Asian, young/old. Call to hear what sounds are
played, who shows up, and what it costs (including drink
specials). Outdoor security provided.... *Tel 202/488–3320.
1111 1st St., SE, Navy Yard Metro, Taxi zone 2E (cabs recommended). Closed Mon. Cover charge.*

Trumpets. Rollicking, mostly male gay bar/restaurant with an
older and somewhat more affluent crowd than elsewhere on
the strip.... *Tel 202/232–4141. 17th and Q streets, NW,
Dupont Circle Metro, Taxi zone 1B.*

Tune Inn. Classic Bar bar inordinately popular with younger Hill
staffers and apolitical Capitol Hill denizens. Irresistible
greaseburgers.... *Tel 202/543–2725. 331 1/2 Pennsylvania Ave., SE, Capitol South Metro, Taxi zone 2D.*

Washington Grill Bar. This lounge in your basic hotel steak-
and-chop house has a great single-malt scotch selection.
Live entertainment on weeknights.... *Tel 202/775–0800.
Sheraton City Centre, 1143 New Hampshire Ave., NW,
Foggy Bottom–GWU Metro, Taxi zone 1B.*

Yacht Club of Bethesda. Practically the only place in town
where older (30 and way up), richer singles can go to pair
off. Everybody is well-heeled and well dressed—except on
casual Wednesday "Dewey Beach Night".... *Tel 301/654–
2396. 8111 Woodmont Ave., Bethesda, MD., Bethesda
Metro. Closed Sun-Mon. Cover charge Fri-Sat.*

enterta

7

nment

Over the past 25
years, Washington
has risen from
provincial
Dullsville to an
important regional
center of the

arts—and you have to credit the Kennedy Center. With six theaters under one two-block-wide roof, the National Symphony, the Washington Opera, Broadway glitz, Important Dramatic Works, and much, much more, the Kennedy Center dominates Washington's cultural-slash-entertainment scene like no institution in any other major American city. When it opened in 1971, culture–starved visitors swiped every fixture and ornament that wasn't nailed down. A $50-million renovation is slated to begin in the summer of 1996, with Concert Hall shut down July through early September, and again February through October 1997; maybe this time they'll get the acoustics right. Eventually all six theaters will be overhauled, which could take five years (or, things being as they are in Washington, may more likely take 15 years).

Washington's classical music scene is more what you'd expect from a city of 600,000 (which it is) than from the capital of a nation of 260 million (which it is). Beyond the Kennedy Center, you probably have to go to a museum, a college, or a church to hear serious music. The dance scene is virtually nonexistent. National rock and rap talent perform at arenas and concert clubs, and hundreds of local groups try gamely to claw their way to the top.

But Washington's jazz scene has been great since the 1930s, when U Street was Harlem's top farm club, and now urban jazz of all kinds is played all over town by cats of all colors. And as one might expect, Washington's most stellar achievements involve the deft manipulation of language. Three satirical revues—Gross National Product, Capitol Steps, Mrs. Foggybottom—have been around longer than some Mall monuments. "Legitimate" theaters produce plenty of road-show plays and revivals, but locals have gradually been groomed to take chances on challenging new work—especially if New York hasn't seen it yet.

Washington has major-league teams in all major sports except baseball—a dearth only slightly ameliorated by the Baltimore Orioles (40 miles away)—and three area minor-league teams. The Redskins obsession reduces the Beltway's only big-time college football team, the University of Maryland, to an afterthought. But Washington is a major center for college hoops, with perennial winners Maryland, Georgetown, George Washington, and half a dozen other Division I teams playing in the area.

Sources

The brawny alternative weekly *Washington City Paper* has categories for Music, Theater, Dance, Comedy, Events, Exhibits, even Performance Art. Easily the most comprehensive listings around, *City Paper* appears on Thursday afternoons in sidewalk paper boxes, bookstores, record stores, office buildings, and libraries all over D.C. and the suburbs. The *Washington Post* runs a terse "Guide to the Lively Arts" box every day, but its Friday "Weekend" supplement lists every concert, club date, play, recital, and dance in the region. It also lists one-of-a-kind weekend events (Civil War re-enactments are big in these parts), outdoor activities including serious sports and nature hikes, and entertainment for kids. The Friday *Post* also lists phone numbers to hear "Sound Bites" of performers in town. The Moonies' *Washington Times* weekend listings are as good as the *Post*'s and they appear one day sooner, in the Thursday morning paper. The gay weekly *Washington Blade* concentrates on theater, art, and goings-on mainly of interest to the gay community. Like *City Paper*, it materializes on Thursdays in boxes and racks all over the metro area. *UR Magazine* (*University Reporter*) is mainly distributed on area campuses, but some copies filter down to bars and shops in nightlife centers like Georgetown, Dupont Circle, Adams-Morgan, and U Street. Music lovers should listen to **WETA** (FM 90.9), an NPR classical music station, where DJs promote local concerts of serious music and "Traditions," Saturday from 8pm to 2am, tells folkies where to go.

The mother of all cultural hotlines, **Time Out Washington** (tel 202/364–8463) informs callers about bar and club appearances, concerts, movie times, pub crawls, and other types of events. It also plays sound bites of 400 to 500 local bands of all musical persuasions and tells you how to find them. Send them your fax number and they'll fax back menu codes and an up-to-date list of Washington clubs. For other phone services, mostly run by radio stations, see Hotlines & Other Basics. To get concert information directly online via **The D.C. Infobase**, have your 9600-or-higher baud modem dial (tel 703/471–5096) for access.

Getting Tickets

Major theaters like the Kennedy Center, the Shakespeare Theater, Warner Theater, and the National Theater handle their own charge-by-phone ticketing, with box-office pickup

WASHINGTON, D.C. | ENTERTAINMENT

any time before showtime. Other theaters and concert halls let you reserve tickets by phone through **TicketMaster** (tel 202/432–SEAT, 800/551–7328) or **Protix** (703/218–6500) for the usual exorbitant surcharges. TicketMaster outlets are also located in Hecht's department stores and other sites. Protix has kiosks in certain Safeway grocery stores; call 703/255–1860 to find out where. Many of the smaller theaters will hold a reservation if you give them a charge-card number—no surcharges.

When box offices and ticket outlets dry up, you can access a thriving industry of **ticket brokers** who might scalp you but somehow come up with (don't ask how) seats for sold-out shows, concerts, and Redskins and Orioles games. Players include **Premier Entertainment** (tel 301/985–6250), **Stagefront Tickets** (tel 301/953–1163), **Encore Tickets** (tel 301/718–2525), **Ticket Connection** (tel 301/587–6850), or **Top Centre**, the only one operating in D.C. (tel 202/452–9040 or 800/673–8422, 2000 Pennsylvania Ave., NW; Foggy Bottom–GWU Metro, Taxi zone 1B), where you can review a list of what's available and maybe, just maybe, negotiate a last-minute bargain when their supply exceeds customer demand. Expect to pay intranasally for your hard-to-find tickets, double or more the regular price. Shop for prices and seat location among the agencies. Real people (and some pros) try to unload tickets via classified ads in the *Washington Post* and *Washington Times*.

TICKETplace sells day-of-show half-price (plus a service charge—10 percent of the ticket's face value) tickets to plays, dance performances, opera, and concerts. Tickets to big sold-out shows won't be available here, but lots of good stuff is offered; it's definitely worth a call. Sometimes next-day half-price tickets are also available. You can call between noon and 6pm (tel 202/TICKETS) to find out what events are available that day and how much they cost, but you can't reserve or buy tickets by phone. Tickets must be purchased—*for cash only*—in the lobby of Lisner Auditorium on the George Washington University campus, two blocks from the Metro station (21st and H streets, NW, Foggy Bottom–GWU Metro, Taxi zone 1A). TICKETplace operates from noon to 6, Tuesday through Friday; 11 to 5 on Saturday. Tickets for Sunday and Monday shows, when available, can be purchased on Saturday. TICKETplace also functions as a full-price, cash-only outlet for TicketMaster, as well as the box office for Lisner Auditorium events.

The Lowdown

The play's the thing... While Washington has many theaters, it has nothing close to a theater district. There's **Kennedy Center**, of course, which gets Washington's most important straight plays at the Eisenhower Theater and big-ticket musicals in the Opera House (*Annie* got started here, *Dolly* recently dropped by to say hello). Kid stuff, experimental work, festivals, and *Shear Madness* (an audience-decides-it comedy-mystery running for nearly a decade), play the smaller upstairs Terrace Theater and Theater Lab. Another five historically and theatrically significant theaters are strewn around the greater downtown area. The **National Theater** has seen its stage studded with stars, from John Wilkes Booth and "Swedish Nightingale" Jenny Lind to Hepburn and Tracy; the Arlington brother-sister act of Shirley MacLaine and Warren Beatty were once, respectively, usherette and stage doorman here. Now managed by Broadway's Schubert Organization, the National presents megahits and pre-Broadway tryouts. The **Warner Theater**, a renovated movie and vaudeville house, presents musical hits that made it big elsewhere. **Ford's Theatre** lay dark from the night Lincoln was assassinated there (April 14, 1865) until Lincoln's birthday in 1968; now completely restored, it specializes in aggressively wholesome new American musicals and plays about "American originals." Intimate **Shakespeare Theatre** brings in medium-name guest stars (Stacy Keach as Macbeth, Pat Carroll as Falstaff) for a four-play season. Each June it produces the Shakespeare Free-for-All for two weeks in Rock Creek Park. The professional **Washington Stage Guild** performs "undiscovered classics" by world-class playwrights—recently *John Bull's Other Island* by George Bernard Shaw and *An Ideal Husband* by Oscar Wilde—in a 150-seat theater within the parochial school of Washington's oldest Catholic church.

When it opened in 1950, **Arena Stage**—boldly located south of downtown by Washington Harbor—defied Washington's color code by seating blacks and whites together. An avatar of the regional (i.e., not New York) theater, its three stages specialize in productions long on political and theatrical courage (this is where *The*

Great White Hope and *K2* originated years ago). The largest of the three troupes along the edgy (in both the artistic and sociological sense) 14th Street Arts Corridor in Adams-Morgan, **Studio Theater** is actually Washington's third largest rep company (after Shakespeare and the Arena). To pay the rent, it produces established modern playwrights and oldies (Tony Kushner, August Wilson, Eric Bogosian, and Anton Chekhov in the 1995–96 season) on its main stage; "free of commercial consideration" envelope-pushers appear on its tiny second-floor Secondstage. The nonprofit, 12-member, professional **Woolly Mammoth Theatre Company** spotlights premières—regional, national, and world—its coup for 1996 being the regional première of Tina Howe's *Birth and After Birth*. One of its 1995 draws was *Rush Limbaugh in Night School*, with Charlie Varon spouting all the right right-wing answers. The **Source Theatre Company** was producing brave new plays in the now-steaming U Street nightlife district back when pre- and post-theater dining was confined to potato chips from the drugstore. Recent hits have included Charles Busch's *Psycho Beach Party*, Harvey Fierstein's *Safe Sex*, and brash revivals such as a *Merchant of Venice* played for laughs. Check out its off-hours programming for really out-there stuff. The **District of Columbia Arts Center** in Adams-Morgan, under executive director B. Stanley, specializes in experimental—nonlinear and ultravisual—productions by new but not necessarily local writers. **Signature Theatre** produces low-budget, highly esteemed dramas and musicals—heavy on the Sondheim—in an industrial section of Arlington; snagging five Helen Hayes Awards (Washington's Tony) in 1995, the most of any local company.

Classical sounds... The **National Symphony Orchestra**, under rookie artistic director Leonard Slatkin, formerly of the St. Louis Symphony, plays home concerts (expect to hear lots from American composers) at the Kennedy Center Concert Hall and summers out at Wolf Trap. The 20-musician **Washington Chamber Symphony**—second-string but first-rate—presents five series a year, including two for families and one just for kids. They play most often at Kennedy Center, with meanders over to the Corcoran Gallery of Art and the Holton-Arms School in Bethesda. The **National Gallery of Art**, **National Building Museum**, **Phillips Collection**, **Corcoran**

Gallery, and other museums (see Diversions) periodically present high-brow entertainment, too.

What's opera, doc?... It was next to impossible to score a ticket to the **Washington Opera** *before* it appointed Placido Domingo artistic director. Now, since almost all tickets are sold in subscription packages, your only hope may be to turn up at the Kennedy Center box office an hour before showtime to troll for returns. The seven-opera season runs from November through March. Classics, premieres, and the occasional superstar appearance—like Samuel Ramey in Boito's *Mefistofele* in 1996—make this the toughest season ticket after the Redskins. Opera buffs might also want to try out the considerably cheaper **Mount Vernon College** Opera in the Chapel series—well-performed productions of little-known operas or twists on old favorites, three each year.

Men in tights... From October through mid-May, the **Kennedy Center** hosts sojourns by world-class companies—in 1995–96 the Joffrey Ballet, American Ballet Theater, Dance Theater of Harlem, and Suzanne Farrell's Ballet Company. The well-respected **Washington Ballet** pirouettes between the Kennedy Center's Terrace Theater and the Warner Theater, with classical and contemporary works and, in December, *The Nutcracker*. Most of Washington's sparse, nonballetic dancing happens at **Dance Place**, a school which also stages powerful modern dance and "community specific" (African, Asian, black, gay, black *and* gay, etc.) performances every weekend of the year.

Longhair-free concert zones... The area represents the northeastern frontier of Bluegrass Country, and folkie concerts still draw crowds. The **Kennedy Center** occasionally books top jazz and pop acts, and ready-for-prime-time comedians. When Sinatra-class show-biz equivalents of national monuments tour, they grace the grand stage of the totally renovated 1924 **Warner Theater**. The biddies who in 1939 vetoed Marian Anderson's concert at **DAR Constitution Hall** (a *Negress!*—gasp!) would surely blush to see their hallowed premises occasionally invaded these days by acts like the Freak Like Me Tour ("For Mature Audiences Only") and multiracial pop acts, among more sedate performances. Reopened in 1994 after a $9 million renovation, the **Lincoln Theatre**, a 1921 movie theater and vaudeville house in the heart of the U Street entertainment district, highlights African American plays, dance, and music; nonblack acts (the Average White Band, for instance) also appear. Campus concert halls—Lisner Auditorium at **George Washington University** and Bender Arena at **American University**—specialize in progressive rock groups with toes in the mainstream.

Out in the suburbs, sports arenas periodically lend their cavernous spaces to pop/rock/rap acts that think they can fill them—all 20,000 seats at **USAir Arena**, an unlovable building on an unappealing off-Beltway site without a whisper of public transportation in Landover, Maryland; and 9,500 seats at **George Mason University**'s Patriot Center out in Fairfax, Virginia.

Kid stuff... **Discovery Theater** in the Smithsonian's Arts & Industries Building presents an ambitious program of original plays and adaptations, puppet shows, storytellers, and musicals, weekdays and weekends throughout the year. The **Kennedy Center**'s Theater Lab and Terrace Theater are venues for straight plays and musicals aimed at and performed by children. Saturday Morning at the National (**National Theater**, that is) uses magic shows, pantomime, storytelling, puppets, music, anything they can think of, in their blatant campaign to get kids "hooked" on live theater, September through May. *Now This! Kids!* is a totally improvised audience participation musical comedy show for kids five through 12 on Saturday afternoons at the Omni Shoreham Hotel. On a more serious (musical) note, the **Washington Chamber Symphony** gears its one-hour Concerts for Young People in the Kennedy Center Terrace Theater to children six and older, and welcomes even younger music lovers (age four and up) to Family Series concerts in the Kennedy Center Concert Hall. **Wolf Trap**'s calendar includes kid-oriented acts, like Raffi and Peter, Paul, and Mary, and a Children's International Festival for three days in September. Almost every day in July and August, the Wolf Trap Theatre-in-the-Woods presents dancers, jugglers, stories, and workshops on music and ballet in a sylvan amphitheater—all free, but reservations are required.

Summer places... Just about everything goes at **Wolf Trap**, from the National Symphony and mainstream rock, folk, and country to full-scale opera, ballet, and

Broadway musicals. This park is probably *the* best thing about Washington summers; seasonal highlights include the Washington Irish Folk Festival in May, Wolf Trap's Jazz & Blues Festival in June, and Movies at Wolf Trap, with the NSO performing scores from films projected on monster screens. About 4,000 people can sit inside the park's Filene Center, while another 3,000 can see the stage from the lawn (which has a special rear section for lawn chairs). Whether or not you spring for pavilion seats, it's a great place for a picnic: bring your own, tap a pretty good selection of concession stands, or order a gourmet picnic in advance, for pickup at Wolf Trap (call Something Special, tel 703/448–0800)—bring your own wine. **Nissan Pavilion at Stone Bridge** is the new kid in town—actually the Virginia countryside 35 miles west of D.C.—and it is a big kid indeed: 10,000 seats under the stark exposed-steel pavilion and 15,000 more on the sloping lawn. Awesome pop/rock/soul acts but, in its inaugural 1995 season, there were awesome traffic and parking problems as well. The **Merriweather Post Pavilion**, between Washington and Baltimore, welcomes mainly the young to performances by major names in rock, rap, and country; families gather for the 10-day Columbia Festival of the Arts in late June–early July. The 4,250-seat **Carter Barron Amphitheater** in Rock Creek Park begins with a two-week Shakespeare Free-for-All in June, then blends an ambitious slate of free and not-free classical, jazz, gospel, and R&B performances. Bring a picnic to eat on the grounds—no serious food is sold on-site—but no food's allowed in the pavilion itself. The **Armed Forces Concert Series** is something you can't get in any other town: uniformed bands from each branch of the service performing marches, patriotic anthems, light classics, and big-band hits at the Sylvan Theater beside the Washington Monument (8pm Tue, Thur, Fri, Sun) and on the east steps of the U.S. Capitol (8pm Mon, Tue, Wed, Fri). These guys and gals are *good*, and there's something wonderful in a dopey way about hearing a crack brass band play outdoors on a summer's eve.

Comedy tonight... If producer George S. Kaufman thought satire was what closed on Saturday night, then he never played Washington. Political satire troupes here just keep going and going and going.... Since 1981, the **Capitol Steps**—a sextet (two gals, four guys) of ex-congressional staffers—have lampooned the mighty in 15 albums, national TV shows, and over 3,000 live performances, nowadays at Chelsea's in Georgetown. Their R-rated musical sketches skewer politicos unmercifully; former president George Bush said they "make it easier to leave public life." (Capitol Steps is named after the notorious site of a tryst between Representative John Jenrette (D–SC) and *Playboy*-centerfold wife, Rita). The titles of **Gross National Product** reviews bespeak its longevity: from *Phantom of the White House* and *Man Without A Contra* through *Bushcapades* to *Clintoons: The First Hundred Daze* and *A Newt World Order*. GNP credits its success not to sharp writing or deft performances but to their wig collection—over 80 wigs, four just for Hillary. They now have a permanent home (an oxymoron when referring to comedy groups) at the Old Vat Theater of the Arena Stage, and on Saturday they run their own Scandal Tours of Washington's naughty parts, led by members costumed as the political buffoons du jour (call 202/783–7212 for reservations). On Saturday nights, the **Marquee Lounge** hosts Mrs. Foggybottom & Friends, which has been around since 1985; Joan Cushing and a cast of other rapier-witted musical satirists have hit targets as shifty as Slick Willie and as broad as the Three Tenors. On alternate Fridays, the Marquee hosts *Now This!*, a totally improvised comedy and music review.

Downtown Washington's reeling stand-up comedy scene has been reduced to two clubs on the K (for Komedy?) Street Corridor: the **Comedy Cafe** above a dead-earnest sports bar, and the local outpost of **The Improv** comedy chain, a virtual Macy's of Mirth. Out in the suburbs, comics "as seen on (Letterman, Comedy Central, HBO, fill in the blank)" appear at **Headliners Comedy Club**, which has taken over not one but two Holiday Inn lounges, in Alexandria and Bethesda. And **Garvin's Comedy Clubs**, a long-time floating gag–a–teria, has settled into a Best Western out in Tysons Corner, Virginia. Are any of these places worth going to? Totally depends on who's at the mike.

The silver screen... Georgetown's **Key Theatre** has four screens for D.C.'s most daring and diverse bill of independent and foreign films; the **Cineplex Odeon Foundry** (seven screens) has Hollywood and independent films at bargain rates; and the **Biograph** runs pure porn in the afternoons, but switches at night to art films—U.S. indies, foreign films, and revivals. The American Film Institute in the **Kennedy Center** shows three or four different movies every day. The main event of the Washington movie season is the **Filmfest DC** (tel 202/275–5000), which, for two weeks in late April and early May, shows carefully chosen movies from around the world, in cinemas all over town.

Some excellent movies are screened in nontheater settings, sometimes for free. The auditorium in the East Wing of the **National Gallery of Art** has free screenings of classic American and foreign films and movies about art, mostly on Saturday and Sunday; films are shown at other museums (**Freer Gallery of Art**, **Library of Congress**, **Hirshhorn Museum of Art**, **National Archives**— for details, see Diversions) on a sporadic basis. The **French Embassy**—an attraction in itself, in its sleek mid-1980s embassy complex on the fringe of Georgetown— screens new and classic French films on alternate Wednesdays ($4). Similarly, the **Goethe Institute** features German films, the new ones often coupled with an appearance by the director ($2).

The sporting life... The NFL **Washington Redskins** are THE toughest ticket in town—even though some media outlets won't print or pronounce the R-name on the grounds of political incorrectness. Until owner Jack Kent Cooke completes his Ahab-like quest for a community where he can build a newer, larger stadium, the 'Skins are stuck in D.C.'s RFK Stadium, a great place to watch a game. Don't even think about buying tickets through normal channels, but follow the advice in You Probably Didn't Know—if the weather's lousy and the team stinks, you stand a decent chance of getting in. The **Washington Bullets**, the closest thing to a professional basketball team in the area, play home games at USAir Arena in Landover, Maryland. For the 1997–98 season the Bullets will get a new fan-chosen moniker ("Bullets" having been deemed unseemly for a city displeased with its "Murder Capital" sobriquet) and a new place to play, the 20,000-seat MCI Center on the block of 6th, 7th, F, and G streets. The hottest team (and toughest b-ball ticket) is the Atlantic Coast Conference **University of Maryland Terrapins** who play in compact Cole Field House in

ENTERTAINMENT | WASHINGTON, D.C.

College Park. John Thompson's Hoyas from **Georgetown University** seldom sell out the huge USAir Arena, where they play. **George Washington University**, ultra-competitive in recent years, plays in the tiny on-campus Smith Center. As for baseball, forget it in D.C.—you'll either have to slog up to Baltimore to catch an Orioles game or go to the **Senators** bar (see Nightlife) to recall the days when Washington *had* a baseball team.

The National Hockey League's **Washington Capitals** currently play at the USAir Arena, but they are also scheduled to relocate to the downtown MCI Center in 1997–98. The **Washington Warthogs** welcome families to high-scoring, pinball-paced Continental Indoor Soccer League matches at the USAir Arena. Between giveaways, mascot antics, Boar Corps cheerleaders, and the parental Dunk Tank, kids may not even know they're at a sporting event. Washington's newest pro team, the **D.C. United** of Major League Soccer, will play its spring and summer 1996 schedule at RFK Stadium.

You must go to Maryland to play the ponies: horserace betting was only recently legalized in Virginia and they haven't opened any tracks yet. **Laurel Park** has three separate thoroughbred seasons, plus harness-racing simulcasts at night. **Rosecroft Raceway**, just outside the Beltway south of D.C., has nightly harness racing and simulcasts all year except Christmas week.

The Index

American University. At this college in far northwest D.C., the Performing Arts department produces ambitious plays, concerts, recitals, and multimedia extravaganzas, October–May. Rock acts and the Eagles basketball team play (but not each other) in Bender Arena.... *Tel 202/885–ARTS (Performing Arts Dept.), 202/885–3267 (Arena). 4400 Massachusetts Ave., NW, Tenleytown Metro, Taxi zone 4A.*

Arena Stage. Prominent regional theater encompasses an 800-seat theater-in-the-round and a 500-seat proscenium stage. A 200-seat cabaret is now weekend home to Gross National Product.... *Tel 202/488–3300. 6th St. and Maine Ave., SW, Waterfront Metro, Taxi zone 2E.*

Armed Forces Concert Series. Summer performances by various military bands.... *Tel 202/767–5658 (Air Force), 703/696–3718 (Army), 202/433–4011 (Marines), 202/433–2525 (Navy), Mid-June–Aug.*

Biograph Theatre. Georgetown cinema has top-rated art films by night, X-rated porn by day.... *Tel 202/333–2696. 2819 M St., NW, Foggy Bottom–GWU Metro, Taxi zone 2A.*

Capitol Steps. Musical political satire troupe performs most Fridays and Saturdays at Chelsea's in Georgetown. Advance reservations recommended.... *Tel 202/298–8222. 1055 Thomas Jefferson St., NW, Foggy Bottom–GWU Metro, Taxi zone 2A.*

Carter Barron Amphitheater. Rock Creek Park setting for theater and concerts, some free, some not, throughout the summer.... *Tel 202/260–6836. 16th St. and Colorado Ave., NW, Taxi zone 3C.*

Cineplex Odeon Foundry. Seven-screen movie complex near Georgetown waterfront.... *Tel 202/333–8613. 1055 Thomas Jefferson St., NW, Foggy Bottom–GWU Metro, Taxi zone 2A.*

Comedy Cafe. Stand-up comedians, some you might even have heard of, upstairs from Fanatics sports bar.... *Tel 202/638–JOKE. 1520 K St., NW; Farragut North, Farragut West, or McPherson Square Metros, Taxi zone 1B.*

Dance Place. Fifteen-year-old school and performance space focuses on cutting-edge programs by resident and visiting troupes.... *Tel 202/269–1600. 3225 8th St., NE, Brookland–CUA Metro, Taxi zone 2C.*

DAR Constitution Hall. A 3,746-seat appendage to the Daughters of the American Revolution world headquarters, just off the National Mall.... *Tel 202/638–2661. 18th St. between C and D streets, NW, Farragut West Metro, Taxi zone 1A.*

D.C. United. The local franchise of Major League Soccer, a start-up ten-team league, will play in 1996.... *Tel 202/333–1880. Robert F. Kennedy Memorial Stadium, 22nd St. between C St. and Independence Ave., NE/SE, Stadium–Armory Metro, Taxi zone 3E. Apr–Sept.*

District of Columbia Arts Center (DCAC). Adams-Morgan institution focuses on emerging experimental theatrical and graphic artists. Friday night Club DCAC features alternative musicians of various ilks. Paid parking nearby, but cabs recommended.... *Tel 202/462–7833. 2438 18th St., NW, Woodley Park–Zoo Metro, Taxi zone 2B.*

Discovery Theater. Weekday and weekend shows for kids.... *Tel 202/357–1500 (voice or TDD). Smithsonian Arts & Industries Bldg., 900 Jefferson Dr., SW, Smithsonian Metro, Taxi zone 1D.*

Filmfest DC. Annual two–week film festival, with movies screened in theaters all over town.... *Tel 202/275–5000. Late April–early May.*

Ford's Theatre. Landmark theater for family-oriented American musicals and biographies of "American originals." *A Christmas Carol runs from the week before Thanksgiving through New Year's Eve. Basement museum about 19th-century theater and Lincoln.... Tel 202/347–4833 (box office), 202/426–6927 (museum). 511 10th St., NW; Metro Center, Gallery Place–Chinatown, or Federal Triangle Metros, Taxi zone 1D. No shows June–Labor Day.*

French Embassy. Presents French films, jazz and classical concerts, plays, and lectures.... *Tel 202/944–6400 (recording), 202/944–6000 (information). 4101 Reservoir Rd., NW, Taxi zone 3A. No programs Aug.*

Garvin's Comedy Clubs. Peripatetic long-running showcase, now ensconced in Tysons Corner on Friday and Saturday nights.... *Tel 202/USA–8880. Best Western Tysons Westpark Hotel, VA Rte. 7 and Westpark Dr., McLean, VA.*

George Mason University. Patriot Center hosts rock concerts.... *Tel 703/993–3270. VA Rte. 123 and Braddock Rd., Fairfax, VA.*

George Washington University. The highly ranked Colonials (both men's and women's squads) hoop it up on-campus at compact Smith Center. The 1,500-seat Lisner Auditorium hosts pop concerts; also home of the TICKETplace half-price ticket counter.... *Smith Center, tel 202/994–6650, 22nd and F streets, NW; Lisner Auditorium, tel 202/994–1500, 21st and H streets, NW, Foggy Bottom–GWU Metro, Taxi zone 1A.*

Georgetown University. Big East home games at the 20,000-seat USAir Arena.... *Tel 202/687–HOYA. USAir Arena, Capital Beltway and MD Rte. 214 (Exits 32 or 33), Landover, MD. Nov–Feb.*

Goethe Institute. Presents German films, guest lectures, and other Teutonic cultural activities.... *Tel 202/319–0702. 1607 New Hampshire Ave., NW, Dupont Circle Metro, Taxi zone 1B.*

Gross National Product. Long-running satirical troupe now playing at Arena Stage's Old Vat Theater.... *Tel 202/488–3300, TDD 202/484–0247. 6th St. and Maine Ave., SW, Waterfront Metro, Taxi zone 2E.*

Headliners Comedy Club. Comics in two suburban hotel lounges, weekends and some weeknights.... *Tel 301/942–HAHA, Holiday Inn Bethesda, 8120 Wisconsin Ave., Bethesda, MD, Bethesda Metro. Tel 703/379–HAHA, Holiday Inn Alexandria, Capital Beltway (I-95) and Telegraph Rd. N., Alexandria, VA, Eisenhower Avenue Metro.*

The Improv. Chain comedy club features national talent. Dinner available for 8:30 shows, eating rates priority seating (though the food's a joking matter).... *Tel 202/296–7008. 1140 Connecticut Ave., NW, Farragut North Metro, Taxi zone 2B.*

John F. Kennedy Center for the Performing Arts. D.C.'s cultural hub has six theaters of varying sizes, configurations, and grandiosity. Concert Hall is the 2,750-seat permanent home to the **National Symphony Orchestra** and the **Washington Chamber Symphony**, with some appearances by the **Choral Arts Society**; the Opera House is the headquarters for the **Washington Opera** (tel 800/87–OPERA), itinerant ballet companies, post- and pre-

Broadway musicals. Major dramatic productions such as the *Kentucky Cycle* are performed in the Eisenhower Theater. The Terrace Theater is the intimate setting for recitals and plays. The Theater Lab features children's theater and, for the last 300 years or so, the comedy whodunit *Shear Madness*. The American Film Institute screens up to four different American and foreign films daily. Kennedy Center is itself an attraction, with guided tours daily between 10 and 1. Rooftop restaurants—the sit-down, coat-and-tie Roof Terrace (reservations tel 202/416–8555), casual Hors D'Oeuvrerie, cafeteria-style Encore Café—have reasonable (not low) prices, reasonable food, outstanding views of river and monuments. Paid parking in underground garage.... *Tel 202/467–4600, 800/444–1324, TDD 202/416–8524, 202/416–8340 (tours). New Hampshire Ave. and Rock Creek Pkwy., NW, Foggy Bottom–GWU Metro, Taxi zone 2A.*

Key Theatre. Georgetown quadriplex for alternative film. Discount parking.... *Tel 202/333–5100. 1222 Wisconsin Ave., NW, Foggy Bottom–GWU Metro, Taxi zone 2A.*

Laurel Park. Race track between D.C. and Baltimore.... *Tel 301/567–4000. MD Rte. 198 and Race Track Rd., Laurel, MD. Open Oct–mid-Apr, July.*

Lincoln Theatre. Restored former movie theater and vaudeville house in the U Street nightlife neighborhood.... *Tel 202/ 328–6000. 1215 U St., NW, U Street–Cardozo Metro, Taxi zone 1C.*

Marquee Lounge. Omni Shoreham Hotel showroom, home to Mrs. Foggybottom & Friends political satire troupe; *Now This!* musical-comedy reviews on alternate Fridays; and *Now This! Kids!* for Saturday matinees.... *Tel 202/745– 1023. Omni Shoreham Hotel, 2500 Calvert St., NW, Woodley Park–Zoo Metro, Taxi zone 2A. Closed August.*

Merriweather Post Pavilion. Summer outdoor pop/rock/rap/ country concerts, about an hour north of Washington.... *Tel 301/982–1800, 703/218–6500 (Protix). Off U.S. 29, Columbia, MD. Memorial Day–mid-Sept.*

Mount Vernon College. "In" series (for innovative, inspiring, inexpensive, in town, etc.) presents pro performances of opera, cabaret, dance, and classical music in in-timate (150 seats) stageless Hand Chapel. Pastoral campus set-ting northwest of Georgetown.... *Tel 202/625–4655. 2100 Foxhall Rd., NW, Taxi zone 3A. Closed July–Aug.*

National Symphony Orchestra. See **Kennedy Center**.

National Theater. A National Theater has occupied the site since 1835. Generous slate of freebies complements big-ticket Broadway shows.... *Tel 800/447–7400 (credit card ticket charge), 202/783–3372 (freebies), 202/628–6161 (information). 1321 Pennsylvania Ave., NW, Metro Center Metro, Taxi zone 1A.*

Nissan Pavilion at Stone Ridge. Modernist megahall— 10,000 seats in pavilion, crawl space for 15,000 on lawn— in wilds of Prince William County presents major names in rock, country, rap.... *Tel 800/455–8999 (information), 202/ 432–SEAT (seats). 7800 Cellar Door Rd. (off I-66 and U.S. 29), Bristow, VA. May–Sept.*

Rosecroft Raceway. Harness racing.... *Tel 301/567–4000. 6336 Rosecroft Dr. (Beltway–I-95, Exit 4A–St. Barnabas Rd., follow signs), Fort Washington, MD. Tue, Thur, Fri, Sat, at 7:30pm, except Christmas week.*

Shakespeare Theatre. Four-play season (three of them by the Bard) in lavish 450-seat theater.... *Tel 202/393–2700. 450 7th St., NW., Gallery Place or Archives Metros, Taxi zone 1D.*

Signature Theatre. Acclaimed professional theater company produces plays and musicals among dingy suburban facto-ries.... *Tel 703/218–6500. 3806 S. Four Mile Run Dr., Arlington, VA.*

Source Theatre Company. Hundred-seat space for bold new plays. Valet parking Friday, Saturday nights.... *Tel 202/ 462–1073. 1835 14th St., NW, U Street–Cardozo Metro, Taxi zone 1C.*

Studio Theater. Large repertory company presents mainstream serious drama and avant-garde performances on two stages. Major renovations planned for 1996–97 season.... *Tel 202/332–3300. 14th and P streets, NW, Dupont Circle Metro, Taxi zone 1B.*

University of Maryland. Top-rated Terps basketball team.... *Tel 800/462–8377, 301/314–7070. Cole Field House, University Blvd. (MD Rte 193) and Stadium Dr., College Park, MD.*

USAir Arena. The 20,000-seat former Capital Centre, for sports and concerts.... *Tel 301/350–3400. Capital Beltway (I-95) and MD Rte. 214 (Exits 32 or 33), Landover, MD.*

Warner Theater. Restored 1924 Art Deco movie/vaudeville house just off the Mall.... *Tel 202/783–4000. 13th St. and Pennsylvania Ave., NW, Metro Center Metro, Taxi zone 1A.*

Washington Ballet. With no home stage of its own, this company's classic and contemporary productions shift between Kennedy Center and the Warner Theater.... *Tel 202/362–3606. Sept, Dec, Feb, May.*

Washington Bullets. Pro basketball team will get new name and return to downtown D.C. for 1997–98 season. Meanwhile, they play at USAir Arena.... *Tel 301/NBA–DUNK, 301/350–3400. USAir Arena, Capital Beltway (I-95) and MD Rte. 214 (Exits 32 or 33), Landover, MD. Nov–Apr.*

Washington Capitals. National Hockey League team, under same ownership as Bullets, will also relocate to downtown D.C. for 1997–98 season.... *Tel 301/386–7000, 301/350–3400. USAir Arena, Capital Beltway (I-95) and MD Rte. 214 (Exits 32 or 33), Landover, MD. Oct–Apr.*

Washington Chamber Symphony. The 20-year-old ensemble performs mostly at Kennedy Center.... *Tel 202/452–1321.*

Washington Opera. See **Kennedy Center**, above.

Washington Redskins. D.C.'s pro football team.... *Tel 202/546–2222, 202/547–9077. Robert F. Kennedy Memorial Stadium, 22nd St. between C St. and Independence Ave., NE/SE, Stadium–Armory Metro, Taxi zone 3E. Sept–Dec.*

Washington Stage Guild. Four plays a season in 150-seat theater in landmark 1904 St. Patrick's School.... *Tel 202/529–2084. Carroll Hall, 924 G St., NW, Gallery Place Metro, Taxi zone 1D. October–June.*

Washington Warthogs. Professional indoor soccer team.... *Tel 301/499–3000 (tickets), 301/350–3400 (information). USAir Arena, Capital Beltway (I-95) and MD Rte. 214 (Exits 32 or 33), Landover, MD. June–Oct.*

Wolf Trap Farm Park. The only U.S. national park for performing arts. Filene Center is the summer site for National Symphony Orchestra concerts and traveling bands; opera; ballet; big-name pop, folk, rock, country, jazz and blues performers. Theatre-in-the-Woods presents free shows for kids in July and August (reservations required, tel 703/255–1827). Nearby, but outside of the park, the Barns of Wolf Trap presents folk, jazz, and chamber music concerts indoors the rest of the year. Wolf Trap Shuttle Bus Express from the West Falls Church Metrorail station (Orange Line) starts running two hours before performances and returns from Wolf Trap before the crack of 11pm.... *Tel 703/255–1827 (recorded information), 703/255–1860 (live information), 703/218–6500 (Protix charge by phone), TDD 703/255–9432, 703/938–2404 (Barns of Wolf Trap). 1624 Trap Rd., Vienna, VA. Filene Center season late May–early Sept.*

Woolly Mammoth Theatre Company. A 15-year-old company staging four innovative plays a year. Free guarded parking opposite entrance.... *Tel 202/462–1073. 14th and Church streets, NW, Dupont Circle Metro, Taxi zone 1B. Closed July–Aug.*

hotlines &
other basics

Airports... **Washington National Airport** (DCA) *(tel 703/ 417–8000)* is Washington's favorite airport, scenically located alongside the Potomac River in Arlington, Virginia, only four miles south of downtown Washington. By Congressional fiat, nonstop flights to and from National may not be more than 1,250 air miles (just far enough to reach Houston and Dallas in voter-heavy Texas), and the only international service is to Toronto and Montreal. National also operates under noise restrictions that all but close it down between 10pm and 7am. National is current- ly in the midst of a major expansion including the con- struction of a new 35-gate main terminal by spring 1997; until then, expect delays, traffic jams, and a shortage of parking. Taxi fares to downtown D.C. average $8–$10 for the 15-minute (traffic willing) ride. **Washington Flyer** *(tel 703/685–1400)* buses run between National and the Downtown Terminal *(1517 K St., NW)* every half-hour (hourly, weekend mornings); fare is $8 one way, $14 roundtrip. **Metrorail** *(tel 202/637–7000, TDD 202/638– 3780)* Yellow- and Blue-Line trains stop at National; fares are $1.10–$1.60 for most downtown destinations. There's a free shuttle bus to the Metrorail station, which will be directly accessible from the new main terminal.

Washington Dulles International Airport (IAD) *(tel 703/661–2700)* is located in the Virginia countryside about 26 miles west of downtown D.C. Dulles, with its sleek Eero Saarinen–designed terminal, has both short- and long-haul domestic flights and international service. Like National, it is in the midst of traffic-snarling terminal and roadway expansion projects (scheduled for completion by fall 1997). **Washington Flyer** *(tel 703/661–8230, 703/528–4440)* operates exclusive taxi service from Dulles and can be called for pickups for return trips; fares average $40 for the hour ride to downtown D.C. **Washington Flyer** buses *(tel 703/685–1400)* run between Dulles and the Downtown Terminal *(1517 K St., NW)* every half-hour (hourly, weekend mornings) for $16 one way, $26 roundtrip. Washington Flyer also runs a half-hourly bus to the West Falls Church **Metrorail** station (Orange Line); the bus costs $8, while Metrorail fare is $1.60–$2.20 to downtown D.C.

Baltimore/Washington International Airport (BWI) *(tel 301/261–1000, 800/I–FLY–BWI)*, 34 miles northeast of downtown D.C., has short- and long-haul domestic service on most major airlines, plus nonstop or direct international service to London, Luxembourg, Frankfurt, Tel Aviv, Toronto, the Caribbean, and South America. **Taxis** cost close to $50 for the ride to downtown D.C.; call Ground Transportation Professionals *(tel 410/589–1100)* for information. **SuperShuttle** *(tel 202/562–1234)* offers hourly van service 6am–12:30am from BWI to the Downtown Terminal *(1517 K St., NW)* for $19 one way, $29 roundtrip. Free shuttle buses connect BWI to BWI Airport Rail Station *(tel 410/672–6167)* where Amtrak *(tel 800/USA–RAIL)* and Maryland Rail Commuter, or MARC *(tel 800/325–RAIL)*, **trains** depart for Washington's Union Station. MARC fares are $4.50 one way, $8 roundtrip for the 40-minute trip; Amtrak charges $10 one way, but does it 10 to 15 minutes faster. Only Amtrak runs on weekends.

Babysitters... WeeSit *(tel 703/764–1542)* will send a sitter to your hotel. Availability varies; call before you leave home if you really need them for a specific time. Rates start at $10/hour for one child, with a four-hour minimum plus a $12 transportation fee.

Buses... Greyhound *(tel 800/231–2222; local fares/schedules, tel 202/289–5154)* offers national service; **Peter Pan**

Trailways *(tel 800/343–9999)* serves the northeast—Baltimore, Philadelphia, New York, Boston, and beyond. Terminals for both Greyhound and Peter Pan are inconveniently located opposite one another at the corner of 1st and L streets, NE, a dubious neighborhood some five blocks north of Union Station and the Union Station Metro station. Fortunately, cabs are usually on hand (Taxi zone 1C). Greyhound also has stations in Arlington, VA *(tel 703/998–6312; 3860 S. Four Mile Run Rd.)*, and Silver Spring, MD *(tel 301/588–5110; 8110 Fenton St.)*.

Metrobus operates to all areas of the city and close-in suburbs, some routes providing 24-hour service (which can be helpful between midnight and 5:30am when Metrorail closes for the night). The Metrobus is the only public transportation to Georgetown and Adams-Morgan, which aren't served by Metrorail. Slow, unpredictable, incomprehensible, user-hostile, Metrobus possesses all the negative mass transit qualities: no route maps are posted at bus stops and drivers have deficient communications skills. Few visitors ever crack the Metrobus code. Many locals are oblivious to the existence of Metrobus. The fare is $1.10 with bus-to-bus transfers 10 cents; Metrorail to Metrobus transfers cost 25¢ (get a transfer from a machine in the station where you board Metrorail); there are no deals for bus-to-rail connections. For routes, schedules, fare information, call **Mr. or Ms. Metro Information Center** *(tel 202/637–7000, TDD 202/638–3780)*.

Car rentals... Major rental car companies are represented at all three airports; National and Budget have counters in Union Station. Many excellent deals are available at the airports for weekend rentals. Call **Alamo** *(tel 800/327–9633)*, **Avis** *(tel 800/831–2847)*, **Budget** *(tel 800/527–0700, TDD 800/826–5510)*, **Dollar** *(tel 800/800–4000)*, **Enterprise** *(tel 800/325–8007)*, **Hertz** *(tel 800/654–3131, TDD 800/654–2280)*, **National** *(tel 800/227–7368)*, or **Thrifty** *(tel 800/367–2277)*.

Convention center... The **Washington Convention Center** *(tel 202/789–1600)* is at 9th and H streets, NW, Gallery Place–Chinatown Metro, Taxi zone 1C.

Doctors and dentists... **Farragut Medical & Travel Care** *(tel 202/775–8500, 815 Connecticut Ave., NW)* offers appointments or walk-in care Monday through Saturday. Call the **Dental Referral Service** of the District of Columbia Dental Society *(tel 202/547–7615)* weekdays

8am–4pm for a referral to a convenient dentist. For dental emergencies call **Dr. Rex H. Hoang** *(Dupont Circle, tel 202/833–8724 or 703/263–5081)*, **Georgetown Dental** *(tel 202/965–2980)*, or **AAA 24-Hour Emergency Dental Care** *(tel 301/770–0123)*.

Driving around... Washington is an awful place to drive. Streets are confusing, and you'd swear the signage was encoded by the CIA. Drivers act as if turn signals are infringements on their right to privacy and red lights are naive suggestions. Parking in many parts of town is scarce and/or costly. (See "Parking", below.) But then, Washington is not L.A.—nobody *has* to drive here. Metrorail goes almost anywhere visitors want to go, almost all the time. Cabs are plentiful and reasonably inexpensive. It's safe to walk in most neighborhoods you'd want to visit. Many people who drive *to* Washington wind up parking their cars in the hotel lot and leaving them there until they go home.

Driving in D.C. requires courage, a bit of chutzpah, some patience, and, most importantly, a detailed city map. Our best advice can be summed up in two words: *Connecticut Avenue*. Connecticut Avenue runs northwest from the White House through Dupont Circle past National Zoo through Chevy Chase, all the way out to the Capital Beltway (I-495). Directions to almost anyplace you want to go begin, "Take Connecticut to..." Know how to reach Connecticut from wherever you are and you'll find the place you want to go.

One other unfortunate fact of Washington driving life is the Capital Beltway (at various junctures I-95, I-395, and I-495), a superhighway and state-of-mind that encircles the city through the Virginia and Maryland suburbs. Every Beltway driver is a lobbyist asserting his own interests in reckless defiance of all others. The most useful thing about the Beltway is that it intersects Connecticut Avenue just north of Chevy Chase, Maryland. Take the Beltway to Connecticut Avenue and from Connecticut south to your final destination—it's seldom the shortest way and never the fastest, but chances are you will arrive.

Emergencies... For **police, fire department, and ambulance service,** call 911 (TTY/TDD callers press space bar or any key). For the **Poison Center,** call 202/625-3333. **24-hour hospital emergency rooms** are at: George Washington University Medical Center *(tel*

202/994–3211; 23rd and I streets, NW) or Georgetown University Medical Center *(tel 202/784–2118; 3800 Reservoir Rd., NW)*.

Events hotlines... Post-Haste *(tel 202/334–9000)* is a *Washington Post* telephone service for information on weather, spectator sports, golf, fishing, restaurants, lottery results, and much more. **Time Out Washington** *(tel 202/ 364–8463)* gives details on bar and club appearances, concerts, movie times, pub crawls, and other events. **Smithsonian Dial-A-Museum** *(tel 202/357–2020)* lists museum hours, special exhibits, and daily events for all Washington Smithsonian museums, plus the National Zoo. **Kennedy Center Performance Information** *(tel 202/467–4600, 800/444–1324)* gives concert details for the Center and lets you charge tickets.

    Various local radio stations operate their own hotlines. **WKYS Entertainment Line** *(tel 202/895–2489)* gives the scoop on movies, Smithsonian events, and concerts by, mainly, black artists. **WAMU Bluegrass Bulletin Board** *(tel 202/885–1234, 800/525–8338)* covers bluegrass concerts and appearances. **WWDC Concert and Information Line** *(tel 301/587–0300)* lists mainstream and alternative rock music attractions. The **WDCU "Jazz 90" Info Line** *(tel 202/274–6490)* features jazz listings, mini-reviews of local plays, and an "Inspirational Update" for religious-oriented events.

Festivals and special events... Washington's biggest event is the **Presidential Inauguration**, which takes place on January 20th every four years. The next one will be in 1997, and whoever wins the election, you can count on a parade, balls, concerts, the whole works. To get tickets to most of the balls you have to know somebody, and hotel reservations will be impossible to land. Other major events include:

Spring: **The Cherry Blossom Festival**, late March through early April *(tel 202/547–1500)*, with a parade, pageants, and a Japanese lantern-lighting ceremony, focusing on the Tidal Basin; the **White House Easter Egg Roll/Spring Garden Tours**, mid-April *(tel 202/456–2200)*; **Filmfest DC**, late April–early May *(tel 202/274–6810)*; **Memorial Day Observance**, late May, which includes wreath-laying ceremonies, concerts.

Summer: **Kemper Open Pro-Am Golf Tournament**, early June *(tel 301/469–3737)*; **Festival of American Folklife**, late June–early July *(tel 202/357–2700)*, in which different countries are highlighted each year on the National Mall, sponsored by the Smithsonian; **National Independence Day Celebration**, July 4, with a parade, concerts, ceremonies, fireworks.

Fall: **DC Blues Festival**, early September *(tel 202/828–3028)*; **Taste of DC**, early October *(tel 202/724–4093)*, a Pennsylvania Avenue restaurant fair; the **Marine Corps Marathon**, late October *(tel 703/640–2225)*, a 26-mile run beginning and ending at the Iwo Jima Memorial.

Winter: **Pageant of Peace/National Christmas Tree Lighting**, early December–early January *(tel 202/619–7222)*, featuring state displays near the National Christmas tree, caroling; **White House Christmas Candlelight Tours**, Dec 26–28 *(tel 456–2200)*; the **Washington Antiques Show**, early January *(tel 202/234–0700)*; **Martin Luther King Jr. Birthday Observance**, mid-January, with various activities around the area.

Gay and lesbian resources... Gay & Lesbian Hotline *(tel 202/833–3234)*; **Whitman-Walker Clinic** *(tel 797–3500, TTY 202/797–4449)* for information and various medical services; **DC AIDS Infoline** *(tel 202/332–AIDS, TTY 202/797–3575)*; **Mattachine Society** *(tel 202/363–3881)*, for rights information and gay assistance info; **Dignity/Washington** *(tel 202/387–4516)*, a Catholic support group; *Gay Community Yellow Pages* *(tel 410/547–0380, 800/849–0406)*; **Gay & Lesbian Information Bureau** *(tel 703/578–4542)*, a computer bulletin board.

Limos... Sedans and limos—stretch, superstretch, and ultrastretch—are plentiful in a city as pompous as Washington. Going rates are $35–$45/hour, often with a three- or four-hour minimum, plus a 15 percent tip. If you can afford the fare, it's definitely the way to go to the airport, for private sightseeing tours, or for day trips to places like Mount Vernon or Annapolis. Call: **Moran Limousine Service** *(tel 202/337–2880)*; **Abo's Limousine** *(tel 301/670–1718 or 800/670–1718)*; or **Manhattan International** *(tel 202/775–1888, 800/336–5503)*.

Newspapers and magazines... The daily *Washington Post (25¢ daily, $1.50 Sunday, tel 202/334–3000)*, the Nixon-toppling newspaper, is close to the middle of the road—both ends of the political spectrum think it's biased against them. The *Washington Times (25¢ daily, $1 Sunday, tel 202/636–3000)*, a right-wing *USA Today*-sized paper published by the Unification Church

(Moonies), at least keeps the nation's capital from being a one-newspaper town. **Washington City Paper** *(tel 202/ 332–2100)* is a weekly alternative tabloid with lengthy muckraking articles and invaluable listings of local events. The weekly **Washington Blade** *(tel 202/7797–7000)* provides serious gay-oriented coverage, available free in paper boxes, office buildings, bars, stores, and libraries. **Metro Weekly** *(tel 202/588–5220)* is a free, weekly, gay-oriented paper focused on arts and entertainment, hard to find outside of gay enclaves.

Parking... Free parking is available on and around the Mall after 10am weekdays, but it's hard to find a spot and you can only stay two or three hours. It may be possible to park in nearby residential neighborhoods—Capitol Hill, for example—and walk a few blocks to Mall attractions, but generally if the neighborhood is close enough and safe enough, only cars with resident decals are allowed to park for more than an hour or so. Metered parking is available on most downtown streets, but these meters gobble up to eight quarters an hour and need to be fed every half-hour or hour.

That leaves paid parking lots, which are plentiful north of the Mall, but expensive. Near-Mall lots charge $4/hour up to $15 a day, although there are plenty of specials in the range of $7 to $10 per day, if you're in before 8 or 8:30am. Prices are lower in lots farther from the Mall, and rates plummet north of Massachusetts Avenue. A lot located north of Mount Vernon Square at the corner of 7th and L streets, NW (which will be replaced by the new convention center if it ever gets built) charges $3.50 a day; the full-day rate at a metered, city-owned lot at 9th and L streets amounts to about the same, but it fills early and you need fistfuls of quarters. These lots are nearly a mile from the Mall, but close to the Mount Vernon–UDC Metrorail station.

Parking illegally is a big mistake in downtown D.C. The District government sees parking fines as a profit center, and traffic cops are the District's most efficient employees (perhaps its only efficient employees). If you get a ticket, you can try to dodge the fine; read *How to Beat a D.C. Parking Ticket*, available for $4.95 at local bookstores or from the D.C. Drivers Association *(tel 202/ 332–2613)*.

Radio stations... On the AM dial, **WTEM** (570) offers all sports (and Imus); **WMAL** (630) has news, sports, and talk shows, notably Rush Limbaugh; talk radio 980 **(WWRC)** offers Ollie North among its hosts. For children's programming, tune in **WKDL** (1050); for jazz, **WJFK** (1300); for soul music and African American-oriented talk shows, **WOL** (1450); for all news, **WTOP** (1500); for hip-hop music, **WPGC** (1580).

FM stations include the local NPR stations, **WAMU** (88.5) and **WETA** (90.9); two noncommercial stations featuring jazz and talk shows, **WPFW** (89.3) and **WDCU** (90.1); conservative talk shows on **WAVA** (105.1); jazz and talk show hosts Howard Stern and Gordon Liddy on **WJFK** (106.7). There's a host of FM music stations—**WKYS** (93.9) for urban contemporary, **WARW** (94.7) for rock oldies, **WPGC** (95.5) for top 40, **WHFS** (99.1) for progressive rock, **WFRE** (99.9) for country music, **WWDC** (101.1) for album-oriented rock, **WRQX** (107.3) for adult contemporary, and **WRCY** (107.7) for country rock.

Restrooms... Compared to some other cities we can think of (New York, Paris, London come to mind), Washington is a good place for finding public restrooms. Most of the museums on the Mall are free to enter and well equipped, and the monuments all have public facilities. On the other hand, Metro stations do not have restrooms, and you'll need a better reason than "I gotta go" to get past security in most government office buildings. For aesthetic reasons we recommend the classic plumbing fixtures in the National Museum of American Art.

Smoking... The sight of all those smokers huddling outside downtown office buildings should be a tip-off—Washington is not a smoker-friendly city. Smoking is banned from public buildings, including museums. In response to guest demand, hotels are constantly upping their inventories of rooms and entire floors for nonsmokers. Larger restaurants have smoking sections, but many don't permit smoking at all. Only a handful of restaurants can be regarded as smoker-welcoming (even for those pariahs of pariahs, cigar smokers). These restaurants include **Les Halles** and **Music City Roadhouse** (see Dining), **Sam & Harry's** *(tel 202/296–4333; 1200 19th St., NW)*, and the **Capital Grille** *(tel 202/737–6200; 601 Pennsylvania Ave., NW)*. A local group called **Smokin'! Tobacco Aficionados of Washington, D.C.** *(tel 202/986–2213 or 202/986–2219)* keeps track of places where smokers of cigars, pipes, and fancy cigarettes can feel at home (assuming they're allowed to smoke at home). Maryland is worse than D.C. A smoker is less of a pariah across the river in Virginia, a big tobacco-growing state where rules and attitudes about smoking are appreciably looser.

Subways... The 90-mile **Metrorail** *(tel 202/673–7000, TDD 202/638–3780)* connects most Washington attractions, hotel clusters, outlying D.C. neighborhoods, and Virginia/Maryland suburbs. Metrorail—Metro for short—does not serve Georgetown (which allegedly turned down the chance to get a Metro station because of the rabble it would bring) or Adams-Morgan. Spotless, safe, efficient, nearly panhandler-free, it's a system where rules against graffiti, eating, and drinking are not only enforced but respected. Metro can make riders of other systems think they've died and gone underground to heaven.

Five color-coded lines—Red, Blue, Orange, Green, and Yellow—operate from 5:30am to midnight weekdays, from 8am weekends. Fares range from $1.10 to $3.25 depending on length of trip, time of day, and day of week; children under four ride free (up to two kids per paying passenger). Higher rush-hour fares (up to a $1.15 difference) are in effect weekdays 5:30am–9:30am and 3pm–8pm on many routes, which explains the crowds you'll see dawdling outside fare gates at 9:29am and 7:59pm and stampeding toward them as 3pm approaches. The $1.10 minimum fare applies at all times to most trips within the downtown area.

Passengers must purchase encoded fare cards before entering the system; fare card vending machines that accept everything from nickels to $20 bills are in every station. Invest in fare card futures if you plan to use Metro a lot—you get a 5 percent bonus for depositing over $10 ($10 buys $10.50 worth of travel) and a 10 percent bonus for more than $20 ($20 gets you $22). A $5 one-day pass—sold at the Metro Center station, the Pentagon, and local supermarkets—is good for unlimited rides after 9:30am weekdays, all day on weekends. For information about Metro schedules, fares, and parking, call **Mr. or Ms. Metro Information Center** *(tel 202/637–7000, TDD 202/638–3780).*

Taxes... **District of Columbia**: general sales tax, 5.75 percent; restaurants, 10 percent; hotels, 13 percent occupancy tax plus $1.50/night surcharge. **Maryland**: sales and restaurant tax, 5 percent; additional 1–10 percent lodging and amusement tax may be imposed by localities. **Virginia**: general sales tax, 4.5 percent; local option for taxes on lodging, restaurants, admissions.

Taxis... Unlike taxis almost everywhere else, D.C.'s don't have meters—at least they won't until 1998, when meters are tentatively slated to make their D.C. debut. For years, D.C. cabs have operated within a bewildering zone system that divides the city into five zones, each of which is subdivided into eight subzones. (Confused yet?) Drivers compute fares according to the number of subzone boundaries the cab crosses in the course of a trip. The current fare for a trip within any subzone is $2.80; travel between subzones within one zone costs $3.20; the fare between any point in Zone 1 and any point in Zone 2 is $4.40. Each zone change after that costs another $1.10, generally. (This system applies only to trips within the District; trips to airports or other destinations in the 'burbs cost $2 for the first half-mile, 70¢ for each additional half-mile). Then there are the surcharges: $1.25 for each additional passenger (six and older); $1 for trips during the 7–9:30am or 4–6:30pm weekday rush hours; $1.25 for use of a trunk; 15¢ for each additional piece of hand baggage (including grocery bags but not briefcases). D.C.'s taxi fare system was imposed by Congress, which gerrymandered zone boundaries to keep fares low for the trips members make the most. Luckily, most of the places out-of-towners go also lie within the cheap fare zones. As confusing as this system may be, it may be metamorphosizing once more: at press time, the D.C. Taxicab Commission had just launched its bureaucratic machinery into action, moving towards a fare restructuring that would add about $1 to $1.50 to each ride.

Unfortunately, not having meters has opened up the game to incessant disputes between drivers (who feel they're underpaid) and passengers (who feel they're overcharged). Passengers get particularly peeved when it costs more to ride a couple blocks across a fare-zone border than it would to travel across the city within one zone. If you know where the boundary line is, get out of the cab before you reach it. Taxicab Zone Maps are posted in all cabs, but they're rudimentary outline maps that may not help unless you're already intimately familiar with Washington street geography. What *will* help is to know the taxi zone of the address you're going to, which is why we list them for every D.C. destination in this book.

Other D.C. taxi quirks: It's perfectly legit for drivers to pick up additional passengers without the consent of the original passengers, as long as the original passenger doesn't have to go more than five blocks out of the way. The driver needs the original passenger's consent if the subsequent passenger has a pet or other animal (other than a seeing-eye dog). Each passenger pays full fare for his or her trip, so it's to the cabbie's advantage to double up.

Washington cabbies cruise major government/business tourist areas and are generally easy to find most times day and night. Off-hours and off-the-beaten-track, for an extra $1.50 surcharge, cabs can be summoned by phone: **Capitol Cab** *(tel 202/546–0200)*; **Diamond Cab** *(tel 202/387–2600)*; **Taxi Transportation Service** *(tel 202/398–0500)*; and **Yellow Cab** *(tel 202/544–1212)*.

The inherent fatalism of the zone fare system (the end is known before the beginning) seems to improve cabbies' dispositions and make them less predatory than cabbies elsewhere. But drivers who speak English and know where they are going are all too scarce. Demand a receipt at the start of the ride, and if you have questions, comments, or complaints, call the D.C. Taxicab Commission *(tel 202/645–6010)*, which is a D.C. government bureau (consider yourself warned).

Tipping... Tipping is a fact of life in Washington. Keep singles on hand for all the porters, doormen, maids, and checkroom attendants you'll encounter. The tip for the concierge is trickier: nothing for basic directions or information, but at least $5 and possibly much more (depending on degree of difficulty) for making restaurant reservations, obtaining tickets, or performing some other delicate service. Restaurant waiters and bartenders get at least 15 percent of the bill, as do taxi and limo drivers.

Trains... Washington's **Union Station** is the southern terminus of Amtrak's *(tel 800/USA–RAIL)* frequent Northeast Corridor service. Between Washington and New York (Penn Station) is a three-and-a-half-hour trip; higher-fare Metroliners make it in 3 hours or less, but only on weekdays. The Washington–Boston trip takes eight hours. The Auto Train carries passengers and their cars between Sanford, Florida (near Orlando) and Lorton, Virginia, 16 miles southeast of D.C. Union Station is in taxi zone 1D, a short, cheap ride to most hotels; there's a Metrorail Red Line station on the lower level.

Travelers with disabilities... Washington is a good city for people with disabilities, partly because it wants to prove it can obey laws (notably the ADA, Americans with Disabilities Act) as well as pass them. The White House has a special entrance for the disabled; the Lincoln and Jefferson memorials and the Washington Monument have elevators for disabled visitors. Handicapped parking is available along the Mall, and museums are designed to comply with federal regulations regarding entrance ramps, elevator service, accessible restrooms and water fountains. The **Smithsonian Institution** distributes a free brochure, "Smithsonian Access," detailing accessibility features, parking, special entrances, and special tours available at all Smithsonian facilities, including the National Zoo; pick up a brochure at any Smithsonian information desk, or contact the Smithsonian Information Center *(tel 202/357–2700, TTY 202/357–1729.* Courtesy discount ID cards are available for visitors with disabilities; call for information *(tel 202/962–1245, TTY 202/628–8973).*

TV stations... Channel 4 (WRC) is the NBC affiliate; **Channel 5 (WTTG)** is Fox; **Channel 7 (WJLA)**, ABC; **Channel 9 (WUSA)**, CBS; **Channel 20 (WDCA)**, UPN; **Channel 26 (WETA)**, PBS; **Channel 32 (WHMM)**, PBS; **Channel 50 (WBDC)**, WB. **Channel 8** on local cable systems features 24-hour local news.

Visitor information... Washington, D.C. **Convention and Visitors Association**: *tel 202/789–7000, fax 202/789–7035; 1212 New York Ave., NW, #600, Washington, DC 20005.* **D.C. Committee to Promote Washington**: *tel 202/347–5644, fax 202/724–2445; 1212 New York Ave., NW, #200, Washington, DC 20005.* **D.C. Chamber of Commerce**: *tel 202/638–3222, fax 202/347–3538; 1301 Pennsylvania Ave., NW., Washington,D.C.* The **White House Visitor Center** *(14th St. and Pennsylvania Ave., NW)* distributes some visitor brochures and maps; visitor centers in major attractions such as the **Capitol Building**, **Smithsonian Castle**, and **Arlington Cemetery** are well stocked. Other options include hotels and concierge/service desks at shopping malls like **Georgetown Park** *(3222 M St., NW).*